Helping Adolescents
with ADHD & LEARNING DISABILITIES

Ready-to-Use Tips, Techniques, and Checklists for School Success

JUDITH GREENBAUM, Ph.D.
GERALDINE MARKEL, Ph.D.

Illustrations by Alice Beresin

JOSSEY-BASS
A Wiley Imprint
www.josseybass.com

Published by Jossey-Bass
A Wiley Imprint
989 Market Street, San Francisco, CA 94103-1741 www.josseybass.com

Jossey-Bass books and products are available through most bookstores. To contact Jossey-Bass directly call our Customer Care Department within the U.S. at 800-956-7739, outside the U.S. at 317-572-3986 or fax 317-572-4002.

Jossey-Bass also publishes its books in a variety of electronic formats. Some content that appears in print may not be available in electronic books.

Library of Congress Cataloging-in-Publication Data

Greenbaum, Judith.
    Helping adolescents with ADHD & learning disabilities : ready-to-use tips, techniques,
and checklists for school success / Judith Greenbaum, Geraldine Markel.
        p.   cm.
    Includes bibliographical references.
    ISBN 0-13-016778-9
    1. Hyperactive children—Education (Secondary)—United States.   2. Learning
disabled—Education (Secondary)—United States.   I. Title: Helping adolescents with
ADHD and learning disabilities.   II. Markel, Geraldine Ponte, 1939–   III. Title.
LC4712.G74 2001
371.93—dc21   00-050765

FIRST EDITION
HB Printing 10 9 8 7 6 5 4 3

Dedication

We dedicate this book to the teachers who strive so hard to make the difference in the lives of students with ADHD and/or LD. Many of these teachers are underappreciated by students, parents, and the community at-large. But not by us. Each student with ADHD and/or LD who graduates from high school is a tribute to a teacher.

We also dedicate this book to parents of students with ADHD and/or LD. These parents are our unsung heroes. They work behind the scenes loving, cajoling, teaching, and arguing with their sons and daughters who have learning and attention problems, in order to help them succeed in school. Some teachers find parents very difficult to work with, but, in actuality, parents and teachers are partners who share the same goals.

And last but not least, we dedicate this book to students with ADHD and/or LD. Few of us understand the courage it takes for these students to go to school day after day (knowing that they are not performing the way the world expects them to). With our support these students can succeed.

Acknowledgments

We wish to express our deep gratitude to our editor, Susan Kolwicz, for her guidance and support.

We want to offer our appreciation to Alice Beresin, whose illustrations enliven the pages of this book and reflect not only her talent, but her understanding of ADHD and LD.

Judy and Geri greatly appreciate the caring and support of their families:

Judy thanks Dan and Alice, Josh and Keren, Sara and Darryl, Susannah, Lisa, Christine and Frank, Rachel and Paul, Wendy, Aaron, Claire, Shoshannah, Hannah, Isabella, Joseph, and last but not least, Dan Roberts.

Geri thanks her husband Shel, and their family: Laura, Joe, and Dylan; David, Stacy, Alex, Jake, Sam, and Danny; Stephen, Ellen, Charlie, and Tim. Of course, the assistance of Asondra Smith can not be overstated.

Special thanks are due to the many students and their families who we have had the privilege of working with and whose stories are shared throughout the text.

Over the years we have valued the exchange of ideas, insights, and challenges presented by classroom teachers and special education consultants. We have enjoyed the opportunities of interacting with professional organizations and community agencies such as the state and national chapters of LDA and CH.A.D.D.

There are a number of individuals we have worked with through the years who deserve our thanks:

- Our colleagues at the University of Michigan, Seth Warschausky, Ph.D., Bruno Giordoni, Ph.D., and Roger Lauer, Ph.D., neuropsychologists, who set the standard in terms of providing comprehensive, clear, and usable diagnostic reports to parents, students, and school staff.

- Robert Chesky, M.D., pediatrician, who worries about the education of children as well as their physical and health needs.

- David Yamamoto, Ione Shea, and Lloyd Holdwick, retired special education directors, who always assumed a "can do" attitude with any problem involving the education of students with disabilities and never lost their focus on the student.

- Lynwood Beekman, Esq., advocate for special education services, provider of legal services to school districts, hearing officer, and mediator, whose devotion to the education of children with disabilities has spanned over 30 years.

- Kathleen Cambria, whose several careers as a school principal and Director of Staff Development at the Washtenaw Intermediate School District, and now, in her retirement as tutor, demonstrate her deep concern about the education of students with LD and ADHD.

- William Miller, Director, Washtenaw Intermediate School District, whose openness to new ideas is moving the W.I.S.D. into the twenty-first century.

- Nona Edsinga at the Citizen's Alliance to Uphold Special Education (CAUSE), who has been a tireless source of information about special education laws and their interpretation.

- Dee Gilvin and the staff of Michigan Rehabilitation Services, who help students with disabilities make transitions and turn more of their dreams into realities.

- The staff of the Student Advocacy Center, who constantly seek to ensure the rights of low income, minority students, and students with disabilities.

Judith Greenbaum
Geraldine Markel

About the Authors

Judith Greenbaum, Ph.D., received her Ph.D. in special education from the University of Michigan. She taught teacher preparation courses in the Department of Special Education and was a Research Associate in the Programs for Educational Opportunity. She is currently involved in consulting with schools and school districts and working with parents in order to design appropriate educational programs for students with disabilities.

Her extensive experience with students with special needs ranges from preschool (Head Start) through college (Washtenaw Community College). This book is based on workshops she has developed for parents and school staff during the last twenty years.

Geraldine Markel, Ph.D., earned her doctorate in educational psychology and a masters' degree in reading from the University of Michigan. While at George Washington University, she earned an educational specialist degree in special education.

Dr. Markel served as faculty in special education and was Director of High School and College Services at the Reading and Learning Skills Center at the University of Michigan. Currently, she is principal of Markel Consulting.

As teacher and consultant, she has worked with secondary and postsecondary students who have learning disabilities, attention deficit disorders, and/or emotional impairments. A popular speaker, consultant, and trainer, she has coauthored numerous articles and instructional materials, including *Quest: An Academic Skills Program* and *The ABCs of the SATs: A Parent's Guide to College Entrance Tests.*

Drs. Greenbaum and Markel have coauthored *Parents Are to Be Seen and Heard: Assertiveness in Educational Planning for Parents of Handicapped Children,* a chapter on crisis prevention; *Crisis Prevention for Parents of Children with Handicapping Conditions; Performance Breakthroughs for Adolescents with Learning Disabilities or ADD: How to Help Students Succeed in the Regular Education Classroom* (Research Press, 1996).

Why We Wrote This Book

Students with ADHD and/or LD can present overwhelming challenges to teachers. Teachers may feel underprepared and overworked. They may feel that some of these students are just dumped in their classrooms without any support. Even when help is provided to teacher and/or student, it is often too little and too late. Still, there are many teachers who are doing wonderful things in their classrooms, despite the odds. Some of them are described in this book.

Each day teachers are offered a chance to make a difference in the life of an adolescent with ADHD and/or LD. Each day, each teacher can choose to use his or her unique talents to enhance the school performance of all adolescents in their classrooms.

We wrote this book because we understand that most teachers need help when planning and implementing programs for students with ADHD and/or LD. We wanted to provide a concise, research-based, practical guide to help them.

We also understand the time constraints under which teachers operate. Although the instructional strategies we suggest may take some planning time, the actual implementation of these strategies will hardly add any time to your day.

This book is both interesting and easy to read. Student case histories are interwoven throughout. You will find an emphasis on whole class instruction and how to integrate the teaching of learning and self-management strategies into the content area. You will be provided with proven, up-to-date, and easy-to-follow guidelines to plan effective programs, utilize effective instructional strategies, and prevent predictable problems.

Four principles for interacting with students reflect our deep commitment to the education of students with ADHD and/or LD.

WHO CAN USE THIS BOOK AND HOW

The primary audience for this book is the committed, busy classroom teacher and special education teacher who want to do the best they can to support students with ADHD and/or

LD. Others who will find this book useful and practical are mental health professionals, preservice and in-service teacher educators, and parents who need an easy-to-read reference of strategies for working with students with ADHD and/or LD. More specifically,

- *Classroom teachers* can use the insights, proven "best practices," and checklists to provide instruction to students with ADHD and/or LD within the context of whole class instruction.
- *Special education personnel* can use this guide in their own consulting with classroom teachers, other school personnel, or parents. They, with counselors and principals, can refer to this resource to plan IEPs or 504 plans, involve parents, or work with individual students.
- *School psychologists, social workers, psychologists, and neuropsychologists* can use this guide to show how diagnostic findings and other information is translated into effective plans and interventions. They can provide it or suggest it as a resource to parents or other professionals.
- *Teacher educators or staff development trainers* can use this resource as a basis for short-term training and a supplement for textbooks which may or may not have as many forms, checklists, practical tips as this guide. Specific chapters may be used as a basis for seminars and workshops.
- *Parents* can use it to help develop educational plans for their sons or daughters with ADHD and/or LD.

CHAPTER OVERVIEWS

Chapter 1 Adolescents with ADHD and/or LD is the most theoretical chapter of the book. This chapter provides you with an overview of these two disabilities including definitions, characteristics, dual and overlapping diagnoses, secondary problems, and commonly used assessment instruments. You will read about predictable problems encountered in the classroom and teachers' roles in confronting these challenges. Learning styles are discussed as they relate to understanding and teaching students with ADHD and/or LD.

We present the profiles and problems of Terry, William, and Marilyn, secondary students diagnosed with ADHD and/or LD.

Chapter 2 Understanding Legal Requirements identifies the underlying premises of legislative mandates and the major provisions of, and differences between, IDEA and Section 504. Constraints affecting IEP and 504 decisions, and barriers to implementation are discussed. In addition, teacher responsibilities implied by law and strategies to comply with the law are described.

Chapter 3 The Learning Environment reviews the components of a supportive learning environment. Teaching philosophy, school climate, the physical environment, and instructional methods and management are discussed. The assumption is that the classroom context sets the stage for learning and that teachers can organize the classroom environment to enhance the learning of students with ADHD and/or LD.

We describe how a middle school teacher welcomes students and parents to the class. We also discuss how teachers arranged the learning environment to help Sonny, a student with ADHD and LD, meet greater success in his large overcrowded school.

Chapter 4 Reading and Writing in the Content Area covers the reading and writing achievements of students with ADHD and/or LD, the types of reading and writing problems they confront, and the relationship between reading and writing. You will find a variety of strategies to enhance reading and writing skills of all students in the content classroom is provided. We have included samples of active reading and graphic organizers. We are recommending a school-wide commitment to improve reading, writing, and study skills in content area classes.

We describe Angelise, a bright 16-year-old with learning disabilities in reading comprehension and expressive language, and Clyde, who has problems with reading decoding. You will see how their problems are addressed in their classes and how they benefit from the strategies and accommodations their teachers provide.

Chapter 5 Teaching Homework-Completion Skills presents the problems of students who do not complete or hand in their homework. We propose strategies that you can use to teach homework completion skills to the whole class. In addition, we have listed possible homework accommodations, ways to prevent homework problems, and how to deal with homework problems when they occur. Sample checklists and action plans are provided for you, students, and parents.

We discuss Brandon, a middle school student with learning disabilities. You will find a list of Brandon's homework accommodations as well as checklists that the entire class can use to improve homework completion skills.

Chapter 6 Teaching Adolescents to Use Self-Management discusses the importance of self-management skills for both learning and behavior, and how students can move to greater self-management by using self-talk, visualizations, self-contracts, checklists, and more. Strategies are outlined for your use within the content area and sample activities and checklists are provided.

We illustrate how self-management skills helped three students: Maria, whose undiagnosed ADHD and frequent school failure convinced her she was stupid; Ophelia, a high school senior with LD in math, who always did poorly on tests; and Christopher who was late to school and class more often than not. We detail how self-management strategies were used to help these students earn higher grades and begin fulfilling their potential.

Chapter 7 Developing IEPs and Section 504 Plans provides you with an in-depth view of the purposes and requirements of IEPs and 504 Plans specifically, how to develop goals and objectives, and issues related to accommodations (e.g., reasonableness and appropriateness). Teacher responsibilities are listed with checklists for teachers and students.

We discuss Monte and Tiffany and show how their IEP or 504 Plans are designed to help them deal with their difficulties and succeed in their classrooms.

Chapter 8 Behavioral Interventions outlines ways you can help students increase behaviors that enhance learning and reduce behaviors that interfere with learning. We discuss positive behavioral supports based on new legal requirements. The assumptions underlying reinforcement and other behavior management techniques within the classroom setting are also discussed. You will find an emphasis on functional assessment and problem prevention. The chapter includes samples of a classroom observation form for functional assessment, a self-monitoring checklist, and a contract.

We introduce Frank, a student with ADHD and emotional problems, and describe how a behavioral support plan helped improve his school and classroom behavior.

Chapter 9 Understanding the Role of Medication provides an overview of the controversies and myths related to medications for ADHD. You will find the uses and possible side-effects of various medications, warning signs for teachers, strategies for monitoring effectiveness, pros and cons, and teacher do's and don'ts.

We meet two students who have made different choices with respect to medication: Cruz, a middle school student with ADHD, who credits Ritalin® with "saving" his life, and Christopher who refuses to take medication because he had a previous drug abuse problem.

Chapter 10 Gifted Students with ADHD and/or LD provides you with definitions and profiles of gifted students with ADHD and/or LD. Myths and facts, the paradoxical nature of students with ADHD and/or LD who are gifted and the difficulty of developing educational plans that address ADHD, LD, and giftedness are discussed.

We present Mike who is gifted and has severe ADHD, and Cory, a high school student who appears lazy and unmotivated, but who is actually gifted but has learning disabilities in reading and written expression.

Chapter 11 Diversity and Parent Involvement provides insights about the legal underpinnings of parent involvement, a definition of parent involvement, and the impact of ethnic and minority status on parent involvement.

We address issues such as socio-economic status, parents' own school experiences, cultural values, communication styles, and the impact of ADHD and/or LD on the family. Strategies are provided to deal with disagreements.

Clyde's mother is introduced. She is a parent who is angry because she has felt ignored by school personnel as she has tried to arrange services for her sixth-grade son who has a severe reading disability.

Chapter 12 Preparing for the Future: Transitions to Postsecondary Settings presents you with an overview of challenges faced by students with ADHD and/or LD as they move from high school to educational or vocational settings. Legislative intent, transition goals and planning, and postsecondary options are discussed. We list the roles and responsibilities of school personnel for preparing these students and provide you with recommendations for the early and ongoing involvement of students and their parents.

We include a letter by Drew, a high school senior, which she wrote as part of her application to college. It effectively explains her disability.

A special appendix, **Problems and Strategies**, identifies common classroom problems and lists strategies to help students with ADHD and/or LD. It provides a quick reference for the busy teacher or parent.

Contents

CHAPTER ONE

Adolescents with ADHD and/or LD—1

Definitions of ADHD—2
Figure 1-1: Specific Problems of Individuals with ADHD under DSM-IV—4
Figure 1-2: Is It ADHD or Something Else?—6
Figure 1-3: Signs of Secondary Emotional Problems of Students with ADHD and/or LD—7

Diagnosis of ADHD—8
Figure 1-4: Commonly Used Assessment Instruments for ADHD and/or LD—9
Figure 1-5: Wechsler Intelligence Scale for Children-III: Description of Verbal Subtests—11

Learning Styles of Students with ADHD and/or LD—10
Figure 1-6: Diagnosing Learning Styles—13
Figure 1-7: Academic Difficulties of Students with ADHD—14

Teacher Roles in the Diagnosis and Support of ADHD and/or LD—16

Learning Disabilities—19
Figure 1-8: Graph of Marilyn's WAIS-III Subtest Scores—21
Figure 1-9: Academic Difficulties of Students with Learning Disabilities—22
Figure 1-10: Warning Signs of Learning Disabilities—25

Language Disabilities—25

Central Auditory Processing Disorder—26

Nonverbal Learning Disabilities—26
Figure 1-11: Nonverbal Learning Disabilities—27

Overlapping Disabilities—28

Multiple Challenges: Adolescence and ADHD and/or LD—28

A Final Word—29

CHAPTER TWO
Understanding Legal Requirements—31

Major Laws Dealing with Students' Disabilities—32

Underlying Premises of IDEA and Section 504—33

Ten Major Provisions of the Individuals with Disabilities Education Act (IDEA)—34
Figure 2-1: Disability Categories Included in IDEA—35
Figure 2-2: Major Provisions of IDEA—36
Figure 2-3: The IEP Process—37

Differences Between IDEA and Section 504—37
Figure 2-4: Major Provisions of Section 504—38
Figure 2-5: Differences Between IEP and Section 504—39

Definitions of Learning Disabilities under IDEA and Section 504—38

Appeals Procedures—40
Figure 2-6: IDEA Appeals Process—41
Figure 2-7: Section 504 Appeals Process—42

Constraints Affecting IEP and Section 504 Decisions—42

Barriers to Implementing IDEA and Section 504—44
Figure 2-8: Legal Responsibilities of Schools and Teachers—43

Teacher Responsibilities Implied by Law—45

Addressing Teacher Questions and Concerns—46

A Final Word—47

CHAPTER THREE
The Learning Environment—49

The Welcome Letter—51

Current Research—52

Predictable Classroom Problems of Students with ADHD and/or LD—53

Components of a Positive Learning Environment—54
Figure 3-1: Ten Components of a Positive Learning Environment—54
Figure 3-2: Strategies to Develop a Supportive Emotional Environment—56
Figure 3-3: Enhancing the Physical Environment—59
Figure 3-4: Monthly Class Calendar—60
Figure 3-5: Student Checklist: A Step-by-Step Guide for Completing Book Reports—62
Figure 3-6: Student Checklist: Elements of Book Reports—63
Figure 3-7: Teacher Checklist: What to Do Before, During, and After a Lesson—66

Monitoring and Assessment of Student Learning—68
Figure 3-8: Tips for Teachers: Helping Students with Classroom Testing—70

Team Teaching—70

A Final Word—72

CHAPTER FOUR
Reading and Writing in the Content Areas—73

Reading: Current Status—74
Figure 4-1: Reading Problems of Students with ADHD and/or LD—75

Writing: Current Status—76
Figure 4-2: Writing Problems of Students with ADHD and/or LD—77

Reading to Write, Writing to Read—78

Whose Responsibility Is It?—79
Figure 4-3: Content Area Reading Objectives for Students—80

Effective Readers and Writers—81
Figure 4-4: Effective Reading Strategies—81
Figure 4-5: Effective Writing Strategies—82

Teaching Reading and Writing in the Content Area Class—83
Figure 4-6: Student Activity: Reading and Writing—85
Figure 4-7: Graphic Organizers for Complex Reading and Writing Tasks—86
Figure 4-8: Student Checklist for a Complex Reading and Writing Task—87

Active Reading and Writing—88
Figure 4-9: Teacher Checklist: Integrating the Teaching of Reading into the Content Area—89
Figure 4-10: Student Checklist: Active Reading—90
Figure 4-11: Student Checklist: Active Writing—91

Reading and Writing Accommodations—93
Figure 4-12: Reading and Writing Accommodations for Students with ADHD and/or LD—94
Figure 4-13: Mike's Writing Checklist—95
Figure 4-14: Angeliese's First Paper for Language Arts—96

A Schoolwide Commitment—97
Figure 4-15: Student Checklist: Active Reading for SAT/ACT-Type Reading Passages—99

A Final Word—101

CHAPTER FIVE
Teaching Homework-Completion Skills—103

Homework, an Unhappy State of Affairs—104

Homework Problems and Their Causes—104

Figure 5-1: Homework Problems Reported by Parents of Students with ADHD and/or LD—105
Figure 5-2: Teacher Checklist: Student Homework Problems—107
Figure 5-3: Homework: Myths and Facts—108

Why Is Homework Assigned?—109
Figure 5-4: Reasons for Assigning Homework—109

Homework Responsibilities of the Teacher, Parent, and Student—110
Figure 5-5: Teacher Checklist: Responsibilities for Homework—110
Figure 5-6: Special Education Teacher Checklist: Responsibilities for Homework—111
Figure 5-7: Parent Checklist: Responsibilities for Homework—112
Figure 5-8: Student Checklist: Responsibilities for Homework—112

Preventing Homework Problems—113
Figure 5-9: Skills Students Need to Complete Homework—114
Figure 5-10: Teacher Checklist: Ten Steps for Teaching Homework Completion—115
Figure 5-11: Student Checklist: Homework Completion—117
Figure 5-12: Student Checklist: My "To Do" List—118
Figure 5-13: Sample Daily Schedule—119
Figure 5-14: Sample Homework Contract/Plan—120
Figure 5-15: Student Survey: What Do You Think About Homework?—121

Providing Support for Homework Completion—122
Figure 5-16: Teacher Checklist: Collaboration Strategies—123
Figure 5-17: Parent Checklist: How to Teach Your Teenager—123
Figure 5-18: Parent Tips: How to Help Students with Homework—124

Providing Homework Accommodations—125
Figure 5-19: Accommodations for Homework—125
Figure 5-20: Christine's Homework Accommodations—126

Solving Homework Problems—126
Figure 5-21: Sample Form: Weekly Homework Report Form for Students and Parents—128

A Final Word—129

CHAPTER SIX
Teaching Adolescents to Use Self-Management—131

Importance of Self-Management Skills—132
Figure 6-1: Self-Management Difficulties of Students with ADHD and/or LD—132

Self Talk—135
Figure 6-2: Student Checklist: Managing Behavior with Self-Talk—136

Visualization—138

Managing Anger—139
Figure 6-3: Student Checklist: Strategies for Managing Anger—140

Managing Attention—140

Managing Test Anxiety—141
Figure 6-4: Student Checklist: Managing Test Anxiety—142

Self-Monitoring—141
Figure 6-5: Christopher's Self-Monitoring Chart: Before Using Strategies—143
Figure 6-6: Christopher's Progress Chart: After Instituting Strategies—144

Setting Goals—145
Figure 6-7: Teacher Checklist: Goal Setting—145
Figure 6-8: Student Worksheet: Getting to School on Time—146
Figure 6-9: Student Schedule: Getting to School on Time—147

Self-Motivation—147

Steps for Integrating the Teaching of Self-Management Strategies in Content Area Classes—148
Figure 6-10: Ten Steps for Integrating Self-Management Strategies into Content Area Classes—150
Figure 6-11: Ophelia's Checklist for Math Tests—151

A Final Word—150

CHAPTER SEVEN
Developing IEPs and Section 504 Plans—153

A Team Approach to the Development of IEPs and Section 504 Plans—155
Figure 7-1: When to Call an IEP Team Meeting—157

Elements of the IEP and Section 504 Plan—158
Figure 7-2: Student Checklist: How to Participate in IEP or 504 Meetings—159
Figure 7-3: Content of the IEP According to IDEA—160
Figure 7-4: Recommended Content of the Section 504 Plan—161
Figure 7-5: Tiffany's Section 504 Plan—162

Responsibilities of the Classroom Teacher—164
Figure 7-6: Responsibilities of the Classroom Teacher at IEP or Section 504 Meetings—164

Responsibilities of the Teacher Consultant and Resource Room Teacher—165
Figure 7-7: Responsibilities of the Teacher Consultant and Resource Room Teachers—165

Responsibilities of the School Social Worker and School Psychologist—166
Figure 7-8: Responsibilities of the School Social Worker and School Psychologist—166

Goals and Objectives—166
Figure 7-9: Monte's IEP Goals and Objectives—167
Figure 7-10: Teacher Checklist: How to Develop Goals and Objectives—168

Accommodations or Supplemental Aids and Services in the Regular Education Classroom—169
Figure 7-11: Types of Accommodations—170

Preparing for the IEP or Section 504 Meeting—169
Figure 7-12: Teacher Checklist: How to Prepare for an IEP or Section 504 Meeting—173

The Well-Run Meeting—175
Figure 7-13: How to Run a Difficult Meeting—176

A Final Word—175

CHAPTER EIGHT
Behavioral Interventions—179

Past Emphasis: Punishment—181

A New Direction: Prevention—181

Behavioral Support Plans—182
Figure 8-1: Teacher Checklist: Writing Behavioral Support Plans—183
Figure 8-2: Observation Form for Functional Assessment—184
Figure 8-3: Frank's Functional Assessment Chart—185
Figure 8-4: Student Checklist: Self-Monitoring—187

Reinforcement—189
Figure 8-5: Sample Reinforcers for Secondary Students—190

Planned Ignoring and Extinction—190

Response Cost—191
Figure 8-6: Points Chart—192

Shaping Behavior and Chaining—193
Figure 8-7: Teacher Checklist: 10 Steps for Shaping Behavior—193

Contracting—193
Figure 8-8: Sample Contract—194

Integrating Behavioral Support Plans for Several Students—195

Stopping Escalation of Negative Behavior—195

Violating Disciplinary Rules or Code of Conduct—196

A Final Word—196

CHAPTER NINE
Understanding the Role of Medication—199

The Teacher's Role—200

Beliefs and Attitudes about Medication—200

Countering Myths—201
Figure 9-1: Medication: Myths and Facts—202
Figure 9-2: Dealing with Negative Parent Attitudes toward Medication—203

Medication Choices—204
Figure 9-3: Medication: Types, Uses, and Possible Side Effects—205

Warning Signs of Side Effects—206
Figure 9-4: Medication: Warning Signs—206

Student Noncompliance—207

The Importance of Monitoring—207
Figure 9-5: Medication: Possible Reactions and Feelings—208
Figure 9-6: Observation Form: Problem Behaviors—209
Figure 9-7: Behavioral Goals—210

Christopher, One Student's Story—211
Figure 9-8: Identifying Christopher's Problem Behaviors—213
Figure 9-9: Strategies for Christopher—214
Figure 9-10: Student Checklist: How to Get to School on Time—215

A Final Word—216
Figure 9-11: Medication: Pros and Cons—216
Figure 9-12: Teacher's Do's and Don'ts about Medication—217

CHAPTER TEN

Gifted Students with ADHD and/or LD—219

Gifted Students with ADHD and/or LD—221
Figure 10-1: Gifted Students: Myths and Facts—222
Figure 10-2: Profiles of Gifted Students with LD: Low Verbal and High Performance Scores—224
Figure 10-3: Profile of Gifted Student with LD: High Verbal and Low Performance Scores—226
Figure 10-4: Profile of Gifted Student with ADHD and LD—227
Figure 10-5: Profile of Gifted Student with ADHD—228

Some Definitions of Giftedness—229
Figure 10-6: Indications of Giftedness—230

Indications of Giftedness and ADHD and/or LD: A Paradoxical Picture—231
Figure 10-7: Indications of Giftedness and ADHD/LD: A Paradoxical Picture—232

Current Status—231

Secondary Emotional Problems—233

Challenges and Opportunities for Teachers—233

Psychoeducational Evaluation—234

Section 504 Plans and Classroom Accommodations—235
Figure 10-8: Accommodations for Gifted Students with ADHD and/or LD—235

Flexible Programming—235

Instructional Planning for the Classroom Teacher—236
Figure 10-9: Teacher Do's and Don'ts—237

Thinking and Self-Management Strategies—236

Student Involvement—238

A Final Word—238

CHAPTER ELEVEN
Diversity and Parent Involvement—241

Legal Underpinning of Parent Involvement—242
Figure 11-1: IDEA Assumptions about Parent Involvement—243

Definition of Parent Involvement—243
Figure 11-2: Parent-Involvement Activities—244

Diversity in the Schools—245
Figure 11-3: Cultural Differences—248
Figure 11-4: Barriers to Collaboration—249

The Influence of ADHD and/or LD on the Family—249

Parent–Teacher Disagreements about the Education of Students with ADHD and/or LD—251

A New Approach to Parent Involvement—252
Figure 11-5: Strategic Planning for Parent Involvement—253
Figure 11-6: Sample Letter to Parents—255
Figure 11-7: Teacher Checklist: Cultural Self-Awareness—256
Figure 11-8: Outreach Activities—258
Figure 11-9: Samples: Reporting Progress to Parents—259

Effective Communication—260
Figure 11-10: Talking to Parents about Student Problems: Do's and Don'ts—262

A Final Word—263
Figure 11-11: The Parent Involvement Checklist—264

CHAPTER TWELVE
Preparing for the Future: Transitions to Postsecondary Settings—269

Why Students Don't Complete High School or Pursue Further Education—269
Figure 12-1: Difficulties of Secondary Students with ADHD and/or LD—271

"A Taste of College," Summer 1995—272

Characteristics of Successful Adults with ADHD and/or LD—273
Figure 12-2: Characteristics of Successful Adults with ADHD and/or LD—274

IDEA Transition Planning Requirements—275
Figure 12-3: Sample Transition Plan—276
Figure 12-4: Teacher Checklist: How to Prepare Students for College Entry—279
Figure 12-5: Special Education Staff Checklist: How to Prepare Students for College Entry—280
Figure 12-6: High School Counselor Checklist: How to Prepare Students for College Entry—281
Figure 12-7: Differences Between High School and College: What to Expect in College—282
Figure 12-8: Parent Checklist: Helping Teenagers Prepare for College—283
Figure 12-9: Student Questionnaire: Preparing for College—285

Postsecondary Support for Students with ADHD and/or LD—288
Figure 12-10: Americans with Disabilities Act (ADA)—289
Figure 12-11: Student Sample Letter to College Admissions Committee—290

Postsecondary Options—291
Figure 12-12: Postsecondary Options—292

A Sense of Completion—292

APPENDICES

A: Problems and Strategies—295

B: Organizations—313

C: Resources—315

D: World Wide Web Sites—317

REFERENCES—319

CHAPTER ONE

Adolescents with ADHD and/or LD

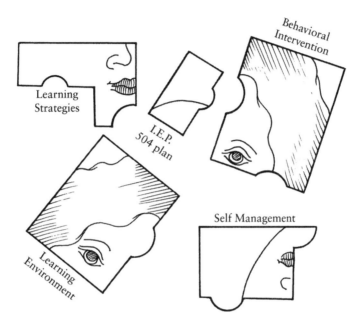

It had been a tough semester for Mr. Briggs, a high school science teacher in a small midwestern city. For some reason, the students in his ninth-grade classes were particularly challenging this fall. In fact, Mr. Briggs was at his wit's end with one student who had LD, severe ADHD, and behavior problems. Because of the student's difficulties, an Individualized Education Planning Team (IEPT) meeting was called in early December to review his program.

Mr. Briggs had taken several workshops on ADHD and LD. He thought he understood how to work with these types of students, and, in fact, he felt that he had been quite successful so far.

However, this student was often very disruptive. The following questions Mr. Briggs asked at the student's IEPT meeting revealed his extreme frustration with trying to reconcile the student's needs with the academic and behavioral standards of the classroom.

- "Are there certain behaviors I should expect of a student with ADHD?

- "At what point and how many times in an ongoing lesson do I tolerate uncontrolled behavior?

- "Specifically, what behaviors should be ignored and what behaviors should be punished?
- "Is spitting on another student on two consecutive days caused by ADHD?
- "Why is a student with LD capable of performing well on one day and not the next?
- "How much time must I spend individualizing for the student with LD?
- "What should I do with the student who reads three to four grades below grade level and cannot read the text?
- "How much should I tolerate a student's refusal to do the work?
- "How should students without ADHD react to uncontrolled and inappropriate behaviors of a student with ADHD?
- "How should a student with ADHD react when repeatedly told to face forward in his seat and stop bothering other students?
- "How much is poor parenting the cause of the inappropriate behavior of a student with ADHD?
- "Is a student's cursing in the presence of twenty-six other students to be excused because that student has ADHD?"

Teachers have many concerns regarding students with ADHD and LD. They have a hard time separating some of the symptoms of ADHD and LD from the symptoms of other problems or disabilities. Many symptoms teachers and parents associate with ADHD or LD are not caused by ADHD or LD. At the other end of the spectrum, many of the symptoms of ADHD and LD are common to all students. When does a behavior cross over from being "normal" to being a disability? How are ADHD and LD diagnosed? What kind of evidence is needed? What other disorders can affect a student's behavior and academic functioning?

In order to answer all these questions, we must first understand the nature of ADHD and LD and how they are diagnosed.

DEFINITIONS OF ADHD

There are several definitions of ADHD and some new hypotheses that are based on brain research. If you are trying to determine if a student with ADHD is eligible for special education services, you must follow the definition in Individuals with Disabilities Education Act (IDEA). If you are trying to determine if the student is eligible for services under Section 504 (of the Vocational Rehabilitation Act of 1974), you can use the definition in the Diagnostic and Statistical Manual of Mental Disorders IV (DSM-IV) as well as that in IDEA. If you are trying to understand the nature of ADHD, some of the new brain-based research can be very helpful.

Both the DSM-IV and IDEA contain definitions of ADHD. Under IDEA 1997 students with ADHD now meet the eligibility requirements for Other Health Impaired (OHI). The IDEA definition of ADHD is:

"having limited strength, vitality, or alertness, including a heightened alertness
to environmental stimuli, that results in limited alertness with respect to the

educational environment, that is due to chronic or acute health problems such as asthma, attention deficit disorder or attention deficit hyperactivity disorder, diabetes . . . (which) adversely affect(s) a child's educational performance."

Under IDEA, a student with ADHD can be considered Learning Disabled or Emotional Impaired if the student meets the eligibility requirements for these categories.

The DSM-IV definition of Attention Deficit/Hyperactivity Disorder is:

- "a persistent pattern of inattention and/or hyperactivity–impulsivity that is more frequent and severe than is typically observed in individuals at a comparable level of development.

- "symptoms . . . have been present before age 7 years, although many individuals have been diagnosed after the symptoms have been present for many years.

- "impairment . . . must be present in at least two settings (e.g., at home and at school).

- "clear evidence" that the impairment 'interferes with developmentally appropriate social, academic or occupational functioning.'

- "the disturbance . . . is not better accounted for by another mental disorder . . ."

Both definitions try to describe the problem behavior of the student, with the DSM-IV definition being more specific. (See Figure 1-1.)

Remember that ADHD is a complex condition. Adolescents with ADHD may differ significantly in the number, combination, and severity of their ADHD problems. Even though they share a label, every student with ADHD and/or LD is an individual.

Some students are very distractible, but not hyperactive or impulsive. They may appear to be "flaky" or "spacey"—like Stacy, a quiet, shy tenth grader who never answers a question in class, rarely is able to locate the homework she completed the night before, and is always late to class.

Other students are constantly on the move. One mother described her son as a 5-year-old: "When Ashanti came into the room, everything fell off the shelves." She says this still happens, although Ashanti is now 13. ADHD is a chronic lifelong disability. People do not outgrow ADHD. They can learn to manage their ADHD so that the effects are minimized.

Although the definitions in IDEA and Section 504 will remain fixed until officially changed, the definition of ADHD is currently in a state of flux as new research adds to our knowledge of brain functioning. No longer do we think of ADHD primarily as a disorder of attention/distractibility (ADD), plus impulsivity, and hyperactivity (ADD-H). New evidence points to ADHD as an impairment of self-regulation or executive functioning.

According to several new theories, a student with ADHD can have deficits in one or more of the following executive functions:

- Behavioral inhibition: inhibiting and regulating verbal and motor responses
- Nonverbal and verbal working memory: recalling and manipulating information
- Activation and maintenance of attention

Specific Problems of Individuals with ADHD under DSM-IV

Inattention

- Makes many careless mistakes; work is messy
- Difficulty persisting with tasks until completion
- Difficulty listening
- Frequent shifts from one uncompleted task to another
- Fails to complete school work
- Difficulty organizing tasks and activities; poor work habits
- Avoids activities that demand sustained mental effort
- Easily distracted by irrelevant stimuli
- Often forgetful of appointments
- Frequent shifts in conversation; not following rules of games

Hyperactivity

- Fidgets; squirms; rocks chair
- Not remaining in seat
- Difficulty engaging in activities quietly
- Appears "on the go, driven by a motor"
- Talks excessively

Impulsivity

- Impatient; difficulty delaying responses; blurts out answers
- Difficulty waiting for one's turn
- Frequently interrupts and intrudes
- Fails to listen to directions
- Grabs objects from others; touches things inappropriately
- Accident prone

Figure 1-1

- Analysis and modification of one's behavior in order to attain a goal and, once the goal is attained, the review of one's behavior
- Management of affective interference: limiting the interference of negative thoughts and feelings in order to complete a task
- Sustaining motivation, energy, and effort in order to complete a task

Executive Functioning: The "Brain's Brain"

The frontal lobe of the brain is the "command center" for goal-directed behavior. Executive functioning is a complex process that enables the student to see a task through from beginning to end by coordinating multiple processes, starting and stopping mental operations, and maintaining motivation and persistence.

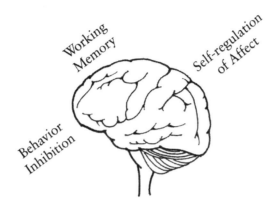

Executive functions aid in completing a task or solving a problem by helping the student:

- Understand the nature of the task or that a problem exists.
- Analyze the task and the setting.
- Determine a goal.
- Consider various strategies that can be used to reach the goal.
- Project the potential success of each strategy.
- Select the strategy that has the greatest chance of succeeding.
- Develop a plan of action.
- Evaluate progress towards the goal.
- Select another strategy and/or modify the plan if the first one is not working.
- Continue monitoring and modifying strategies until the goal is attained.
- Analyze the strategies and plan that were used and how well they worked.

Working memory is part of the complex nature of executive functioning, and involves retrieving and manipulating information in short- or long-term storage. It includes the internalization of speech and visualization in order to self-direct problem-solving behavior. (See Chapter 6 on self-management.)

Focusing and maintaining attention is a part of executive functioning, although problems with attention can also be a part of other disorders. When trying to determine just what is causing attention problems, it is important to remember that attention is also influenced by lack of sleep, task difficulty, motivation, processing speed, anxiety, auditory processing deficits, visual processing deficits, and language ability. (See Figure 1-2.)

Is It ADHD or Something Else?

- Is the work too difficult?
- Is the work boring or uninteresting?
- Is the work challenging enough?
- Are there problems understanding oral directions?
- Are there problems with short- or long-term memory?
- Is there a reading disability (e.g., poor decoding, slow rate, poor comprehension)?
- Is it the student's personality (e.g., high energy, impulsive)?
- Is there too much independent seat work in class?
- Are there large blocks of unstructured time?
- Is the classroom too chaotic, noisy?
- Does the student lack some essential skills (e.g., organization, time management, math calculations, basic writing)?
- Is it depression or anxiety?
- Is it the side effects of some medication?
- Is it learned helplessness, chronic failure syndrome?
- Is it perfectionism, avoidance of failure syndrome?
- Is it slow processing speed?
- Is it sleep deprivation?
- Is it hypothyroidism?
- Is it a seizure disorder?
- Is it oppositional defiant disorder?
- Is it obsessive compulsive disorder?
- Is it a conduct disorder?

Figure 1-2

Prevalence

Because of poor identification practices, ADHD is both overidentified and underidentified. Research shows that ADHD is often overidentified in the upper middle class, well-educated population, and underidentified in lower socio-economic groups. For upper socio-economic groups ADHD may be seen as a refuge for underachieving or poorly behaved students. Lower socio-economic students, on the other hand, are more apt to be labeled emotionally or mentally impaired than ADHD. Although ADHD appears to be more prevalent in boys than girls, current research suggests that it is underidentified in girls.

The reported prevalence of ADHD varies greatly from state to state and from country to country, due to both poor identification practices and differences in the definition of ADHD.

The prevalence of ADHD is estimated at between 3 to 5 percent of the school-age population, although some estimates go as high as 20 percent. Students showing characteristics of ADHD now make up the largest percentage of students referred for diagnostic evaluation.

Comorbidity

ADHD commonly occurs with other disorders. Forty to 65 percent of students with ADHD are estimated to have Oppositional Defiant Disorder (ODD). Twenty-five to 40 percent of students with ADHD are estimated to have Conduct Disorder (CD). It is estimated

---

Signs of Secondary Emotional Problems of Students with ADHD and/or LD

- Withdrawn for long period of time
- Shows no interest in others
- No peer group or friends
- Avoids teachers, friends, and parents
- Rarely acts independently, rarely initiates activities
- School attendance or achievement generally very poor
- Doesn't work at all in school
- Runs away from school or home
- Frequently argues with teachers; is defiant
- Frequently fights; physically abuses others; verbally abuses others
- Alcohol or drug abuse
- Looks or acts anxious, depressed, or lethargic
- Unable to respond with apparent pleasure to praise or rewards
- Irritability or frequent, excessive anger
- Dangerous activity with guns or other weapons
- Talks about or threatens committing suicide
- Extreme risk-taking
- Spends every afternoon and weekend watching television, listening to music, or playing computer games

Figure 1-3

that 25 to 60 percent of students with ADHD have Learning Disabilities and close to 30 percent have a major depressive disorder or anxiety disorder. A student with one of these disorders is eligible to receive special education services under the Emotional Impaired label.

Although a student with ADHD can be defiant at times, a student who frequently resists school work and is unwilling to conform to teacher demands can be diagnosed as having ODD. When more serious problems are involved—such as serious violations of school rules, cruelty to other humans or animals, deceitfulness, or deliberate destruction of others' property—the student may have CD.

Students with ADHD often develop school-related anxiety or depression due to their inability to perform up to their and their parents' and teachers' expectations. They may refuse to do school work or even to go to school for fear of failure. (See Figure 1-3.)

Sleep disturbance may be a part of ADHD or a separate entity, in and of itself. Many students with ADHD complain of chronic insomnia. Their minds race and they can't get to sleep. They have great difficulty waking up in the morning and are often late to school. They often fall asleep in school.

Students with ADHD are at great risk for substance abuse problems. It has been suggested in the past that individuals with ADHD may turn to alcohol or drugs as a way of self-medicating themselves.

DIAGNOSIS OF ADHD

Both IDEA and Section 504 specify that students with disabilities must be evaluated by a multidisciplinary evaluation team. Evaluations can include ability and achievement testing by a school psychologist, evaluation by a school social worker, teacher observations and checklists, parent reports and checklists, student self-report, and outside evaluations by neuropsychologists and psychiatrists. The school district is responsible for the evaluation of a student with possible ADHD, but outside neuropsychologists and psychiatrists may have more evaluation tools with which to conduct in-depth evaluations and rule out other disorders. (See Figure 1-4.)

It is important to discover if attention and impulsivity problems are caused by ADHD or by other problems or disabilities. Some of a student's problems may be traced to ecological factors in the classroom (e.g., noise, unstructured environment).

The Wechsler Intelligence Scale for Children (WISC-III) and the Wechsler Adult Intelligence Scale (WAIS-III) attempt to measure a student's global intellectual abilities. These tests are probably the most widely used instruments for assessing students for learning and attention problems.

Two areas of ability are assessed by the WISC-III—verbal and performance. Each area is divided into six subtests. The average score for each subtest (50th percentile) is 10. The test yields three scores: a full-scale score, a verbal score, and a performance score. (See Figure 1-5.)

Achievement tests such as the Wechsler Individual Achievement Test (WIAT) or the Woodcock–Johnson III Tests of Achievement (WJ-III) are designed to assess school-related skills. The student's performance on these tests is compared with that of other students in

Commonly Used Assessment
Instruments for ADHD and/or LD

Intellectual Ability

- Wechsler Intelligence Scale for Children (WISC-III or WISC-R)
- Wechsler Adult Intelligence Scale Revised (WAIS-III) for students 16 years of age or older
- Kaufman Brief Intelligence Test (KBIT)

Achievement

- The Woodcock–Johnson III Tests of Achievement (WJ-III)
- Kaufman Test of Individual Achievement (K-TEA)
- Test of Written Language (TOWL)
- Wechsler Individual Achievement Test (WIAT)
- Wide Range Achievement Test-3 (WRAT-3)
- Peabody Individual Achievement Test-Revised (PIAT-R)
- California Verbal Learning Test (CVLT)

ADHD

- Test of Variables of Attention (TOVA)
- Connors' Parent Rating Scale-Revised
- Connors' Teacher Rating Scale-Revised
- ADD-H Comprehensive Teacher Rating Scale (ACTeRS)
- Attentional Capacity Test (ACT)
- Connors' Continuous Performance Test (CPT)
- Gordon Diagnostic System (GDS)
- Conners' Rating Scales for Parents, Teachers, and Students
- Attention Deficit Disorders Evaluation Scale (ADDES)

Memory Function

- Rey–Osterreith Complex Figure Test
- Wide Range Assessment of Memory and Learning (WRAML)
- Wechsler Memory Scale III
- California Verbal Learning Test (CVLT)

(continued)

Figure 1-4

2

Visual–Motor Skills

- Developmental Test of Visual–Motor Integration (VMI)
- Finger Tapping
- Rey–Osterreith Complex Figure Test
- Bender Gestalt Test
- Finger Tapping Test
- Grooved Pegboard Test

Executive Functioning

- Wisconsin Card Sorting Test
- Trail Making Tests A & B
- Freedom from Distractability Index of the WISC-III (working memory)

Fluid and Crystalized Intelligence

- Horn Groupings of the WISC-III

Emotional

- Personality Inventory for Children-R
- Connors' Rating Scales for Parents, Teachers, Students
- Child Behavior Checklist

---

the same grade across the country. The scores provide a percentile rank and a grade-level equivalent. The student's scores on the WISC-III are compared with scores on one of the achievement tests in order to help determine if the student has ADHD and/or LD.

Evaluation is not a one-time event. It is an ongoing process in which you, the teacher, continue to evaluate student functioning long after the psychologist submits his or her report. Through this type of diagnostic teaching, you may be able to uncover significant information that will help you fine-tune your teaching strategies. The parent should also continue to evaluate student functioning.

LEARNING STYLES OF STUDENTS WITH ADHD AND/OR LD

The diagnostic process yields information about the student's weaknesses and strengths as far as learning is concerned. Students with weaknesses in auditory processing generally learn best by using their visual processing strengths, and vice versa. Sometimes "hands on"

Wechsler Intelligence Scale for Children-III: Description of Verbal Subtests

The *Verbal* scales measure verbal fluency, verbal memory abilities, and the degree to which a person has benefited from education.

- **Information:** An indication of how observant and experienced the student is in the world around him or her. Indicates the student's fund of general verbal knowledge about the world. This is influenced by education.

- **Similarities:** Student identifies similarities between pairs of objects or concepts. It is a measure of concept formation.

- **Arithmetic:** A timed test. Shows how the student computes mathematical problems without paper and pencil. Measures auditory processing, numerical reasoning, and attention to task.

- **Vocabulary:** Students define words of increasing difficulty and their major uses. Measures general overall verbal knowledge.

- **Comprehension:** Measures the response to common-sense questions. An indication of problem-solving, social knowledge, and practical judgment.

- **Digit Span:** Students are asked to repeat forward and backward a series of digits of increasing length. Measures auditory recall and attention. Also measures working memory and the ability to make mental manipulations. Low scores may also suggest anxiety.

The *Performance* scales measure visual–motor ability, ability to work in concrete situations, work quickly, and evaluate visuospatial information. These are much less influenced by education.

- **Picture Completion:** The student identifies what parts are missing in a picture. Measures visual acuity, alertness, logical reasoning, and perceptual vigilance. The student must pay attention to detail, differentiating the essential from nonessential detail.

- **Coding:** A timed paper-and-pencil task. The student replicates a specific code pattern, which provides a measure of the speed of learning and of the ability to solve problems involving spatial relationships. Measures the ability to work well under pressure and dexterity in eye–hand coordination.

- **Picture Arrangement:** The student arranges a series of pictures into a sequence so that they tell a sensible story. Measures visual–perceptual skill, social understanding, sequencing ability, cause-and-effect relationships, and integration of thinking. Student is required to look at parts and organize it into a coherent whole.

(continued)

Figure 1-5

- **Block Design:** The student arranges blocks to duplicate a two-dimensional design. Measures abstract thinking and nonverbal problem-solving. Student uses visuospatial skills to analyze a pattern into component parts. This task requires self-management and self-correction. It is usually correlated with general intelligence.
- **Object Assembly:** A timed task. Students are required to put the pieces of a puzzle together without prior knowledge of the topic. Measures visual–motor skills and the ability to distinguish the whole from its parts. Shows the ability to plan and organize one's approach. Requires visuospatial analysis and synthesis.
- **Symbol Search:** A timed test. The student is provided with a symbol and is required to scan a line of symbols to find a match to the designated symbol. Measures speed of information processing, visual-motor coordination, and spatial visualization.
- **Mazes:** Measures fine-motor skills, coordination, planning abilities, and problem-solving abilities (optional subtest).

is the best approach to teaching a student with LD. The strengths of the student with LD and/or ADHD can be considered his or her learning style.

Strictly speaking, we all have our own learning styles. Visual learners need to see things written down or in graph form before fully understanding them. Auditory learners prefer to listen to new information rather than read it. Depending on their strengths, students with ADHD and/or LD need a specific type of input when they are learning new information.

In addition to preferred input, students with ADHD and/or LD also have their own styles of processing information. Some are global thinkers who need to see the whole picture before they begin to learn the details involved. Sequential processors prefer to begin with the first piece of information and gradually add to it until the picture is completed. Still others, analytical processors, like to be presented with the whole picture and then break it down into its component parts. In addition to a student's preferred way of receiving information, learning is also affected by his or her learning environment and emotional and physical needs. (See Figure 1-6.)

Many students with ADHD and/or LD cannot learn at all using a sequential approach because they don't know to what they are building. Other students may not do well with an analytic approach because they are too disorganized. Many students, particularly those with visual and visuospatial strengths and verbal weaknesses, first need to see the whole picture. Some students who are visual learners have reading problems because they have language problems. These students also may need graphic organizers to help them organize and remember what they have read. Graphic organizers can also help these students with writing assignments. (See Figure 1-7.)

The psychologist's recommendations should include suggestions for you about how to adapt the learning environment of your classroom and your instructional methods in order to help these students learn.

Learning Styles

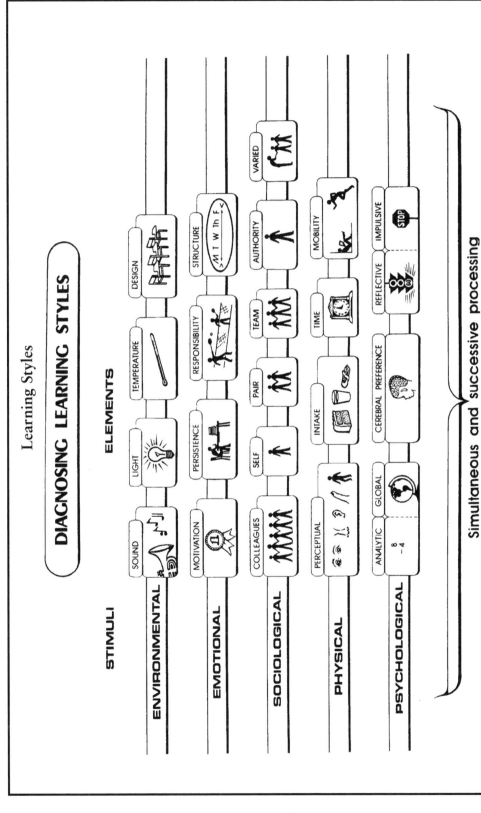

DIAGNOSING LEARNING STYLES

STIMULI

ELEMENTS

ENVIRONMENTAL — SOUND · LIGHT · TEMPERATURE · DESIGN

EMOTIONAL — MOTIVATION · PERSISTENCE · RESPONSIBILITY · STRUCTURE

SOCIOLOGICAL — COLLEAGUES · SELF · PAIR · TEAM · AUTHORITY · VARIED

PHYSICAL — PERCEPTUAL · INTAKE · TIME · MOBILITY

PSYCHOLOGICAL — ANALYTIC / GLOBAL · CEREBRAL PREFERENCE · REFLECTIVE / IMPULSIVE

Simultaneous and successive processing

Figure 1-6

From Carbo, M., Dunn, R., & Dunn, K., *Teaching Students to Read Through Their Individual Learning Styles* © 1991 by Allyn & Bacon. Reprinted by permission.

Academic Difficulties of Student with ADHD

Listening and Speaking

- Mishears, misunderstands
- Doesn't listen to what others are saying
- Interrupts
- Talks excessively
- Inappropriate verbalizations (e.g., tongue clicking, humming)

Reading

- Skips words, sentences, lines of text
- Loses place
- Difficulty remembering what was read
- Slow reading rate

Arithmetic

- Incomplete mastery of basic facts such as addition or multiplication tables
- Confuses symbols and formulas
- Difficulty sequencing steps when problem-solving
- Many careless mistakes

Time

- Dawdles, often late to class or to school
- Poor time management (e.g., doesn't leave enough time to complete tasks)
- Procrastination: late to begin long-term projects or papers
- Assignments handed in late or not turned in at all
- Needs more time with transitions and to settle into new situations
- May only be able to produce when "under the gun" and in fear of failing

Memory/Cognition

- Poor short-term, working, and long-term memory
- Difficulty remembering oral directions
- Frequently loses things (e.g., pencils, assignments, books, keys)
- Doesn't anticipate and plan
- Doesn't prioritize (effort allocation)

(continued)

Figure 1-7

Written Expression

- Copies incorrectly from the board
- Stream of consciousness writing
- Poor punctuation
- Poor sentence structure including run-on sentences, incomplete sentences
- Poor paragraph construction including lack of a main idea
- Poor organization (e.g., lack of logical sequence of paragraphs)
- Lack of clear statements including main idea or summary
- Omits words
- Slow writing or copying

Social/Emotional

- Easily angered, frustrated
- Becomes overexcited, has difficulty settling down
- Is frequently teased
- Has few friends
- Inappropriate social interactions
- Anxious, stressed about school
- Poor judgment
- Perfectionism
- Can't inhibit behavior when he/she should
- Frequent physical complaints including headaches, stomach pains, etc.
- Unable to modulate reactions to others

Motor Activities

- Fidgets, makes noise, stretches, taps desk, often out of seat
- Unable to navigate around school or neighborhood, gets lost
- Accident prone
- Inappropriate gestures, grimaces
- Intrudes into others' private space

Test-Taking

- Misreads directions
- Doesn't read all options
- Selects the first answer that seems right; doesn't check other answers
- Has difficulty working under time pressure

TEACHER ROLES IN THE DIAGNOSIS AND SUPPORT OF STUDENTS WITH ADHD AND/OR LD

Even though you do not have to know how to administer most of the evaluations that are used, you have a strong role in diagnosis. Part of your role in the referral process is to give the school psychologist a list of your concerns and observations. Asking the parents and the student to list their concerns is also important. The two main questions to ask the psychologist are: "What are the primary reasons for this behavior?" and "How does this student learn best?"

Your role in the evaluation process is to contribute your professional observations and opinions, and collect samples of the student's work that can illustrate your observations. It is also important to collect work samples that illustrate how well the student can work in certain situations. Remember, the psychologist only spends a few hours with the student. You have a wealth of information to contribute.

You can discover important information about the student's perceptions of the problems by asking the student such questions as:

- What is the easiest and most difficult part of this course?
- Do you understand the material? If not, what parts did you find difficult?
- Do you have problems taking tests? What are they?
- Do you have problems completing your homework? What are they?
- Do you think the textbook is difficult or easy to read? Why?
- When and under what conditions are you the most successful?
- Do you have difficulties with writing? What are they?

You could also give the student a commercially prepared self-evaluation questionnaire to complete (e.g., Levine, 1997).

Observe the student as he or she works on an academic task in your classroom. Also observe the student in another class to see how the student behaves in a different setting. One of the goals of the observations is to discover the conditions under which the student works best (and most poorly). You can also observe how the student attacks a task or deals with frustration. Behavior checklists and rating scales can help you report the student's behavior in a more systematic way.

You also have a strong role in developing Individualized Educational Plans (IEPs) and 504 Plans for students with disabilities in your class. (See Chapter 7 on developing appropriate IEPs and 504 Plans.) However, your most important responsibility is to translate psychoeducational evaluations and recommendations into appropriate teaching strategies.

In order to fulfill your role effectively, you will need to become familiar with the names and general purposes of the most common diagnostic tests and understand how to interpret the results. You should expect the psychologist to explain test results and to make recommendations as to how you should proceed. But if things are not clear, you must question the psychologist at length regarding test results.

When going over the results of ability testing, it is important to remember that tests such as the WISC-III do not measure such attributes as creativity and motivation. A student who scores relatively low in an area may have the motivation and persistence to overcome the challenges he or she faces. A highly creative student may not do well at all because the answers he or she gives may not fit the "correct" answers upon which the test has been normed.

Standardized achievement tests don't always measure the things you consider important or focus on the types of responses you feel are adequate. Standardized tests are good for comparing a student with a national sample of students in the same grade. For in-depth measurement of a student's achievement, your own evaluation instruments—based on the content you have taught—may be the best measures of achievement.

If the student has a language problem, the tests may not be a good measurement of either ability or achievement because students have to have good auditory processing and expressive language skills to answer the test questions. The same holds true if the student is a slow processor and responds slowly to the questions. This student will do badly on timed tests even though he or she may be quite bright.

Terry's Diagnosis

Terry is a tenth-grade student at a small alternative high school. He has poor grades including D's and E's. He says that he is a very slow reader. He also says that he has attentional difficulties. Terry is currently in psychological treatment for depression.

The psychologist reports that Terry's level of intellect falls in the high-average range (IQ Full Scale Score 115) eighty-fifth percentile, including average-range verbal scores and superior performance scores. Academic achievement levels generally fall within the average range with a significant discrepancy between level of intellect and reading and written expression. His ability as measured by the WISC-III and his achievement as measured by the WIAT are as follows:

- *WISC-III Verbal and Performance Tests*

Information	10	Picture Completion	11
Similarities	12	Coding	12
Arithmetic	12	Picture Arrangement	11
Vocabulary	11	Block Design	17
Comprehension	11	Object Assembly	15
Digit Span	12	Symbol Search	16

- *Summary of WIAT Subtests and Composite Scores*

	%ile	Grade Equivalent
Spelling	30	7.3
Reading Comprehension	32	7.1
Numerical Operations	66	10.4
Written Expression	25	6.9
Writing	23	7.2

Although he is in the tenth grade, Terry's achievement level is around seventh grade, around the thirtieth percentile, except for Numerical Operations. (There are significant discrepancies between the results of the WISC-III [Ability] and the WIAT [Achievement]).

According to the report, "There are no indications of significant ADHD features. Processing speed generally falls within the superior range. Significant strengths were noted in the nonverbal sphere throughout the evaluation." However, the psychologist notes that Terry's psychological/behavioral profile supports the need for ongoing therapy for depression.

Terry has learning disabilities in both written expression and reading. His attention and processing difficulties are secondary to his depression. Terry's grades in school are a reflection of his LD and his depression. These affect all his courses, since all require reading, writing, and concentration for academic success.

William's Diagnosis

William is also a tenth-grade student. He attends a large urban high school and has a summer job as a swimming instructor. He is currently failing a number of subjects because of missing or incomplete assignments and poor test grades. Like Terry, William also reports that he has problems with attention.

The neuropsychologist reports that William's level of intellect includes a high-average verbal score (113) and an average performance score (99). His academic achievement levels fall generally in the average range. His WISC-III and WIAT are as follows:

- *WISC-III Verbal and Performance Subtest Scores*

Information	14	Picture Completion	13
Similarities	14	Coding	5
Arithmetic	12	Picture Arrangement	9
Vocabulary	11	Block Design	10
Comprehension	10	Object Assembly	12
Digit Span	10	Symbol Search	8

- *Summary of WIAT Subtests and Composite Scores*

	%ile	Grade Equivalent
Spelling	45	8.6
Reading Comprehension	42	11.3
Numerical Operations	73	12.5
Written Expression	70	12.9
Writing	58	11.0

Several WISC-III composite scores indicated problems with memory. The Kaufman composite, Freedom from Distractibility, indicated problems with attention. The results of the Test of Variables of Attention (TOVA) also indicated that William had problems with attention.

The psychologist continues, "The profile does indicate attentional difficulties including slow processing speed (TOVA), significant variability in response time on a continuous performance test (TOVA), and aspects of memory falling significantly lower than would be predicted from level of intellect." Parents' ratings of behavior and attention are also consistent with ADHD.

Although William is capable of above-grade-level achievement in a nondistracting, one-on-one situation, his ADHD greatly affects his functioning in a class situation.

Further testing indicates that William has "a discrepancy between impaired memory for discrete verbal information (e.g., word lists) and relatively intact memory for verbal material in context (e.g., stories). This is commonly observed in individuals with attentional difficulties and is tied to the role of attentional processes in memory." William has ADHD. He does not have LD.

In reporting the findings of psychological evaluation, the evaluator must state whether or not, in his or her judgment, the test is a valid assessment of the student. The evaluator also reports on his or her observations of the student. Generally you would expect to see "He remained focused throughout the evaluation. He was alert with good endurance. He was cooperative and put forth good effort. In general, results are believed to be an accurate reflection of current levels of functioning."

In the case of students with ADHD and/or LD, the evaluator often states that the results of the WISC-III are underestimates of the student's ability. The test scores are strongly affected by attention, slow processing, emotional states such as depression, and auditory and expressive language functioning.

If the student cannot maintain focus, he or she will not be able to answer correctly. If the student processes information slowly, he or she will not be able to answer in a timely fashion. If the student has language problems, he or she will not be able to fully understand the questions and directions and/or have difficulty responding correctly.

Comments such as the following mean that the test results are probably an underestimation of the student's ability: "During this evaluation he was fidgety, restless, hyper verbal (he was unable to refrain from interrupting, going off on verbal tangents, making editorial comments about the testing process). His performance was inhibited by his excessive mental activation and free flight of ideas."

LEARNING DISABILITIES

By definition, students with ADHD and Learning Disabilities have at least average intelligence. Some are quite gifted. These students all have the ability to learn, but they may learn "differently." These students have difficulty learning in more traditional classroom settings, such as:

- Large group instruction
- A lot of independent seat work
- Noisy rooms
- Lecture format
- Paper-and-pencil tests as the primary basis for grading

Although most people believe there is only one definition of Learning Disabilities (the definition found in IDEA), there are several fully accepted definitions of Learning Disabilities. These are the definitions developed by: the National Joint Committee on Learning Disabilities (NJCLD), the Interagency Committee on Learning Disabilities (ICLD), and the American Psychiatric Association in their Diagnostic and Statistical Manual of Mental Disorders IV (DSM-IV). Thought generally similar, these definitions vary somewhat from the definition of LD found in IDEA.

The IDEA 1997 definition of Learning Disabilities is:

"A disorder in one or more of the basic psychological processes involved in understanding or using language, spoken or written, that may manifest itself in imperfect ability to listen, think, speak, read, write, spell, or to do mathematical calculations. The term includes such conditions as perceptual handicaps, brain injury, minimal brain dysfunction, dyslexia, and developmental aphasia. The term does not include a learning problem which is primarily the result of visual, hearing, or motor handicaps, of mental retardation, of emotional disturbance, or of environmental, cultural or economic disadvantage."

The second part of the definition states that the student must be in need of special education services. The student who is to be served under IDEA must meet both parts of the definition.

The law refers to a "severe discrepancy" between ability (or potential) and achievement in order to make the determination of LD, but does not specify what is "a severe discrepancy." Thus, the definition of severe discrepancy can vary from state to state.

The NJCLD definition of LD includes problems in self-regulatory behaviors, social perception, and social interaction, as part of the significant difficulties the student may have in the acquisition and use of listening, speaking, reading, writing, reasoning, or mathematical skills. The NJCLD definition goes on to say that learning disabilities may occur with other disabilities such as emotional impairment. LD is presumed to be related to central nervous system dysfunction.

The ICLD definition of learning disabilities is similar to the NJCLD definition and also includes social disabilities.

The DSM-IV includes Reading Disorder, Mathematics Disorder, and Disorder of Written Expression under the definition of Learning Disorders. In addition, the DSM-IV—under the definition of Communication Disorder—defines Expressive Language Disorder, Mixed Receptive–Expressive Language Disorder, Stuttering, and Phonological Disorder.

In the DSM-IV, a student is considered as having a Learning Disorder if his or her achievement, as measured on standardized tests, is substantially below that expected for age, schooling, and level of intelligence and the learning problem interferes with academic achievement or activities of daily living. "Substantially below" is generally defined as a discrepancy of two standard deviations between ability and achievement.

Other definitions of learning disabilities refer to significant discrepancies between the verbal and performance scores on the WISC-III or between subtest scores on the WISC-III. A 12-point or greater discrepancy between performance and verbal scores is considered significant. A discrepancy of nine or more points among the subtests is also significant. Such discrepancies are observed in the profile of Marilyn, a high school senior. (See Figure 1-8.)

Graph of Marilyn's WAIS-III Subtest Scores

WAIS-III

Full Scale IQ Score: 109

Verbal Tests
Verbal IQ Score: 100

Performance Tests
Performance IQ Score: 121

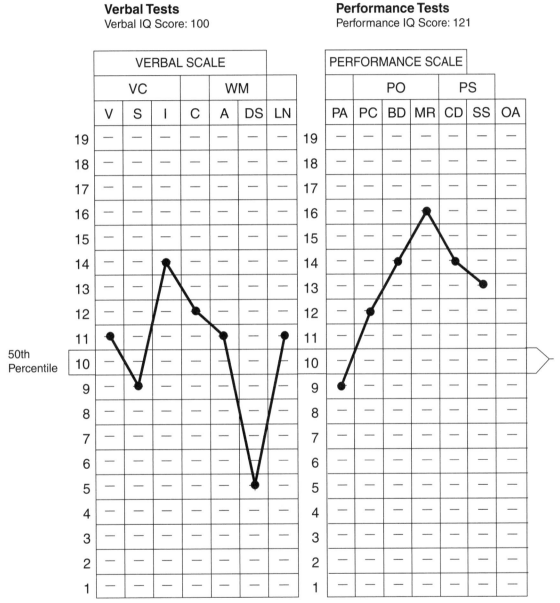

Figure 1-8

Academic Difficulties of
Students with Learning Disabilities

Listening and Speaking

- Difficulty understanding oral language
- Does not remember numbers or words in sequence
- Confusion between like-sounding words
- Fails to grasp word meanings
- Problems following verbal directions
- Inability to select or understand main ideas from oral conversation or lectures
- Problems in expressing ideas in understandable ways (e.g., language mumbled, starts and stops in mid sentence)
- Word-retrieval difficulties
- Slow processing
- Cannot relate a story in proper sequence
- Cannot listen and take notes simultaneously

Reading

- Slow reading rate
- Poor comprehension
- Poor retention
- Difficulty locating main ideas and themes
- Poor vocabulary
- Difficulty decoding words, poor mastery of phonics
- Confusion of similar sounding/looking words

Arithmetic

- Incomplete mastery of basic facts such as addition or multiplication tables
- Understands how to solve problems but makes many careless mistakes
- Copies numbers and signs incorrectly or reverses sequences of numbers
- Difficulty solving story problems because of reading difficulties
- Disorganized approach to solving problems
- Confuses symbols and formulas
- Poor retention of rules and formulas
- Difficulty remembering sequence of a process

(continued)

Figure 1-9

- Can do math in his or her head but can't write it down
- Does better with higher order (e.g., concepts, application) than lower level problems (e.g., rote learning)

Time

- Poor grasp of time, often late, dawdles
- Difficulty moving from one task or activity to another
- Procrastinates
- Poor planning, prioritizing
- Does not allow enough time to complete tasks

Memory

- Difficulty with retention of information
- Poor retrieval skills
- May have better short-term than long-term memory skills or vice versa
- Inconsistent according to type of material (e.g., may not be good at remembering dates but can remember faces)
- Poor visual or auditory memory

Written Expression

- Slow writing
- Poor spelling
- Poor sentence structure including run-on sentences, incomplete sentences
- Poor paragraph construction including lack of a main idea
- Poor organization (e.g., lack of logical sequence of paragraphs)
- Lack of clear statements including main idea or summary

Social/Emotional

- Unable to discriminate or understand nonverbal behavior (e.g., gestures, facial expressions, symbols)
- Poor social judgment, doesn't learn from experience
- Problems discriminating or understanding social discourse, humor, or changes in tone of voice
- Poor awareness of own feelings
- Insensitive to others' feelings, lack of empathy

(continued)

- May be excluded, rejected, lonely
- May be rigid and inflexible: can't deal with alternatives, nonroutine events

Visual–Motor

- Difficulty copying words from the board
- Slow writing
- Poor penmanship; poorly formed letters, inappropriate size
- Poor memory for visual material
- Gets lost
- Poor spatial judgment

Test-Taking

- Cannot read directions or the questions
- Slow processing
- Cannot remember facts or formulas
- Slow writing of essay questions

Although many students have these discrepancies—and these discrepancies by themselves do not constitute evidence of a Learning Disability under IDEA—they are warning flags that the student may have LD.

Most students with learning disabilities have underlying language problems. A large percentage of these students have a history of delayed or atypical language development. However, some students with reading disabilities have underlying visual-processing problems. They may have difficulty remembering the shapes of letters and words. They may have problems with visual tracking. These types of problems are largely correctable as students get older. Language-based problems are harder to overcome. (See Figure 1-9.)

Difficulties with visual–motor or visuospatial skills often go hand-in-hand with learning disabilities. Students with these difficulties may write very slowly and illegibly, make many mistakes when copying assignments from the chalkboard, and have great difficulty taking notes during lectures. These types of writing problems differ in nature from problems with expressing thoughts, opinions, and ideas in written form.

Whenever a student who you think is bright is underachieving, you should suspect learning disabilities. Whenever you face a student who is particularly disruptive or emotionally impaired, the student should be tested for underlying learning or language disabilities. (See Figure 1-10.)

Once again, you need to remember that Learning Disabilities manifest themselves differently in different individuals. Although two students may both have dyslexia, they may have it to varying degrees. One may be four or more grades behind in reading. The other may be reading near grade level, but very slowly. The response of these students to having

---

Warning Signs of Learning Disabilities

- Bright student, low achievement test scores
- Large differences among course grades in different subjects
- Poor performance in reading-dependent subjects; better in science and math
- Discrepancy among student's grades and the amount of effort the student exerts
- Decline in performance as student progresses in school
- Spending an unusually long time on homework
- History of retention in grade
- Preschool language disorders, even if corrected
- Procrastination
- Psychosomatic disorders
- Acting-out behavior
- Refusal to go to school
- Problems with basic skills: spelling, grammar, punctuation, calculation

---

Figure 1-10

dyslexia may vary. One may be quite self-aware of his weaknesses and strengths. The other may try to hide his dyslexia and not want any special help. Teaching strategies that may work for one may not work for the other.

Students with learning disabilities may also have problems with executive functioning. They can have difficulties with time management, working memory, planning, and organization.

Prevalence

While the DSM-IV reports the prevalence of what they call Learning Disorders as between 2 to 10 percent of the school-age population, estimates of prevalence range between 3 to 30 percent. At this time, most professionals agree on a 10- to 12-percent prevalence rate.

LANGUAGE DISABILITIES

There is a large overlap between LD and language disabilities. Language disabilities can affect both academic and social behavior. Students with language disorders frequently have problems with reading comprehension and written expression and these, in turn, can affect all of their academic subjects.

More specifically, students with expressive language disorders have difficulty expressing ideas verbally and/or in written form. They may have difficulties with word retrieval. They may have difficulty answering questions in class and may need additional time to formulate answers. Their writing is similarly affected. They write little, often in incomplete sentences with little punctuation and poor grammar.

Auditory processing problems can present even more formidable obstacles to learning. These problems can affect how students understand the world around them. Students with auditory processing problems may have difficulty understanding or remembering verbal instructions, and have difficulty following other verbal material such as lectures and discussions. They may have difficulty answering questions in class because they don't understand or remember the questions. It may take a student with an auditory processing problem such a long time to process auditory information that, while the teacher continues to talk, the student is still trying to decipher what the teacher said previously.

Language disabilities can also present barriers to the natural development of social interaction and conversational skills. Students with language disabilities may:

- Have difficulty "getting" jokes.
- Misinterpret what another person is saying and react inappropriately.
- Have difficulty expressing emotions verbally.
- Have frequent misunderstandings with their friends and family.
- Have few friends.
- Be quick to anger.

CENTRAL AUDITORY PROCESSING DISORDER

Students with Central Auditory Processing Disorder (CAPD) may develop behavior problems because they perceive the world as chaotic and unpredictable due to their difficulties with language. These students appear to respond to all sounds equally, whether speech or background noise. They have difficulty making sense out of what they hear. They can misinterpret what others are saying. They may have problems with reading due to their difficulty with sounds. Because they have difficulty with auditory processing, they may give up trying to decipher what is being said and appear inattentive.

Students with CAPD often have problems with sensory integration. They may have problems with tactile defensiveness, in which touch can cause discomfort, or imbalance, due to problems in the vestibular system of the inner ear.

A student with CAPD might have a borderline or low-average Verbal Score and a high-average or superior Performance Score on the WISC-III.

NONVERBAL LEARNING DISABILITIES

Nonverbal Learning Disabilities are essentially disabilities related to self-awareness and social interaction. Although it would seem that these disabilities have little to do with academic success, the contrary is true. These subtle but serious disabilities can affect academic as well as social functioning. (See Figure 1-11.)

Nonverbal Learning Disabilities

Language and Cognition

- Poor pragmatic speech
- Difficulty understanding abstractions, tend to be concrete thinkers
- Impaired memory for visual material
- Difficulty with visualization
- Difficulty seeing "the big picture"
- Poorly modulated tone of voice and fluency

Social/Emotional

- Difficulty interpreting facial expressions
- Difficulty expressing feeling
- Difficulty adapting to novel and complex situations
- Difficulty appreciating humor and incongruities
- Social withdrawal
- Unaware of own feelings
- Poor social judgment and social problem-solving skills
- Poor social interaction skills
- Difficulty picking up nonverbal social cues
- Difficulty integrating or learning from past experiences
- Unaware and invasive of others' personal space
- Difficulty establishing and maintaining friendships
- Difficulty recognizing faces
- Frequently excluded
- Frequently thought of as obnoxious; frequently teased
- Frequently interrupts
- Can't take turns

Academic Behavior

- Overreliance on rote behaviors
- Difficulty understanding subtleties and implications when reading/listening
- Difficulty with cause and effect
- Poor visual/spatial organization
- Difficulty analyzing and predicting events and behavior

(continued)

Figure 1–11

Perceptual Motor

- Abnormalities in tactile perception, body orientation
- Poor psychomotor coordination
- Difficulty in creative thinking, imagination, idea generation

---

OVERLAPPING DISABILITIES

Many of these disabilities overlap. Since some of the symptoms overlap, it is sometimes difficult to ascertain whether a student has Central Auditory Processing Disorder or Nonverbal Learning Disabilities or whether a student has dyslexia or a language disability. These distinctions are important because the treatment can vary depending on the student's problem. However, it is possible to distinguish what the underlying disability is through careful observation and evaluation.

If it is determined that the student has a language disability, the student is eligible to receive special education services under Speech or Language Impaired.

When assessing a student who is thought to be emotionally impaired, it is important to include an assessment for learning disabilities. A large percentage of students who are diagnosed as emotionally impaired have been found to have underlying learning or language disabilities. Students with LD should be tested for ADHD—over half the students with LD have ADHD. Since a major depression can masquerade as LD, and since some students with LD and/or ADHD become depressed or anxious, it is important to assess the student's emotional status.

One of the most important things to remember is that, more often than not, you cannot attribute the student's difficulties to only one source, such as emotional impairment, ADHD, or "poor parenting." It is not an either/or situation (e.g., LD or EI). Students frequently have several problems (e.g., ADHD *and* ODD) and each problem must be addressed.

MULTIPLE CHALLENGES: ADOLESCENCE AND ADHD AND/OR LD

During adolescence students confront greater academic challenges, often at a faster pace. Adolescents find themselves in a new type of school environment, one that is more impersonal and more demanding. Academic, social, and emotional expectations and pressures increase—often without the necessary increase in social judgment, study skills, and problem-solving ability on the part of the student.

Adolescents can become enmeshed in the battle between their wish for autonomy and their need for some type of guidance and control. They strive for independence while being dependent on the emotional and financial support of their parents and the guidance of their teachers. While they are developing a new grown-up identity, they may not want to give up the comforting aspects of childhood.

This same independence/dependence battle explains, in part, the decline of school grades and the increase in teacher perception of "behavior problems." It may appear as if the adolescent student is saying: "I'll only do what I feel like doing."

Because adolescents increasingly identify with peers, the influence of adults is further lessened. Peer pressure assumes a greater influence in their lives than ever before, often exasperating both parent and teacher.

Thrown into this mix is the adolescent's need for acceptance and a sense of belonging in the face of large, impersonal, middle schools and high schools.

ADHD and/or LD make adolescence a more challenging, sometimes overwhelming, experience. Both of these disabilities can interfere with the accomplishment of the normal developmental tasks of adolescence. Students with LD and/or ADHD are generally less mature emotionally than students without these learning problems. Their sense of acceptance by peers, parents, and teachers may have been eroded long ago. Their self-esteem may have been similarly eroded.

Already suffering the pangs of adolescence, the insecurities and difficulties of these students are compounded by constant reprimands for behaviors they can't seem to control, even when they try. It is not uncommon to hear one of these students say plaintively: "What have I done now?"

Poverty and minority status have strong effects on adolescent behavior. An "at risk" adolescent is faced with a much more difficult challenge than the "average" adolescent.

Many adolescents falter under the onslaught. In middle school we can see a decline in grades, academic motivation, and self-esteem, and a temporary increase in family conflict.

However, this is not true of all adolescents. Research tells us that adolescents, even "at risk" adolescents, can weather the years between 11 and 18 quite well if they:

- Attend quality schools.
- Receive stable care from a competent adult.
- Are involved in church and/or other community activities.
- Have good learning and problem-solving abilities.
- Are involved in school activities.
- Feel that their effort and hard work can make a difference.

As we can see, quality schools are at the top of the list. Schools and teachers can make a great deal of difference in an adolescent's life. We sell ourselves short when we think that there is little we can do to help these students.

A FINAL WORD

Let us try to answer some of Mr. Briggs's questions from the beginning of this chapter. Several answers are quite simple. No, spitting on another student and cursing are not symptoms of ADHD. Although impulsiveness *is* a symptom of ADHD, the student can be held accountable for what he or she actually says.

The behaviors that should be ignored are behaviors not under the control of the student at this time *if* they are relatively minor. Such behaviors might include jiggling, rocking, talking to oneself, etc. If a behavior not under the student's control cannot be ignored, the student must be taught the appropriate behavior. (See Chapter 8, Behavioral Interventions.)

A student's constant refusal to do the work should be investigated by the teacher to determine the cause. Is the work too difficult? Is the student depressed? Does the student have other learning problems? The teacher can turn to the special education staff or the counselor for help in answering these questions. The student may need additional support from special education staff to function appropriately in the classroom. The same thing holds true if a student constantly disrupts the classroom or bothers the other students while the teacher is trying to teach.

The laws state that the amount of time the teacher spends individualizing for a student with LD should be "reasonable" and not cause "undue hardship" for the teacher. Although the specifics of these terms are undefined, the teacher is clearly protected against spending too much time on one student with ADHD and/or LD.

The reaction of other students to the uncontrolled or inappropriate behavior of a student with ADHD and/or LD depends on the classroom climate the teacher has developed. If the teacher is understanding of weaknesses, and values each student's contribution to the class, the other students will behave similarly.

ADHD and LD often mask a student's strengths. We are so focused on the student's weaknesses and needs that it is hard to believe that a student who has such difficulty in school could also have many areas of strengths. One of the most important things we can do as teachers is to uncover the strengths of these students and nurture them. We can help these students take pride in their strengths and help the other students respect the student with ADHD and/or LD for the things he or she *can* do.

Students with LD and/or ADHD may not learn in traditional ways, but they can learn. It is up to us as teachers to help them find the way.

CHAPTER TWO

Understanding Legal Requirements

There are many students in my class who need extra help. I do the best I can. I don't have time to individualize for everyone.

—Middle school teacher

We can't help him because he doesn't meet the definition of Learning Disabilities.

—High school teacher

I refuse to put up with this student's constant disruptions!

—Middle school teacher

The teachers are already giving him extra help. Why do we need to be so formal? The teachers will think you are criticizing if you insist on having a 504 Plan.

—Middle school principal

I don't care what the assessments say, this student is just plain lazy. It's not fair to help him when I have other students in my class who need help more.

—High school teacher

How can I help the other students who also have learning problems but who don't qualify for Special Education services?

—High school teacher

Teachers and principals care about the students in their school and want them to be successful. But many often do not understand the laws governing the provision of services to students with disabilities. This is understandable. The laws are complex and are often not written clearly. Laws are also interpreted differently by different school districts.

It is important, however, that you understand these laws just as it is important that you understand the disabilities of some of your students. The attitudes, concerns, and questions quoted above illustrate the difficulties some teachers and principals have in understanding what the laws require of them when it comes to educating students with disabilities.

MAJOR LAWS DEALING WITH STUDENTS' DISABILITIES

Students with disabilities are protected by three major federal laws: the Individuals with Disabilities Education Act (IDEA), Section 504 of the Vocational Rehabilitation Act of 1973, and the Americans with Disabilities Act (ADA). The ADA and Section 504 are largely the same; however, in planning educational programs for children with disabilities, we generally refer to Section 504.

In addition to the federal laws, each state has a special education law that echoes or exceeds federal law. Federal and state guidelines memoranda and policy statements provide further clarification of the laws. As with any laws, these laws are open to interpretation. There is a large body of case law that seeks to define, more specifically, the rights and responsibilities of schools, parents, and students.

Mandating the provision of special education services to students with disabilities is a relatively new concept. Federal and state special education laws went into effect in the mid 1970s. However, the full implementation of these laws often took many years. Section 504 was ignored for almost twenty years and only now is being implemented. Very few school personnel or parents are aware of this law or the school's responsibilities for educating the student with a disability under this law.

All of these laws were written to help "normalize" the lives of people with disabilities. The Education for All Handicapped Act (EHA) of 1971 was written because children with disabilities were largely excluded from school and were often confined to institutions. This law mandated that these children be provided an education at public expense. Section 504 banned discrimination against people with disabilities. These laws helped parents move disabled children back into their homes where they could now be assured of an education, a chance to work, and a chance to participate in all life's activities.

These benefits hold true for students with learning disabilities (LD) and/or attention deficit hyperactivity disorder (ADHD). Before the laws were passed, these students were either in general education classes where they failed or in special classes or separate schools with children who were retarded or seriously emotionally disturbed. Half of them dropped out of school.

Today, most of these students are beginning to succeed in ways we thought impossible two decades ago. The federal and state laws have made all the difference.

UNDERLYING PREMISES OF IDEA
AND SECTION 504

There are three major premises in both IDEA and Section 504, underlying the school's responsibility for the education of a student with disabilities. These are: (1) a free appropriate public education (FAPE), (2) an individualized education program (IEP), and (3) placement in the least restrictive environment (LRE).

Free Appropriate Public Education (FAPE)

All students with disabilities are entitled to a FAPE. This means that the student's public school education—with its attendant aids and services—must be free of charge, appropriate for the student's needs, and provide enough support to the student so that he or she can progress in school. In cases where there is disagreement between school and parents, a Hearing Officer may be called in to help define exactly what an appropriate educational program is for that particular student. Most of the disagreements between parents and schools hinge on the "appropriateness" of the student's education.

Some states, notably Michigan, state that special education and related services are provided to help the student reach his or her "maximum potential." Because it may result in greatly increased financial burden for the schools and because "maximum potential" is so difficult to define, this phrase will probably be eliminated as amendments are made to existing laws.

Individualized Education Program (IEP)

Individualization was a startling concept when EHA and Section 504 were first passed. Individualization recognized the fact that all students are not the same, that each student has a different pattern of strengths and weaknesses, and that there are many different learning styles. Although the curriculum and syllabus are the same for every student in the class, the instructional methods and materials the teacher uses are individualized based on student needs.

Least Restrictive Environment (LRE)

Special Education law makes a strong statement regarding placement, which is echoed by Section 504: Students are to be educated to the maximum extent feasible in general education settings with their nonhandicapped peers. This is called the "least restrictive environment." Any removal from the general education classroom can be done only if the student cannot, with supports and services and accommodations, profit from the general education classroom.

This strong thrust toward general education placement does not mean that all students with disabilities must be educated in the general education classroom all the time. The placement and program must be appropriate for the particular student.

The reason for the strong commitment to placing these students in general education class is twofold. There was (and still is) a questionable overrepresentation of African American and Hispanic students, especially boys from any background in special education classes, removed from the mainstream.

Research demonstrates that students with disabilities make more progress both socially and academically in general education classes than they do in special education classes. If these students are to function in the mainstream of the community, they need to learn how to function in the mainstream of school.

In the past too many students were removed from the mainstream because their teachers found them disturbing or considered them too difficult to teach. Preservice teachers were taught that students with disabilities would be "better off" in special education classes with teachers specifically trained to help them. In the last 25 years, as our knowledge about these students has continued to grow, we have learned more about their ability to learn and more about how to teach them.

Today, more than 85 percent of students with disabilities are educated in the mainstream. Unfortunately, many students are just "dumped" in the general education classroom with no support, regardless of the appropriateness of the placement.

TEN MAJOR PROVISIONS OF THE INDIVIDUALS WITH DISABILITIES EDUCATION ACT (IDEA)

IDEA was designed to meet the educational needs of students with disabilities. Specific categories of disabilities are defined and students must meet eligibility requirements. (See Figure 2-1.)

IDEA is a comprehensive and complex law. It is not necessary to know every detail unless disagreement arises. What is important to understand is the *spirit* of IDEA: It was written to help children with disabilities receive a good education.

The ten major provisions are:

1. An individualized education program (IEP) must be developed for each eligible student based on the student's particular needs and strengths.

2. A multidisciplinary evaluation team (MET) comprised of teachers, school psychologists, school social workers, and parents meets to examine various types of information about the student in order to make a recommendation regarding the student's eligibility. Information must be gathered from various sources: observation, testing, teacher and parent reports, and outside evaluations.

3. The IEP team—consisting of, at the least, an administrator responsible for the provision of general and/or special education services, a general classroom teacher, a person who can translate evaluation data into teaching strategies, and a parent—meets to develop the IEP for the eligible student. The committee considers the recommendation of the MET and determines if additional information is needed. Other persons such as an occupational therapist or a family advocate can be invited to the meeting at the discretion of the school and the parents. All decisions are made by the IEP team, generally by consensus.

There are two parts to meeting eligibility requirements. It is not enough to prove that the student has a disability. IDEA also requires that the student with a disability must

---

Disability Categories Included in IDEA

- Autism
- Mental Retardation
- Emotional Disturbance
- Specific Learning Disability
- Traumatic Brain Injury
- Visual Impairment

- Hearing Impairment
- Orthopedic Impairment
- Other Health Impairment
- Speech and Language Impairment
- Developmental Delay
- Multiple Disabilities

Figure 2-1

be "in need of special education services." Section 504 states that the disability the student has must "substantially limit one of life's major activities."

4. A Behavioral Support Plan, based on a functional assessment of student behavior, must be developed for a student whose behavior interferes with learning.

5. A continuum of alternative educational placements—which ranges from full-time placement in the general education class with a minimum of special education and/or related services to full-time placement in a special school—must be available to the student. However, the least restrictive environment must be considered in every placement decision.

6. The full participation of parents in the IEP process must be ensured. Parents are to speak for the child. If parents are not available, a surrogate can be appointed who can serve *in loco parentis* in the development of the educational program.

7. The IEP must include a description of the student's current functioning, how the student's disability interferes with his or her progress in the general education class, the amount and type of special services and supports the school will provide, and measurable goals and short-term objectives that are monitored regularly to ensure student progress. The IEP is carried out by both special and general education staff.

8. Accommodations, or program modifications in the general education classroom, are listed in the student's IEP. In IDEA, accommodations are listed under "Supplemental Aids and Services in the General Education Classroom." These accommodations must be "reasonable" and not cause "undue hardship" to the school or teacher. This is usually translated as meaning that the accommodations must not be too costly or require too much of the teacher's time to implement.

9. Parents are to be actively involved in the development of the IEP and serve as equal partners to school personnel. Student evaluation cannot take place without parent consent. IEP team meetings must be held at a time convenient for the parents. Parents must be given the choice to agree or disagree with the IEP and a chance to appeal the decisions of the IEP team.

10. IDEA has an appeals process that can be used by parents if they disagree with any of the recommendations of the IEP team. Parents must be informed of the appeals process and of the timelines under which the appeals operate. (See Figure 2-2.)

Major Provisions of IDEA

- Free appropriate public education, ages 3 to 21
- Twelve disability categories with strict eligibility requirements
- Multidisciplinary Evaluation Team
- IEP team includes at least: one parent, one regular education teacher, special education teacher, representative of local educational agency, someone to translate evaluations into instructional methodology, others as invited
- Written Individualized Education Program (IEP)
- Behavioral Support Plan, as appropriate
- Continuum of special education services
- Time lines
- Related services:
  - —Transportation
  - —Evaluations
  - —Social work
  - —Physical therapy
  - —Occupational therapy
- Supplemental aids and services in regular education (Accommodations)
- Transition services
- Procedural safeguards:
  - —Protection against extended suspensions
- Parent communication and training
- Appeals procedures
  - —Hearings
  - —Mediation
  - —Complaints

Figure 2-2

The law includes a description of the IEP process in order to ensure parent involvement, team decisions, and the development of an appropriate IEP for the student. (See Figure 2-3.)

The IEP Process

- An individualized education program (IEP)
- A multidisciplinary evaluation team (MET)
- The IEP team
- All decisions are made by team or committee
- A continuum of alternative educational placements
- The full participation of parents in the IEP process
- Measurable goals and short-term objectives
- Accommodations, program modifications, supplemental aids and services in the general education classroom
- Support for the general education teacher
- An appeals process

Figure 2-3

DIFFERENCES BETWEEN IDEA AND SECTION 504

Both IDEA and Section 504 include accommodations to be carried out in the general education classroom as well as special education and related services. Both laws also have policies relating to student disciplinary procedures.

Although both laws have similar provisions, there are differences between them. One of the major differences between IDEA and Section 504 is how they define disability. (See Figure 2-4.)

Section 504 has a noncategorical definition of "Handicapped" that includes "any person who has a physical or mental impairment which substantially limits one or more major life activities; or has a record of such impairments; or is regarded as having an impairment." Under this broad definition, an obese person is considered handicapped, for example, as is someone with a temporary handicap such as a broken leg. Also included in the definition are Learning Disabilities and ADHD not meeting the definitions in IDEA. All categories listed under IDEA are also included.

Section 504 states the individual asking for accommodations must also be "otherwise qualified." Essentially, this means that a student who uses a wheelchair and who applies for admission into a music Magnet School must meet the entrance requirements in music. (See Figure 2-5.)

Major Provisions of Section 504

- Civil rights law
- All ages
- Includes employment, transportation, housing, recreation, and education
- Noncategorical definition
- Eligibility and service decisions made by committee
- 504 Plan carried out by both general education and special education staff as needed
- Reasonable accommodations, not causing undue hardship
- Requires district to develop 504 policy and procedures
- A district 504 coordinator
- Appeals process
- If no district 504 Plan in place, special education law is followed
- Individual must be otherwise qualified

Figure 2-4

Schools and teachers have much more experience with IDEA than Section 504, so it is much more likely that the student with a disability will receive an appropriate education under IDEA. A student with a disability who doesn't neatly fit a category under IDEA may be able to receive services under Section 504. Since Section 504 is more flexible and less bureaucratic, 504 Plans are much less expensive to develop and implement than IEPs.

Students who are ineligible for services under IDEA are often eligible for services under Section 504. Some eligible disabilities covered by Section 504 and not covered by IDEA are: obesity; temporary handicap; allergies; academic, social, or emotional problems not meeting IDEA definitions; learning disabilities and ADHD not meeting IDEA definitions; and alcohol and drug abuse (if student is not currently using either).

DEFINITIONS OF LEARNING DISABILITIES UNDER IDEA AND SECTION 504

Under IDEA, a student has LD if he or she does not achieve commensurate to his or her age or ability levels and has a severe discrepancy between ability and achievement in one or more of the following areas: Oral Expression, Listening Comprehension, Written Expression, Basic Reading Skill, Reading Comprehension, Mathematics, Calculation, or Reasoning.

Differences Between IDEA and Section 504

IDEA	Section 504
• IDEA is an education law intended to provide free appropriate education.	• Section 504 is a civil rights law intended to prevent discrimination.
• IDEA affects the education of children ages 3 through 21. (Some state laws provide services from birth through 26.)	• Section 504 affects both adults and children with disabilities from birth to death.
• IDEA provides for many educational services including physical, occupational, and speech therapy.	• Section 504 is broader in scope, providing for housing, transportation, work, recreation, education, extracurricular activities, and summer programs.
• IDEA regulations are very specific, with strict eligibility requirements and evaluation procedures, and specific services to be provided.	• Some students are eligible for services under Section 504 who are not eligible for services under IDEA.
• IDEA specifies the right of parents to participate in the development of an educational plan.	• Section 504 does not specify the right of parents to participate in the development of the 504 Plan. However, generally, parents are included in 504 planning as "best practice."
• IDEA spells out rigorous procedural safeguards.	• "Due process" is assumed in Section 504 and must be written in state and local 504 Plans.
• IDEA provides much more protection for a disabled student regarding suspension and expulsion.	• School districts have much greater administrative latitude under Section 504 and less accountability.
	• Section 504 makes no reference to the specifics of an education plan, such as the inclusion of goals and objectives or the development of a Behavioral Support Plan.

Figure 2-5

In Section 504 a student with LD or ADHD fits under the general category of "handicapped" as a person who has a mental impairment that substantially limits learning.

The following are categories in IDEA under which a student with ADHD can receive services:

- *Specific Learning Disability,* if student meets criteria for LD eligibility.
- *Other Health Impairment.* ADHD is considered a "chronic impairment which includes heightened alertness to environmental stimuli resulting in limited alertness with respect to education."
- *Emotional Disturbance,* if student has, "over a long period of time" and "to a marked degree," an inability to learn that cannot be explained by sensory, intellectual, or health factors; or "inappropriate types of behavior or feelings under normal circumstances."

APPEAL PROCEDURES

There are procedures under both laws for appealing the decisions made by the IEP team or 504 planning committee and for filing complaints if the law is not being followed. However, because IDEA is an education law and Section 504 is a civil rights law, the procedures differ.

Appeal Procedure for IDEA

IDEA spells out two separate appeals procedures. The first procedure, which includes *hearings and mediation,* is for disagreements regarding student eligibility, the appropriateness of a student's IEP, payment for an outside evaluation, and amendment of student records. The second procedure, *complaints,* is for violations of law, rules and regulations, or state or local plans. Complaints and requests for a hearing can be filed simultaneously, although through different parts of the educational system.

There is a "stay put" provision under IDEA that states a student is to remain in his or her current placement throughout the appeals process, with an exception for emergency situations. Parents can have legal recourse only after the appeals procedures in IDEA are exhausted.

Most hearings result in educational programs that benefit students with LD or ADHD. In this regard the Hearing Officer may side with the school or the parent. Unfortunately, the hearing process can be costly, time consuming, and emotionally draining for all participants. It is an adversarial process that must not be entered into lightly.

Mediation is a much more "friendly" process. It is a negotiation process in which the mediator meets separately with each party. When successful, it results in a compromise with which both school and parents can live.

The complaint process, in which the Compliance Officer investigates the complaint by talking to each party separately, is also a much more "friendly" process than a hearing. (See Figure 2-6.)

IDEA Appeals Process

Hearings

- Written request to Special Education Administrator
- Reasons:
  - —Student eligibility for services
  - —Appropriateness of IEP
  - —Payment for outside evaluation
  - —Amendment of student records
- Mutually agreed-upon Hearing Officer
- District pays administrative costs of hearing
- Must take place no less than 15 nor more than 30 calendar days after request
- Decision no later than 45 calendar days after request
- Decision can be appealed for state-level review
- "Stay put" provision for student during appeal process

Mediation

- Written request to Special Education Administrator
- Takes place before hearing
- No effect on hearing timelines
- If no agreement, can proceed to a hearing

Complaints

- Reasons: violation of law, rules, or local or state plan, not following IEP
- Letter of complaint to local Compliance Officer
- Compliance Officer responsible for investigating complaint
- Investigation completed within 21 calendar days of receipt of complaint
- "Stay put" provision for student
- May be appealed to state level

Figure 2-6

Section 504 Appeals Process

- Written request to school principal and school 504 coordinator
- Can be appealed to district 504 coordinator
- May request impartial hearing
- Simultaneous complaint can be filed with regional Office of Civil Rights
- Based on a violation of "equal educational opportunity"
  —Failure to provide appropriate program
  —Procedural violations
  —Inadequate facilities, underfunding, overcrowding
  —Unreasonable delay

Figure 2-7

Appeals Process for Section 504

Appeals under Section 504 also involve two procedures. The first is through the school district's 504 Coordinator and may involve a state-appointed Hearing Officer. The second appeal is to the Regional Office of Civil Rights claiming that the student has been denied "equal" educational "opportunity." (See Figure 2-7.)

CONSTRAINTS AFFECTING IEP AND SECTION 504 DECISIONS

It would be simplistic to say that all decisions made by IEP Teams or 504 Committees are based only on what is best for the student. Although this is the law's intent, there are several system constraints that strongly affect the educational decisions that are made.

Most decisions are made with an eye on cost. The education of students with disabilities costs more than that of nondisabled students. In particular, cost strongly affects the continuum of services that are offered to a student. Although an IEP Team may say full-time placement in the mainstream is in the child's best interest, the decision may have been made because it is much less expensive to place the student in the mainstream than to maintain a Resource Room in a particular building in which the student might be more appropriately placed part of the time. It is also less expensive for a teacher consultant or speech and language pathologist to see a student two times a week rather than five times a week which would, of course, be more helpful.

There is a shortage of speech and language pathologists, school social workers, school psychologists, and occupational and physical therapists in many school districts. The shortage of psychologists means that there can be long delays before a student is evaluated and placed. The shortage of occupational therapists, physical therapists, and speech and language consultants limits the amount of therapy available to each student who needs it. The caseloads of these staff are usually very high and often involve students in two or three school buildings. Shortages often occur because school districts may try to save money by hiring very few ancillary personnel.

Union contracts can also affect IEP or 504 decisions. Because their function is to protect teachers, union contracts often specify the number of students with disabilities who can be placed in one class. If a student with LD or ADHD needs to be in a particular class and that class already has its quota of students with disabilities, that student is usually not placed there by the IEP (although this is illegal).

Legal Responsibilities of Schools and Teachers

- Schools must evaluate students suspected of having a disability.
- IEP meetings must be held at a time convenient for both parents and school personnel.
- Parents must be invited to IEP/504 meetings and any other meeting in which their child's education is discussed.
- Parents must be involved in developing the IEP/504 Plan.
- IEPs must be written.
- Parents must be informed of their rights under law.
- IEP and 504 Plans must be followed by the school and/or teacher even if the particular teacher was not involved in developing the plan or disagrees with it.
- Parents may bring others, such as advocates, with them to an IEP/504 meeting.
- Classroom teacher(s) must attend IEP/504 meetings if invited.
- Strict confidentiality of student records must be maintained.
- Parents are allowed to see all their child's records and make copies.
- Parents can challenge their child's records and either ask the school to remove a particular record or add a note to the record explaining their disagreement.
- Parents or teachers can request a new IEP/504 meeting to develop a new plan if the old one is considered inappropriate for some reason.
- Timelines in the law must be followed.
- Classroom teachers are required to make the accommodations set forth in IEPs or 504 Plans.
- Classroom teachers are required to individualize lessons and activities for students who have IEPs or 504 Plans.
- Implementation of all plans must begin on the date of initiation.
- The IEP team must develop an appropriate program for the student regardless of what the schools currently offer.

Figure 2-8

BARRIERS TO IMPLEMENTING IDEA
AND SECTION 504

A major barrier in the implementation of the IEP is the lack of communication between general education teachers and special education teachers. Unfortunately, this is usually due to the fact that the general education teachers believe they alone determine the specifics of how and what to teach. Even when special education teachers offer their help, many general education teachers do not take it. In fact, many general education teachers do not even read the student's IEP. Special education staff are often seen, and see themselves, as second-class citizens.

Although IDEA is generally being implemented in most of America's schools, Section 504 is not. This is interesting because the laws were written within two years of each other. The lack of implementation of Section 504 until recently illustrates how a law can be on the books and still not be followed. Unfortunately, we have many laws like this. It is only when challenges in the form of lawsuits are made that implementation of these laws is begun.

One of the main reasons for the lack of implementation of Section 504 is, again, a financial one. Special Education services are funded by federal and state statutes as well as local millage. Section 504 has no special funding sources. Funds needed for implementation of 504 come out of the general education budget.

There is an ongoing controversy as to who will pay for any special education services or personnel utilized in a 504 Plan: general education or special education? There is a corollary question: If the student is receiving teacher consultant services, can the teacher consultant count the student on his or her caseload as part of the special education services that the consultant provides?

As of now, most teacher consultants cannot count the student with a 504 Plan as part of his or her caseload. This means either the teacher consultant does not provide services to the student or provides services on a catch-as-catch-can basis.

There is great variability among the states—and among school districts within a state—in the use of 504 Plans. There seems to be no rush by the schools to implement Section 504. Little training is provided to teachers regarding the specifics of the law and their responsibilities under it. Other barriers to implementation of Section 504 are:

- The parent's lack of awareness of Section 504.
- School personnel who do not know the requirements of Section 504.
- The lack of implementation of 504 Plans by classroom teachers.
- The lack of monitoring of these Plans regarding their appropriateness.
- Often no district or building 504 Coordinator has been appointed; if one does exist, many teachers do not know who that person is.
- Many parents do not know who to contact regarding a request for a 504 Plan for their children.
- Often no record is kept regarding a parent's request for a 504 Plan or for a denial of eligibility by a 504 Committee.
- Many school districts do not think Section 504 requires them to evaluate students.

- Often due-process procedures are either not written or not communicated to parents.

It is clear that schools are responsible for implementing both IDEA and Section 504. In fact, under IDEA, federal special education funding can be withheld until a violation of the law has been corrected; a state can withhold state funding from a local district for the same reason. Under IDEA, schools are not just supposed to educate students with disabilities—they are supposed to seek out and identify children with disabilities who are not being served in order to help them progress in school. This means that teachers, too, have the obligation of identifying these students. (See Figure 2-8.)

TEACHER RESPONSIBILITIES IMPLIED BY LAW

Teachers are required by law to carry out the provisions of the student's IEP or 504 Plan. The teacher also has responsibilities implied by law to help provide an appropriate education for the student. These responsibilities are:

- Being familiar with a student's IEP or 504 Plan, accommodations required, goals, and objectives.
- Understanding of student's psychoeducational evaluations and the affect the student's disability has on progress in the general education classroom.
- Consulting with special education staff for suggestions regarding instructional methods, materials, and accommodations for the student.
- Having the same responsibility for students with disabilities in the class as they have for other students.
- Involving students with LD and/or ADHD in all classroom activities.
- Communicating frequently with parents regarding student progress and responding to parent concerns.
- Helping parents understand child's problems.
- Informing parents of their rights regarding their child's educational program.
- Planning for accommodations, instructional methods and materials, learning environment modifications, etc., for the student with LD and/or ADHD before the first day of school.

It is true that the laws require a great deal of teachers, but IDEA specifically mentions that the IEP can contain supports for the classroom teacher, such as:

- Training in area of need, e.g., information regarding a specific disability
- Instructional aide in classroom and/or personal aide for student
- Consultation with special education staff regarding methods and materials to use with a student

- Team teaching with special education teacher
- Special education and related services provided in the classroom
- Special arrangements for particular students

In addition, the schools can arrange for community volunteers to be placed in the classroom or for older students to serve as tutors or mentors for students with LD and/or ADHD. Teachers can arrange to provide support for each other by sending a student who is disturbing others to another class until the student is able to settle down.

If a student with ADHD and/or LD is constantly disrupting the class, his or her educational program is inappropriate in some way. A new IEP team meeting or 504 committee meeting should be called to consider changes to the existing plans, such as a change in the amount of special education services, and/or moving the student to a different class or a different teacher.

It is important to remember that the laws protect teachers from having to provide "unreasonable" accommodations or those that cause "undue" hardship.

ADDRESSING TEACHER
QUESTIONS AND CONCERNS

Let us try to answer the teachers' questions posed at the beginning of this chapter:

- It is important to have written 504 Plans to help all present and future teachers provide appropriate accommodations. It is also important to have written plans to document a student's disability. For example, a student must present documentation of at least a two-year history of test accommodation in order to qualify for accommodations on SAT and ACT tests.

- A teacher must follow a student's IEP or 504 Plan regardless of whether or not the teacher believes the student has a disability. It is important to remember that the student's eligibility was determined after careful evaluation by a team of professionals in addition to the student's parents.

- Teachers are required by law to individualize for students with IEPs and 504 Plans regardless of what the teacher is doing for the other students. Most teachers instinctively individualize for all students in some way.

- As we have shown, students with LD may be able to be served by Section 504 if they do not meet the definition of LD under IDEA.

- It is unreasonable to expect a teacher to put up with a student's constant disruptions. The teacher should refer the student for further evaluation, and a new IEP team meeting or 504 Planning meeting should be called to provide the student with the services he or she may need.

- The laws are careful to balance teacher rights with the needs of students with disabilities. Some people may interpret the laws in ways that infringe on teacher rights, but this can be rectified.

A FINAL WORD

The laws *are* complex, but understandable. They include supports for student, parent, and *teacher*. Many modifications of the learning environment and requirements, such as individualized instruction, are good for all students. Most student accommodations are easily integrated into the general education curriculum with little effect on the teacher's time. When problems arise, there are school staff who can consult with the classroom teacher to help make things work.

Although this chapter has focused on the law and its provisions, we must not allow this focus on the law to interfere with the education of the student. It is important for you to understand the laws, but no decisions should be made solely to satisfy the law. Educational considerations should always be uppermost in your mind.

As a classroom teacher you have a wealth of information and experience at your fingertips. You have taught many students with learning problems in the past and you will teach many more in the future. Essentially, IDEA and Section 504 merely codify what you know and what you are already doing in your classrooms. The laws were written by teachers, school administrators, and parents—all of whom are responsible for the education of students with disabilities.

CHAPTER THREE

The Learning Environment

Welcome

Dear Parents and Students,

Welcome to sixth grade and to Monroe Middle School. This is a big step for many of you. Many things will be new and different and will take some time to get used to. I will do everything possible to make this transition as easy as possible.

I hope this information will help you understand the coming year a little better. Please take time to read it and go over it together.

Parents, if you need to contact me with questions or concerns, please dial 555-3298 and ask to speak to me. I am usually available in the mornings from 7:00 to 7:30 A.M., during my conference period from

10:20 to 10:45 A.M., and after school at 2:20 P.M. You can also e-mail me at sjones@monroe.k12.mich.use

Teacher expectations for a successful year:
1. Come to class every day.
2. Be on time.
3. Turn in homework at the beginning of class.
4. Listen in class.
5. Be prepared. Have supplies, materials, and books ready.

Field trips:
• Sixth-grade field trip to Chicago in May.
• October—Visit my family's farm for nature/plant study sessions, and pumpkins for Halloween.
• High School pool for three afternoons of drownproof swimming classes in the Spring.
• Greenfield Village in May to reenact school life in the mid 1800s.

Book reports:
Each month there will be a topic for book choice. I must approve the book chosen. Parents, encourage your child to read every day so he or she doesn't end up with three-fourths of the book left to finish in the last week. I suggest you help your child organize the number of pages to be read each day or week. Reports are due the last day of the month.

Other main projects and activities:
The first major one will be in October with our Native American unit. Students will work in small groups for this project. We will have a Trade Fair with our Explorers unit. I will inform you in advance of these dates. There will be a major research paper due in the Spring.

Homework:
Yes, there will be daily homework. Parents, check your child's daily planner. We will take time to write assignments at the end of the Language Arts block. I will also institute a homework hotline that you can call after school. Spelling work will be daily except Friday.

Tests:
All tests will be announced at least two weeks before the test. I will provide study guides for all tests. I will give out test alerts the night

before major tests. Parents, you can help your child be more successful by being aware of the tests, and by helping him/her to study and review. Students will receive extra credit if they study and if you sign the test alert form and return it the day of the test.

Spelling:

Each Monday students will take a pretest. The words may come directly from our sixth-grade spelling book because it gives patterns and general spelling rules. Some weeks the words will come from the Social Studies or Science block. The final spelling test will be on Fridays. Assignments will be as follows:

Monday: Write each misspelled word five times.

Tuesday: Write sentences with each of the spelling words.

Thursday: Study for test.

Reading:

Our reading program consists of four components:

- eight required classroom novels (we will be reading these together)
- individual silent reading (20 minutes every day, book of choice)
- book reports on required novels
- books I read aloud to the class

Students may bring a snack for mid-morning break. I allow closed container water bottles in their desks as long as they don't create a problem. I want the students to be comfortable in my class and to understand what is expected of them. Parents, I also want you to feel free to contact me with any concerns you might have. With all of us working together, we should have an interesting and enjoyable year.

Sincerely,

Mrs. Jones

THE WELCOME LETTER

This sample welcome letter continued with a request for parent help in the classroom and guidelines for homework. The last page was a list of expectations for student behavior that includes persistence, creativity, responsibility, and caring.

It is clear that this teacher wants to get the year off to a good start. The letter underscores several key elements of a supportive learning environment:

- welcome to students and parents
- expectations of students
- overview of topics to be covered in class, field trips, special projects, tests
- routines: daily homework, monthly book reports, weekly spelling tests, daily teacher conference times
- information for parents

The teacher invited the parents to a meeting just before school started in September to discuss the newsletter and extend a welcome. She met briefly with Clyde's mother after the meeting. Clyde's mother, the angry parent you will meet in Chapter 11, said after the meeting, "I can't believe this. All these years. She seems really nice and she knew about Clyde's problems, too!"

The fact that the teacher had welcomed *her* into the school ("They used to hide when they saw me coming!") and had taken the time to read Clyde's IEP and understand Clyde's severe reading problem actually moved Clyde's mother to tears. The teacher ended her conversation with Clyde's mother by saying that she would do all in her power to make this year a successful one for Clyde.

This teacher clearly understood the impact a positive learning environment can have on student achievement.

CURRENT RESEARCH

In past practice, learning problems were thought to lie almost entirely within the student. The emphasis in the classroom was on "fixing" or changing the student through teaching and discipline. Some students were thought to be "unteachable" in regular education classes due to the severity of their problems. Others hung on by the skin of their teeth.

Current research has demonstrated the important role the learning environment can play in fostering the learning of *all* students—those with ADHD and/or LD, in particular.

Studies show that learning is enhanced when:

- Students feel a sense of belonging in the school and class.
- A personal relationship is established between teacher and students.
- Students have opportunities for social interactions with their peers.
- Teaching styles match students' learning styles.
- Teachers have positive expectations of students.
- Students are provided with structure, predictability, and clear expectations.
- New learning is related to what the students already know.
- Learning is made relevant to students' lives.
- Learning and thinking strategies are taught in the content area classroom.
- Student motivation is increased through reinforcement, success experiences, and high-interest tasks.
- Parents and schools work together for the benefit of the students.

In several studies, high school students were asked how their teachers could make learning easier for them. Their comments indicated that:

- They find learning from textbooks boring.
- They prefer hands-on learning.
- They want more strategy instruction.
- They would like teachers to adapt the pacing of instruction to student needs.

Based on these and other studies, there is a new emphasis not only on arranging the learning environment to enhance student learning, but also on the prevention of many learning and behavior problems that stem from an ill-considered learning environment. Far too many students with learning and attention problems are failing—not because of their own inadequacies—but because an inconsiderate learning environment makes learning difficult for them.

The learning environment of students with or without ADHD and/or LD has a significant effect on their:

- ability to concentrate
- willingness to approach and persist at a challenging task
- confidence in their own ability
- ability to work independently
- feelings of acceptance and value
- level of frustration

Making the learning environment more conducive to learning can mean the difference between success or failure for students with ADHD and/or LD.

PREDICTABLE CLASSROOM PROBLEMS OF STUDENTS WITH ADHD AND/OR LD

The problems that students with ADHD and/or LD have are predictable, in most cases, given the nature of these conditions. Teachers who have had these students in their classes know what most of these problems are, despite individual differences. Every year these same problems will repeat—only the faces and personalities of the students will change. You can plan ahead for these students and prepare the learning environment in advance.

It is not just students with ADHD and/or LD who have predictable problems. Many other students in the class have similar problems. For example, students of low socio-economic status and immigrant children may have difficulties with standard English. These students may also have significant experiential and educational gaps when dealing with mainstream culture and school requirements. In actuality, unique learning needs are the rule rather than the exception.

Teachers who anticipate the diverse needs of their students can plan and organize a flexible environment that supports many types of students. This type of environment also allows for a more natural incorporation of accommodations for students with ADHD or LD when they are needed.

COMPONENTS OF A POSITIVE LEARNING ENVIRONMENT

When considering how to design a more positive learning environment, you need to take into account current research findings, current best practice models, the predicted needs of the students in your classrooms, the required curriculum, and your own teaching experiences.

There are ten components of a supportive learning environment for students with ADHD and LD. (See Figure 3-1.)

Inclusive Teaching Philosophy

Before beginning to redesign the learning environment, you need to examine your own teaching philosophy when it comes to students with ADHD and/or LD in regular education classes. Philosophy involves a system of values and beliefs that provide a basis for interpreting the world. Our teaching philosophy influences the roles, responsibilities, and goals we, as teachers, adopt for ourselves. In this case we must uncover our values and beliefs about educating students with ADHD and/or LD in our classes and possibly modify them.

Just as some students have a "won't do" attitude toward learning, some teachers have a philosophy that closes the door to learning for students with ADHD and/or LD. As James Baldwin said:

"The only people in the world who can't be fooled are children. A child knows if you despise him, and if you despise him, you cannot teach him." (Keynote Address,

---

Ten Components of a Positive Learning Environment

- Inclusive teaching philosophy
- Caring and motivating emotional environment
- Grading for effort and progress
- Authentic learning and assessment
- Effective organization of the physical environment
- Structure and predictability
- Varied methods of presentation
- Flexible programming
- Varied grouping of students
- Strategic teaching

Figure 3-1

February 21, 1980. National Invitational Symposium on The King Decision. Wayne State University, Detroit, Michigan)

The following beliefs about teaching students with ADHD and/or LD can be incorporated as a part of your overall teaching philosophy:

- I want to help these students learn.
- These students belong in my class.
- These students are capable of learning what the other students are learning.
- It is my responsibility to develop a positive learning environment and modify my teaching strategies to help these students learn.
- I will ask for help for myself or the student from a learning specialist or teacher consultant, if necessary.

Caring and Motivating Emotional Environment

Teacher perceptions and attitudes toward individual students influence the other students' perceptions and attitudes—and influence the targeted student's feelings about himself or herself. When you stress the strengths and contributions of all students in the class—including students with ADHD and LD—the other students will not see these students as "different."

Student learning takes place in a social context. The attitudes and perceptions of their peers are very important to the development of a student's self-concept.

Adolescents with ADHD and/or LD need understanding, acceptance, reinforcement, and respect. They are more willing to meet a challenge, take a risk, and work hard when they know that you (and the other students) are in their corner. You can accomplish this by communicating the following to the student:

- I understand you.
- I respect you.
- You are a worthwhile member of my class.
- We will all help each other.
- We will take pride in the progress of every student.

There are many other strategies that can be used to develop a supportive emotional environment. (See Figure 3-2.)

Motivation is the key to learning. It is the positive attitude that keeps you going when the going gets rough. Many students with ADHD and/or LD have lost their motivation because of the continuing struggle they have in understanding the rules and attaining the goals of learning. Without motivation, students cannot achieve, even with high ability. In fact, strong motivation can overcome a certain lack of ability.

Your and the other students' caring, respect, and encouragement can greatly enhance a student's motivation to learn. Your enthusiasm for learning is contagious and can help motivate students to learn. Reinforcement and reward are also motivators as are topics of interest to the student in an area in which the student is particularly strong.

Strategies to Develop a Supportive Emotional Environment

- Develop a class or team spirit.
- Cheer everyone's progress and little successes.
- Model and reinforce the idea that everyone is different and has his or her own pattern of strengths and weaknesses.
- Provide hope and encouragement for students who encounter difficulties.
- Turn mistakes into learning experiences.
- Do not shame or reprimand students in front of the class.
- Emphasize zero tolerance for bullying and teasing.
- Help students with LD and/or ADHD to become a part of classroom groupings.
- Rotate class jobs and class leadership among all students in the class.
- Model and encourage helping behavior and service.
- Greet each student by name when he or she enters the classroom.

Figure 3-2

Student motivation is enhanced when you arouse curiosity about and an interest in the new material to be learned. To increase student motivation:

- Select tasks and activities at an appropriate level of challenge or difficulty.
- Adapt tasks to students' interests.
- Explain or demonstrate the link between effort and outcome.
- Allow students opportunities to make choices.
- Increase the amount of time you spend interacting with students.
- Increase the opportunities for creativity, divergent thinking, analyzing, and applying new information.

Grading

Course grades, like a worker's wages, are the rewards for a job well done. They are indicators of value, reinforcers of good work, and motivators to continue working or work even harder. They are a source of pride to student and worker.

Unfortunately, most students with ADHD and/or LD receive relatively low grades: C's and D's. Few receive A's, regardless of how intelligent they are or how hard they work. Usually the reason is the student's learning problems.

Grades can serve to motivate and involve a student or, conversely, to "turn off" that student. If students think that no matter how hard they try, they will never be able to achieve at an A or B level, they will eventually stop trying.

Usually students with ADHD and/or LD are already working harder than other students. They spend much more time on their homework. They struggle to read the textbook. They struggle to control or hide their learning problems. However, since only a finished product is valued or graded, their effort or progress goes largely unnoticed. Since we know how important reinforcement is to student motivation to learn, we need to take a serious look at the biggest reinforcer of all: grades.

Although most schools have grading policies, few have policies that set guidelines for adapting grading procedures for students with disabilities. Few see the need. But anyone who has worked with a student who is finally managing to stay focused for a longer period of time but whose grades are still low, can see the bitter disappointment caused by a low grade on a test or an interim report.

Most teachers already include homework completion and class participation as part of the course grade. Is it possible to include effort and progress also?

The solutions are not simple. If we only grade on student progress, how will the student know whether or not he or she has acquired enough knowledge and skills to move to the next grade or pass a statewide assessment? Many schools give two grades—one for progress and one for actual achievement. There may be two honor rolls as well. Some schools give a combination grade, weighting progress as well as mastery.

Many teachers emphasize progress and effort in their classes through a variety of reinforcement methods. A strong team spirit can help support those students whose grades do not yet reflect the progress they are making.

When students understand how grades are assigned:

- They report less stress related to grades.
- They understand how to improve their work.
- They begin to monitor, adjust, and improve their work.

Authentic Learning and Assessment

Authentic learning is not textbook learning; it is usually not classroom learning, either. It refers to learning in the real world about real-life situations, and solving real-life problems. Focusing on relevant and practical issues can be highly motivational to students, and can lead to a great sense of accomplishment when a task is completed.

Students with ADHD and/or LD flourish in such a setting. Authentic learning brings the freedom to develop a creativity and potential that may have been overlooked in more traditional settings. Inherent in this approach is the opportunity for hands-on learning, to move around a bit, to take breaks as needed, to vary activities, and to actively contribute to the group.

Authentic learning and assessment require the student to use higher-level thinking skills such as application, analysis, and synthesis. Students enjoy the interaction with each other, seeing the fruits of their labor.

Authentic learning, dealing with real problems in a real world, can enhance learning for all students. Community-based learning—working or volunteering in monitored settings in the community—can greatly increase students' motivation to learn. Motivation is enhanced when students:

- Create a finished product either individually or in a group.
- See how their work fits into the larger picture.
- Work as a team towards the same clear goal.
- See the work they have done actually put to use.
- Receive immediate feedback directed to improving what they are doing.
- Are provided with concrete rewards in the form of wages and/or praise for a job well done.

Effective Organization of the Physical Environment

A supportive emotional environment includes a physical environment that is inviting, organized, and conducive to learning. Sometimes this kind of physical environment is hard to come by, as the following description illustrates.

> Sonny is a student with ADHD and LD in a large, overcrowded suburban high school. He is rapidly becoming very frustrated because he is having great difficulty getting to class on time. He has a hard time understanding what the teacher expects him to do. His Language Arts class is particularly difficult for him.
>
> When the bell rings to signal the beginning of Language Arts class, many students are still in the hallway, frantically pushing and shoving their way to class. Sonny finally rushes into class two to three minutes late. The class has already begun work. Sonny leans over the desk of the girl beside him to ask what page they are on when a student rushes between them to scramble to a seat near the front. Students continue to straggle into class for a few more minutes.
>
> The room is a sea of students, wall to wall, front to back. Desks are everywhere. Sonny has to stand up to locate the teacher, who is leaning over a student's desk at the side of the room. The chalkboard is covered in math problems from the previous class. Raising his voice above the din, Sonny calls out, "What page are we on?"

Systematic thought and preparation are required if teachers are to avoid the problems that tend to occur when classrooms are crowded and noisy, students don't know what to do and can't find materials, and the teachers themselves are rushed and harried.

There usually is little you can do regarding lighting, ventilation, or room temperature, except continuously asking the maintenance staff for help. Union negotiations limit class size, although there are still far too many overcrowded classrooms. In some areas, schools can hardly keep up with the influx of new students; in others, new buildings are being built, but not fast enough. Many school buildings in urban areas are in various stages of decay, with leaky ceilings, crumbling paint, and broken toilets becoming more common.

There are some things, however, that you can do to make even the worst surroundings more usable and inviting. (See Figure 3-3.)

Enhancing the Physical Environment

- Invite students and parents to help work on a more appealing environment (e.g., paint, fix, move furniture, build shelves, etc.).
- Remove unnecessary distractions.
- Hang posters of heroes and motivating mottos.
- Include several plants.
- Provide a quiet space or corner.
- Keep one wall or corner free of visual distractions.
- Provide a file draw or box for students' use. These files can contain student work and portfolios, copies of worksheets, topic outlines, old tests, etc.
- Provide a bulletin board to post student progress and other student contributions.
- Have a suggestion box—and use it.
- Post classroom rules.

Figure 3-3

Student desks can be arranged in different configurations depending on the task at hand. Generally speaking, students with ADHD and/or LD may be less distractible if the desks routinely are in rows, although these students do enjoy occasional variety. Regardless of the way desks are arranged, clear aisles should be maintained for safety and noise control.

Structure and Predictability

The noise and chaos of an overcrowded school were not the only problems Sonny had to face as a student with ADHD. Many students with ADHD and/or LD have difficulties with Language Arts courses, even without the constant talking and moving of chairs of an overly large class. Language Arts teachers complain that these students are frequently off task. In fact, these students often appear to do no work in class, and students who are not working often talk to or bother other students.

Assuming the student with ADHD and/or LD is capable of doing the work, why isn't he or she working? Is he or she lazy, unmotivated, a troublemaker? Or does the student have problems with attention, organization, time management? Some of these students don't know how to begin a task. Some students with ADHD and/or LD do not know how to break down large tasks into small steps. When the Language Arts teacher tells the class to begin planning their papers, the student with ADHD and/or LD may not know what to do. The unstructured thinking and creativity that is inherent in a Language Arts class may prove the undoing of students who have organizational problems and/or who cannot work independently.

These same students may have little or no problems in math or computer classes. These classes, by their very nature, tend to be more structured. New learning is built on previously learned material. Practice is an integral part of learning. There are specific ways to solve problems and specific rules to follow.

Structure does not mean that every student is doing the same thing at the same time, however; structure means predictability. Each student knows what is expected of him or her at any given time. Rules and routines are set up for certain class activities so that the student does not have to try to remember or reinvent ways of doing things. It is particularly helpful if you provide clear expectations for what constitutes competent work and appropriate behavior. It is important that the student knows the consequences of rule infractions.

Scheduling tasks and activities on a class calendar and teaching students to write their assignments in their assignment book every day provides the organization students need to help juggle the many school-related activities in which they are involved. Provide students with a checklist of steps that can help them complete tasks during large blocks of unstructured time. These checklists can be used for planning a long-term project, or listing tasks and activities students should begin working on as soon as they enter the classroom or any other unsupervised or unstructured situation.

Clyde's teacher presented an overview of class assignments and activities in her Welcome Letter (refer to the beginning of this chapter). She followed it up by scheduling all activities on a monthly calendar, providing checklists of step-by-step procedures for writing a book report, and a checklist to help ensure that the critical elements of a book report are

Monthly Class Calendar

			October			
	Monday 1	Tuesday 2	Wednesday 3	Thursday 4	Friday 5	Saturday 6
	SELECT A BOOK		CHECK BOOK WITH TEACHER	READ 10 PAGES STUDY FOR TEST	HOMEWORK READ 20 PAGES SPELLING TEST	
Sunday 7	Monday 8	Tuesday 9	Wednesday 10	Thursday 11	Friday 12	Saturday 13
	SPELLING PRETEST	READ 10 PAGES	READ 10 PAGES	STUDY FOR TEST	READ 20 PAGES SPELLING TEST	
Sunday 14	Monday 15	Tuesday 16	Wednesday 17	Thursday 18	Friday 19	Saturday 20
	SPELLING PRETEST			STUDY FOR TEST	SPELLING TEST	
Sunday 21	Monday 22	Tuesday 23	Wednesday 24	Thursday 25	Friday 26	Saturday 27
	DUE: OUTLINES REPORTS--BEGIN REPORTS – REPORTS			VISIT FARM	SPELLING TEST	
Sunday 28	Monday 29	Tuesday 30	Wednesday 31			
	BOOK REPORTS DUE					

Figure 3-4

addressed. Figures 3-4, 3-5, and 3-6 are examples of calendars and checklists that provide structure and predictability to the student's day.

There are many reasons why rules, routines, calendars, and checklists support student learning. These aids provide the structure that can:

- Help students develop good work habits.
- Put some tasks and activities on automatic pilot.
- Help students use time efficiently.
- Provide students with guidelines and blueprints for completing a task.
- Increase the students' feelings of control.
- Reduce the need for students to depend on others for direction.
- Provide a feeling of safety and increase comfort level.
- Aid memory.
- Provide students with a sense of purpose and accomplishment.
- Reduce student uncertainty, anxiety, and stress.

The most important function of structure is to free the student from extraneous concerns so that the student can focus on learning new material and demonstrating what he or she has learned.

Methods of Presentation

State and local school districts identify the knowledge and skills they consider critical for student learning. However, teachers determine the instructional methods they will use in their classroom. Teachers control the way they present new information to the students.

Marshal McLuhan said, "The medium is the message." (*The Medium Is the Message: An Inventory of Effect,* with Quintin Fiore and Jerome Angel, Bantam Books, New York, 1967) This means that *how* something is taught is as important as *what* is taught. If students are to understand what is being taught, the methods used to teach new information must be made compatible with the way students learn.

As academic standards are being raised throughout the United States, it becomes critical to analyze these standards and the curriculum itself for any possible mismatch with the needs of students with ADHD and/or LD, and then to develop strategies that will help these students bridge the gap. Some instructional alternatives are better suited to the needs of individual students with ADHD and/or LD than others. The method of presentation—whether lecture, discussion, demonstration, self-paced/independent, or hands-on—can support or hinder learning. If a student is a visual learner and the material is presented orally, for example, the student will have great difficulty understanding and remembering what is being taught. Mixing methods, appealing to several different learning modalities, e.g., auditory, visual, kinesthetic, can help these students understand, organize, and remember new information.

Remember, your teaching style affects the student's ability to understand and remember new material, and affects student motivation to learn.

Student Checklist: A Step-by-Step Guide for Completing Book Reports

Book Title: _____

Due Date: _____

1. Select a book.

2. Preview or look it over to make sure you can read it and that you are interested in it.

3. Check with the teacher.

4. Read ____ pages per day or read ____ pages per week. (Divide the number of pages in the book by the number of days available for reading.)

5. Fill out an index card or form before, during, and after reading with information about the book.

6. Check assignment: What does the teacher want me to write about? What questions need to be answered?

7. Brainstorm (list) the points you want to make.

8. Arrange the points into an outline.

9. Add details, examples, supporting evidence, or quotes to the outline.

10. Edit the outline: Add or omit sections.

11. Check outline with the teacher.

12. Write the introductory paragraph.

13. Write the body of the report.

14. Write the concluding paragraph.

15. Go over the report. Ask yourself questions, such as:
    —Does this make sense?
    —Should I add something here?
    —Should I reorganize the paper?
    —Is the conclusion based on the information in the paper?
    —Does the introduction say what the paper is about?

Figure 3-5

Student Checklist: Elements of Book Reports

Book Title: _____

Author: _____

Setting of Book:

   —where (place): _____

   —when (time): _____

Main Characters:

   —name: _____

   —description: _____

   —point of view: _____

   —name: _____

   —description: _____

   —point of view: _____

Plot:

   —main event #1: _____

   —main event #2: _____

   —other events: _____

Possible questions to answer:

- What was the problem or conflict presented in the story?
- How was the problem resolved?
- What was your opinion of the book? Why? Give examples.
- What other ending could this book have had?
- Compare a main character from this book with a character from another book.

Figure 3-6

Flexible Programming

Most secondary schools follow a lockstep curriculum based on graduation require-ments set by the state. The students must take biology before chemistry, for example, or al-gebra before geometry. But some students with ADHD and/or LD with strengths in the visual–spatial area might do better taking geometry before algebra. Allowing a student to take a course out of sequence requires a lot of creative thinking on the school's part, but should be considered if the student is doing poorly and getting very frustrated with an in-troductory or prerequisite course.

Allowing a student with severe problems to take fewer courses is another option to consider. Taking fewer courses allows students more practice and study time. It also helps prevent the buildup of stress that so often accompanies students with ADHD and/or LD.

Home-based learning, carefully coordinated with the school, can individualize learn-ing for a student having difficulty in a large school or classroom or with a particular teacher. Home-based learning can also help the student who is very stressed by school.

Taking courses at another school or in a local community college can provide addi-tional learning opportunities for students who are bored or who dislike the particular school they are in.

For example, Sonny, who was getting D's in Language Arts because of his disorganized stream-of-consciousness writing, was finally allowed to take a twelfth-grade law course in which he was very interested. Because the law course required a lot of clearly structured writing, it was an acceptable substitute for ninth-grade Language Arts. Sonny received a high B in the course.

Grouping of Students

Humans are social creatures, and this is particularly true of adolescents. Since adoles-cents are so interested in establishing social relationships, it becomes particularly important for you to consider the grouping of students as part of the learning environment. Students can work together in small groups of various sizes, although some instruction takes place in large groups and some students occasionally prefer to work independently. Both small- and large-group discussions have been shown to enhance learning and recall. Generally students prefer to learn from discussions rather than from lectures or texts. Discussions can also hold the attention of students with ADHD better than lectures or texts.

Cooperative learning groups, carefully selected so that each member has some-thing to contribute, can be used as vehicles for group projects. It is important to monitor these groupings to ensure that the students share the work rather than one or two stu-dents doing all the work. Bright or gifted students may prefer to work in homogeneous groups. Occasionally students of similar ability can be members of one group to enhance the equal contributions of all members, but this should be the exception rather than the rule.

There is a downside to large- or small-group instruction for students with ADHD. Due to their distractibility, these students may prefer self-paced learning or working in pairs.

Some topics or tasks lend themselves more naturally to group learning than others. A paper requiring an opinion or an evaluation may be greatly enhanced by group discussion prior to writing or during the revision stage. Practicing using newly learned skills can be done individually.

Many students prefer to study for tests in a small-group setting. As long as progress is made and the group doesn't deteriorate into time-wasting activities, this is an excellent way of understanding and remembering important information. Group study sessions can make learning fun.

Strategic Teaching

Strategic teaching means the teaching of strategies that will help students learn and remember new information in an efficient manner. No longer should you be content for students to struggle to learn a long list of unrelated material for a test, and then forget it within a short time. You want to teach students how to organize, remember, and write about new information. You want students to be able to use new information they have learned to enhance their lives. Students must get into the habit of using learning and thinking strategies when they approach any new learning task. In the words of the old adage: *"Give me a fish and I eat for a day. Teach me to fish and I eat for a lifetime."*

The teaching of learning and thinking strategies is integrated into the teaching of new material in content area courses. You should teach students how to use the following strategies:

- checklists
- charts and maps
- reading and writing strategies (see Chapter 4)
- homework completion strategies (see Chapter 5)
- visualization and self talk (see Chapter 6)
- test-taking strategies

Specific strategies for learning specific content can be developed as needed. Strategic teaching emphasizes the importance of thinking and planning before starting a task and of checking back after a task to see that it is completed accurately. (See Figure 3-7.)

As students acquire a set of learning strategies, they can select from among them those that will help with a particular learning task.

Research has shown the positive effect of strategic teaching on student learning, especially those students with ADHD and/or LD. The needs of students with ADHD and/or LD for individualization, organization, structure, help with focusing attention, and help with remembering new information can be addressed by teaching them specific strategies.

To teach learning strategies, do the following:

- Describe how the strategy can help learning.
- Describe the strategy.
- Model the strategy using content material.
- Provide time for rehearsal and guided practice.
- Model how the strategy can be used in other situations or for other tasks.

Teacher Checklist: What to Do
Before, During, and After a Lesson

Before a Lesson

☐ Announce what the students are going to learn.

☐ Describe the purpose for learning the information or skill.

☐ Discuss how the information or skill can be used or when it can be used.

☐ Ask/discuss what the students already know about the topic.

☐ Ask/discuss how this topic fits into what is already known.

☐ List key words/concepts for the day on the chalkboard.

☐ Develop some questions about the topic.

☐ Provide advance organizers.

☐ Preview materials (e.g., headings, chapter summary, and questions).

☐ Instruct students to listen for the answers to questions, the main ideas, and vocabulary.

During a Lesson

☐ Use visual clues.

☐ Use auditory clues (e.g., "most important," "number one," etc.).

☐ Provide hands-on models.

☐ Allow time for students to think.

☐ Provide short, clear directions.

☐ Provide examples.

☐ Check for understanding.

☐ Encourage discussion.

After a Lesson

☐ Summarize or ask students to summarize what was learned.

☐ Review the purpose for learning the information or skill.

☐ Ask/discuss what additional questions or information the students want to know.

(continued)

Figure 3-7

- [ ] Relate the lesson to homework assignments.
- [ ] Discuss how assignments are to be completed.
- [ ] Ask students to discuss and share information, reactions, and opinions.
- [ ] Review examples of projects or tasks.
- [ ] Provide positive feedback to students.
- [ ] Integrate rewards and recognitions for effort and progress.
- [ ] Set the stage for the next lesson.

Notes

_____

_____

_____

_____

_____

_____

_____

_____

_____

_____

MONITORING AND ASSESSMENT OF STUDENT LEARNING

Too often decisions about instructional methods are based on habit, intuition, myth, or stereotype. Teachers need specific information about student effort, progress, and mastery upon which to base instructional decisions.

You need to monitor and assess student progress in the classroom in order to determine how well instructional methods are meeting student needs. "Should I go over this again? Do the students need more practice? Are they ready to go on to more difficult material?"

Monitoring and assessment give you information you can use to provide feedback to students regarding their performance. Feedback can tell students whether or not they have learned the information you deem important, what they need to relearn or practice, and what they are doing well. Feedback also provides students with information about their progress from the beginning of the year.

Assessment data can be used to determine how an individual student is doing relative to the other students in the class or to other students at the same grade level in other schools. Statewide assessment data can be used to determine if the student has mastered the curriculum set forth by the state. National assessment data is often used to compare students, teachers, and schools across the nation. The results of state and national assessments are often used to determine student eligibility for a college scholarship, or as gatekeepers guarding the entry of students into elite programs or schools.

State assessment data can also be used to determine how well a school is doing in relation to others in the state or the amount of the state's contribution to a local school district. Occasionally the data collected is used inappropriately to assess a teacher's performance or to determine teacher salaries.

It is important to consider the purpose of assessment when selecting or developing an assessment tool for classroom use. Classroom assessment can have several different purposes, and several of these purposes can be combined in one assessment instrument to:

- Measure individual student progress.
- Measure individual student mastery.
- Compare students in class.
- Determine if instructional methods are meeting student needs.

There are several different types of assessment you can choose from when developing an assessment instrument.

- Authentic assessment seeks to document learning through the application of knowledge to the real world (e.g., solving problems, conducting experiments, making demonstrations, preparing reports).
- Portfolios are compilations of students' work that document the knowledge and skills learned over time in the classroom. Portfolios can also include examples of work outside the classroom, such as descriptions of volunteer work and other after-school activities.

- Demonstrations, models, projects, and products are used with increasing frequency to allow students to use a hands-on approach to assessment rather than taking a paper-and-pencil test.
- Teacher-made tests are designed for a particular class and reflect the importance the teacher places on certain topics or aspects of a topic. These tests can include information from the textbook, from class discussion, from outside reading, and from homework. They vary from class to class, as well as in the form they take, their length, and their difficulty.
- Textbook-based tests reflect the importance placed by the author of the text on certain topics in the book.
- Criterion-referenced tests are prepared in order to assess the quality or the quantity of information that a student has mastered. If all the students have learned all the material, then all of the students will get an A.
- Norm-referenced tests are prepared so that students can be compared with each other and ranked. A certain percentage of the class will get an A, a B, or a C, regardless of the amount of information the students have mastered.

In deciding on what type of instrument to use for a particular topic, you must still decide the following:

- Should the test reflect material covered in the textbook, the lectures, and/or class discussion?
- How often should testing take place?
- How should I score each question or part of the test?
- What accommodations will I have to make for the students with ADHD and/or LD?

Whatever decisions are made, you should ensure that:

- The directions and questions are written clearly and simply.
- Scoring procedures and criteria are also clear.
- The students know specifically what the assessment covers.
- The questions are interesting.
- Students are given a choice of questions to answer.
- The questions utilize analytic, creative, and practical (application) aspects of knowledge, not just recall.
- Clear, specific, immediate feedback is provided to students regarding their performance.

Students with ADHD and/or LD often do not understand what will be on the tests, what to study, how to answer questions, or how to divide their time so as to maximize their score. You can teach test-taking strategies so that the students can become efficient and effective test takers while focusing on demonstrating mastery. (See Figure 3-8.)

Tips for Teachers: Helping Students with Classroom Testing

- Allocate time to provide direct instruction on test taking.
- Discuss the purpose of testing and how test scores relate to grades.
- Show samples of different types of test questions.
- Create a variety of items, some that require:
    —recognition only (e.g., matching)
    —recall with some clues (e.g., multiple choice)
    —recall with no clues (e.g., fill in)
    —summarization in the student's own words (e.g., short answer)
    —summarization, organization, and problem-solving (e.g., essay)
- Review different types of test directions with the class; circle key words.
- Show how to circle key words in multiple-choice or short-answer questions.
- Demonstrate how to plan and organize answers to essay questions.
- Conduct a review of a completed test and explain how answers can be improved.
- Review their tests with the students and help them decide how they can improve on the next test.
- Work with students to show their individual strengths and weaknesses on a test and how they can improve through study and practice.
- Show where the answers to questions can be found (e.g., text versus notes).
- Administer a practice test.
- Remind students of a test at the beginning of the week and the night before.
- Provide a sheet for parent report. If a student studied at least 15 to 30 minutes, then he or she gets extra points on the test.

Figure 3-8

TEAM TEACHING

You are an important part of the learning environment; however, there may be several other adults also present in many classrooms. These may be paraprofessionals and community volunteers as well as other teachers and support staff. Team teaching is one of the best ways to meet the needs of students with ADHD and/or LD. In team teaching, the regular education teacher is joined by a special education teacher or a social worker or a psychologist to provide instruction.

Involving Other Teachers

There are several different types of team-teaching arrangements.

- Each teacher can share responsibility for lesson planning and teaching, with each presenting part of the lesson to the whole class while the other teacher helps individual students.
- The general education teacher can present the content of the lesson and the special education teacher can teach learning strategies to the whole class.
- The special education teacher can adapt teaching material and suggest teaching strategies to the general education teacher.
- The class can be divided in half and each teacher can adapt a lesson to the needs of the group.

Unfortunately, team teaching can be a logistical nightmare. There are never enough special education teachers to go around, so the special education teacher tends to team in specific subjects, such as Language Arts. In many schools most of the students with LD and/or ADHD are placed in one or two classes in each subject that are then team-taught. As long as half the students in the class are general education students, these classes are considered mainstream classes.

Team teaching can serve as an excellent transition between resource room placement and full-time general education placement. Many general education students with learning problems also benefit from team teaching.

Using Paraprofessionals and Volunteers

If used wisely, paraprofessionals and classroom volunteers can be of great help to students and teachers. Some paraprofessionals and volunteers have college degrees, while many do not. Most are high school graduates without any special expertise. That is why you must carefully supervise these classroom helpers.

Generally, you present a lesson to the whole class and the paraprofessional helps an individual student by:

- helping the student learn new material
- providing additional practice
- helping the student focus attention
- cuing and prompting the student
- implementing modifications designed by the special education teacher
- encouraging the student to socialize appropriately with other students
- acting as scribe for writing
- reading to the student

- preventing behavior problems, and/or removing the student from the room if the behavior interferes with the learning of other students

You must remember that many paraprofessionals and volunteers do not have the skills to teach the student new material or modify behavior. It is your responsibility to train these helpers when they are lacking appropriate skills.

Some paraprofessionals and volunteers do not work well with some students. There may be a personality clash or the volunteer may not have enough information to meet the needs of the student. If you feel there is a mismatch or if a student or parent complains, the situation should be investigated. Sometimes additional training can solve the problem.

A FINAL WORD

The learning environment has a tremendous effect on student learning. Regardless of what goes on in other parts of the school, you are in charge of the learning environment in your classroom. You can engineer an environment conducive to learning by modifying the physical environment, providing a supportive and caring emotional environment, providing structure and predictability, and modifying teaching materials and methods to meet students' needs. Even in a rundown overcrowded school, you can have a positive impact on the physical environment of the classroom.

Remember Sonny? His teacher brought up the overcrowding and distractions in her classroom at a staff meeting. She was joined by other teachers with similar problems. Together the staff came up with some solutions for that particular classroom. It was clear that the scheduling of classes and rooms was an issue, so another larger room was found for Sonny's class. With careful thought, several other classes were moved to larger quarters, enabling ten desks to be removed from the original classroom. The school librarian agreed that students like Sonny could use the library as a quiet work space.

Sonny's teacher was able to arrange a learning environment that made an important improvement in Sonny's performance. Suggestions like these can benefit all students, not just students with ADHD and/or LD.

CHAPTER FOUR

Reading and Writing in the Content Areas

The tall, slender young girl slipped silently into the room moments before the bell rang. She sat as still as a statue appearing lost in a trance. Finally, after the teacher had been talking for a minute or two, she stirred, reached down to her backpack and pulled out her notebook and a pen.

Angeliese is a bright 16-year-old with learning disabilities in reading and expressive language. Her reading comprehension is affected by the difficulty she has discerning the organization and structure of what she is reading. These difficulties with organization are also noticeable in her speaking and writing. Although her rambling speech often appears off-target, there is a fine mind at work here, as evidenced by the astute comments imbedded in what she says. Her reading is very slow because it takes her a long time to assimilate what she has read. Essentially, in both her reading and writing, she appears to not be able to distinguish "the forest for the trees."

Clyde has problems with reading decoding. Although he is in seventh grade, Clyde reads at a beginning third-grade level. He appears to be a visual, hands-on learner. He is active in his local 4H club and is very knowledgeable about farm animals. He has recently won several awards at the County Fair. He also loves to help his father repair farm machinery. Although Clyde says that he likes school, he is getting extremely discouraged. Despite his average IQ scores, Clyde is failing every subject except science because of his learning disabilities in reading.

Students like Clyde and Angeliese, with ADHD and/or LD, bring a variety of reading problems into the content area classroom. Virtually all students with ADHD and/or LD have some problems with reading. Students with LD who have severe decoding problems usually can get very little information out of middle or high school texts. Because they have great difficulty reading test questions as well as directions, they do very poorly on tests. Word problems in math are also difficult, even though they may be quite capable in math.

Students with ADHD who are able to read middle or high school texts may have a slow reading rate and/or trouble concentrating on the reading material. They read and reread and may skip words, read words inaccurately, or skip entire lines of text. They frequently lose their place due to extraneous sights and sounds. They lose books and assignments and are generally stressed by the effort it takes them to read and concentrate. All of these students have great difficulty keeping up with their assignments in *all* academic courses.

READING: CURRENT STATUS

Unfortunately, society tends to view people with reading difficulties as having limited intellectual abilities. As teachers see many of their students with ADHD and/or LD failing or barely passing courses due to reading problems, they question whether these students really belong in the mainstream courses they are teaching.

Secondary school teachers find it difficult to teach students who cannot read the grade-level text. They cannot understand how these students can pass the course if they have difficulty reading, writing, and taking tests. (See Figure 4-1.)

It is not just students with ADHD and/or LD, however, who are reading below grade level. In secondary schools only one-third of the students read and write at levels that assure them academic success and future job skills. Another one-third of the students are functionally illiterate.

The reading proficiency among secondary students ranges from below fourth grade to beyond twelfth grade. A student who is reading below the fourth-grade level cannot read a seventh-grade textbook. Students reading at a fourth- or fifth-grade level can gain minimal information from the text, but they often misread or misunderstand what they have managed to read. To compound their reading problems, these students read little outside of school or avoid reading altogether.

Reading problems, like other learning problems, do not reside wholly within the students. Part of the problem can be traced to the method used to teach reading in the early grades. We know now that the whole language approach to teaching reading, which was used 10 to 20 years ago, is not adequate for many students. Teachers who combine a whole language approach with the teaching of phonological awareness are much more successful in teaching reading to elementary school children.

The textbooks the students are required to read in middle school or high school are often to blame for some reading problems. Textbooks are often poorly written and poorly organized. They may be written several grades above course-grade level and/or present ideas that are too complex for students with little experience of the subject matter to master.

Reading Problems of Students with ADHD and/or LD

Basic Skills

- Poor decoding skills
- Poor general vocabulary
- Slow reading rate
- Skipping words and lines of text
- Poor organizational skills

Comprehension/Retention

- Lack of background information
- Difficulty understanding directions
- Poor understanding of the structure of reading materials (e.g., headings, sub-headings, paragraphs)
- Difficulty selecting and using appropriate strategies and skills
- Difficulty understanding specific concepts
- Difficulty locating the main idea and important information
- Difficulty remembering facts, details, directions, etc.
- Difficulty expanding or extending ideas
- Difficulty relating current assignment to previously learned material
- Difficulty understanding deeper meaning or significance
- Difficulty making inferences

Self Management

- Difficulty maintaining concentration while reading
- Procrastination
- Loses assignments and/or books

Figure 4-1

Many schools use reprints of articles that are written above grade level, duplicated in blurred or tiny print with no headings or reading aids.

Another part of the problem is that students entering middle school are not used to reading expository texts and are unfamiliar with their structure and organization. These students do not understand the importance of subtitles, information presented in boldface type, visuals and graphics, or questions at the end of the chapter in helping them comprehend and remember the information presented. Unfortunately, many textbooks do not have organizational aids, and reading comprehension suffers accordingly. Even when study aids are included, some teachers do not use them.

Cognitive and metacognitive strategies that can enhance the comprehension and retention of expository material are rarely taught in middle and high schools. It has long been assumed that the teaching of reading is not the responsibility of the secondary school classroom teacher.

However, because it has become abundantly clear that our students read quite poorly, reading improvement has become an important educational issue. The federal government has given the states money to hire additional teachers to teach reading. States have adopted tough reading and writing standards for secondary school students after assessments have shown how badly short of the mark these students fall.

WRITING: CURRENT STATUS

Most students with a reading problem also have a writing problem, since both are language based. (See Figure 4-2.)

A limited reading vocabulary directly affects written expression. Students who know little about a topic cannot write about it. Clyde is a prime example of such a student. His dyslexia greatly limits the amount of information he can get from his textbooks; this, in turn, hinders his academic writing. In addition, Clyde's decoding problems are evident in his spelling, which is so bad as to be indecipherable.

Angeliese hardly writes at all. She doesn't take notes in class. She says that she remembers all that is being said. Even though she is well-read and contributes eagerly to class discussions, she has not handed in a paper all semester. Her learning disabilities in written expression are so severe that she doesn't even try to write anymore.

Mike, who you will meet in Chapter 10, is an exceptionally bright student with severe ADHD. His stream-of-consciousness writing, although reflecting wide-ranging intellectual interests, is disorganized and extremely difficult to understand. He gets D's and F's on his long, rambling papers and does not understand why.

It is estimated that well over 40 percent of students with ADHD have reading and writing problems. These are directly attributable to problems with distractibility and organization. A student with organization problems, who has difficulty with the organization of print material, will have difficulty with the organization of written material.

Students with ADHD may lack the focus and patience to develop a theme or be so overwhelmed by the sheer number of their ideas that they cannot select the few to include in their papers. They keep losing their train of thought. Due to their impatience and impulsivity, they often do not want to take the time to develop an outline, locate supporting evidence, or edit their papers. They often develop writer's block because they have been so unsuccessful with their writing and are unable to correct it.

Students with LD have writing problems that are directly attributable to their disabilities. They can have problems expressing themselves in writing, difficulty with the fine-motor skills affecting handwriting, and/or the extremely poor spelling attributable to dyslexia. Many of these students know what they want to say, but the physical act of forming letters

Writing Problems of Students with ADHD and/or LD

Writing

- Poor planning
- Poor editing
- Poor organization
- Problems with expressing or explaining ideas verbally or in writing
- Problems thinking of enough to say
- Difficulty building a logical argument
- Low fund of information
- Poor use of technical or mature vocabulary
- Problems with word retrieval

Handwriting

- Slow writing
- Poorly formed letters and words
- Messy writing (e.g., erasures, crossing out of words)

Grammar and Spelling

- Run-on sentences or fragments
- Incorrect punctuation
- Incorrect verb tenses
- Subject–verb disagreement
- Incorrect spelling, capitalization

Self Management

- Procrastination
- Writer's block
- Perfectionism
- Losing assignments
- Problems breaking assignment into smaller parts

Figure 4-2

and words, with speed and accuracy, is beyond them. They even have great difficulty copying from the chalkboard.

A large percentage of all adults have written language problems, largely because they never learned to write correctly. They use poor grammar and punctuation. They capitalize nouns when they shouldn't and vice versa. When they do write, they write very little. They often become quite anxious when they have to write for public consumption. These problems exist despite the fact that these adults may be able to speak very well.

Almost all students have some difficulty with the mechanics of writing. In addition, like students with ADHD and/or LD, they often lack the skills and strategies needed to write effectively. Strategies and skills they lack include:

- knowing how or where to begin a writing assignment
- knowing how to organize a paper
- deciding between ideas to include and those to discard
- generating content and expanding on ideas
- understanding the need to review and edit what they have written
- understanding why the teacher doesn't like what they have written
- knowing how to improve on what they have written

Often students attempt to write about a topic they do not fully understand. Instead of getting more information on the topic, spending more time in thinking things through, or changing topics, many students will turn in a poorly conceived paper, not realizing what is missing.

Many students have the mistaken belief that all great writers write only when they are inspired. The students also believe that great writing springs fully formed from the writer's head, needing no editing or change. These students believe that their writing problems are caused by a lack of inspiration. These false assumptions need to be addressed directly by showing students anecdotal evidence from great writers and examples of their many drafts and editorial comments.

Many students say their writing problems are caused by the fact that they cannot write as fast as they think. They try to excuse their uncompleted assignments by complaining that it takes them such a long time to write that they cannot finish on time. They also complain that, although they have good ideas, they tend to forget them when it comes time for writing.

Middle and high school Language Arts teachers do teach writing to their students. However, they often focus on the mechanics of writing, rather than on the problem-solving and higher-level thinking skills necessary to generate an adequate paper.

READING TO WRITE, WRITING TO READ

Reading is an active thinking process during which the reader tries to extract meaning from texts by using a variety of learning strategies. For too many students, however, reading is not an active process. Ask students how they read and they reply, shrugging their shoulders, "I just open the book and start to read."

Their eyes go over the words, but they do not absorb the message of the text. They do not use a conscious or intentional thinking process to understand, organize, and remember what they have read.

Writing, like reading, is also an active thinking process. It is a problem-solving task that requires the writer to construct meaning by generating and organizing ideas, and adapting the result to the needs of the reader. Reading involves the extraction of meaning; writing involves the construction of meaning. Writing has the added purpose of communicating meaning to an audience.

Academic reading and writing are in many ways interdependent. One reads in order to gain information that one will use for writing. Writing presupposes that someone will read what is being written and involves an understanding of what the reader needs to know about a topic.

Similar thinking strategies and skills are needed for both. Students need to:

- Understand the purpose of a specific reading or writing assignment.
- Activate what they already know about the topic in question.
- Solve problems as they go along.
- Organize their thoughts and ideas.
- Summarize.
- Review.

WHOSE RESPONSIBILITY IS IT?

Whose responsibility is it to teach secondary students to read? Many of us who teach content area courses feel that teaching reading is not our job. We are concerned because we feel that we do not know how to teach reading to adolescents, especially those with ADHD and/or LD. We worry that we will not have enough time to teach both reading and content in the number of minutes allotted to each class.

Most of us feel that these students should have learned to read in the early grades. Many of us feel that any secondary students who need remedial help should receive it from reading specialists or special education staff.

On the other hand, we all expect to teach writing skills and provide students with feedback on the papers they write.

However, regardless of whose responsibility it is to teach reading and writing at the secondary level, we are all faced with a sizeable percentage of students whose lack of reading and writing skills greatly interfere with school success. None of us wants to sit idly by as our students fail.

Although the teaching of remedial reading and writing to students like Clyde is the responsibility of specialists, you can do much to enhance content-related reading and writing skills in addition to making reading and writing accommodations for students with ADHD and/or LD. Specifically, you can:

- Understand the particular reading and writing difficulties of your students with ADHD and/or LD.

- Provide instruction to all students on how to extract meaning from the course text-book and other required reading materials.

- Provide instruction to all students on the type of writing required by the course and provide examples of effective writing.

- Teach students skills and strategies from which they can select to help them with a particular reading or writing task.

- Provide students with checklists and graphic organizers for both reading and writing.

- Appeal to a variety of learning styles when teaching reading and writing strategies.

- Give students alternative assignments that allow them to tap into their areas of interest and expertise.

- Select well-written, interesting, and relevant reading materials at the appropriate level of difficulty.

Since textbooks differ from field to field—and students have little experience with expository writing—reading and writing objectives need to be developed for all content area courses. (See Figure 4-3.)

Content Area Reading Objectives for Students

- Increase understanding of content area technical vocabulary.
- Improve comprehension of text material.
- Improve retention of text material.
- Increase the fund of content-related information.
- Select and apply appropriate strategies before, during, and after a reading task.
- Integrate information gained from reading and discussion, note-taking, test-taking, and writing.
- Increase the use of visual aids in texts, including maps, graphs, timelines, charts, illustrations and diagrams.
- Increase performance on classroom, standardized state-wide, or college admissions tests.
- Understand the purpose of the assignment.
- Demonstrate the use of advanced reading skills, including:
    —making inferences and interpretations
    —agreeing or disagreeing with the author's point of view
    —differentiating fact from fiction or propaganda
    —critically analyzing literary or technical material

Figure 4-3

Specific reading and writing objectives for a student with ADHD or LD are listed in the student's IEP. Reading and writing accommodations to help students benefit from regular class placement are listed in both IEPs and 504 Plans.

EFFECTIVE READERS AND WRITERS

Research on effective readers and writers tells us how they approach a reading or writing task. Effective readers and writers make sure they understand the assignment and what they must do in order to complete the task. They plan the strategies they will need to use; monitor their progress, attention, and motivation while working; and review and rethink what they have done when the task is completed.

Effective Reading Strategies

Thinking Strategies

- Identify the purpose of the reading assignment.
- Activate relevant background knowledge and experience.
- Preview the organization and content of the text.
- Use the structure of the text as a guide to determine important concepts.
- Identify or generate questions that need to be answered.
- Read to answer questions.
- Adjust reading speed according to the purpose of the assignment and text difficulty.
- Reread to enhance comprehension.
- Use context clues for word meaning.
- Take notes, make outlines, use graphic organizers.
- Paraphrase.
- Summarize.
- Review.

Self-Management Strategies

- Activate attention.
- Self-motivate.
- Monitor attention.
- Monitor comprehension; use self-talk and visualization.
- Use self-instruction to refocus.

Figure 4-4

Effective readers try to understand the purpose of the reading assignment. Is it to list important events leading up to a war? Is it to gather information to support a particular point of view? Is it for pleasure?

Effective readers adjust how they read and how fast they read according to the purpose of a reading task. If the purpose is to gain in-depth knowledge, reading rate slows and the reader frequently checks his or her comprehension. If the purpose of reading is pleasure, reading speed can be much faster and some specific word meanings are not necessary. (See Figure 4-4.)

Effective Writing Strategies

Thinking Strategies

- Identify the audience and what the audience needs to know.
- Activate background knowledge and experience.
- Identify or generate questions that need to be answered.
- Locate additional information, if needed.
- Discuss topic with others.
- Brainstorm important ideas and concepts.
- Relate ideas to each other.
- Add and delete ideas to help clarify and focus.
- Organize ideas.
- Add specific facts and examples.
- Make sure you have answered important questions.
- Write an outline.
- Write first draft. (Review and discuss.)
- Revise and reorder so the reader can understand.
- Review/check that there is an introduction and summary or conclusion.
- Write final draft.
- Edit.

Self-Management Strategies

- Activate attention.
- Self-motivate.
- Monitor attention.
- Use self instruction to refocus.

Figure 4-5

Similarly, effective writers know that the purpose of a writing task regulates what they need to write and how they must write it. If the writer is writing for a reader who knows nothing about the topic, the writer must first present a certain amount of background information. If the writer is writing for a reader who knows something about a topic, the writer does not need to go into too much detail. If the writing is for the purpose of self-expression, the writer writes only for himself or herself and many of the conventions of expository writing can be ignored.

Effective writers employ the same self-management strategies as effective readers. Their thinking strategies are similar, with a few notable additions: brainstorming, and maintaining a sense of audience. (See Figure 4-5.)

Effective readers and writers know that the selection of appropriate thinking and self-management strategies is the key to effective reading and writing.

TEACHING READING AND WRITING IN THE CONTENT AREA CLASS

Your decision to teach students the skills they need to be effective readers and writers is an important one. It can make the difference between success and failure for your students with ADHD and/or LD. When content area teachers coordinate their teaching and guided practice of these skills, all student learning is greatly enhanced.

Based on the research, you can focus on teaching specific strategies to improve reading and writing in content area classes. Many of these strategies are currently being taught in some content area classes; some important ones are not.

In addition to teaching specific reading and writing strategies, there are other things you can do to help improve student reading and writing. Adjust your method of presentation and provide the structure students with ADHD and/or LD need in order to become better readers and writers. As with all the learning strategies in this book, all students will benefit from the teaching of reading and writing strategies in the content area class. There are ten major adjustments in instructional methodology that you can make.

1. *Teach students to utilize questions on the topic before beginning a reading or writing assignment.* Questions can help students focus on the critical aspects of the topic. These questions can be the questions at the end of the chapter or the questions you give the students for assignments and test preparation.

2. *Provide time for students to discuss what they have read.* Discussion can greatly enhance reading comprehension. Most students prefer class discussions over reading the text because they often think the text is boring. Many students get more information from discussions than they do from reading. Students with ADHD who have difficulty focusing their attention on a reading task are much more able to cue in to a class or small-group discussion where specific points are being emphasized and questions answered. Discussions can help students with LD focus on important points as well as help with comprehension.

3. *Provide time for students to discuss what they are thinking of writing.* Discussions can help students clarify ideas prior to writing and can also help students determine what

the audience wants to know. After writing, discussions with other students can help the student edit what he or she has written, adding further explanatory material and/or deleting confusing or unnecessary detail.

4. *Tie reading more closely to writing.* If students read in order to gather information for writing, they have a purpose for reading. If students are consciously aware that what they write will need to be understood by a reader, their writing will become clearer and more focused.

   You can tie writing directly to reading by giving students a writing assignment based on a particular reading. This is often done on statewide or national achievement tests. For example, students may be asked to agree or disagree with the author or to extend the author's line of thinking to another situation. The student then reads for the specific purpose of writing a paper.

5. *Teach students how to read a variety of expository texts.* Vocabulary, text structure, and content vary from course discipline to discipline. Text structure within a discipline can also vary. Teaching students how to locate the main ideas from a variety of texts can greatly enhance reading comprehension.

6. *Teach students how to write for a variety of audiences.* If students write in order to be understood by a particular audience, the content and organization of their papers will be enhanced. Providing students with an authentic audience for whom to write, such as another student, a new immigrant or one's grandmother, will help the students decide what to include in their papers and what is not needed.

7. *Activate students' prior knowledge of the topic before reading and writing.* When you activate what the students already know about a topic, you help stimulate thought, enhance comprehension, and help students remember new material.

8. *Teach students how to use the illustrations and charts in the text to enhance comprehension.* Many students are visual learners and may respond poorly to text. The text illustrations and charts carry the same message as the text and can help visual learners learn much the same material as the readers do. Students with reading difficulties greatly benefit from these learning aids.

9. *Teach students how to use graphic organizers.* Graphic organizers can help students organize their thinking prior to and during reading and writing. The use of a prepared chart, for example, allows students to examine, record, and remember main ideas and relationships during reading. (See Figure 4-6.)

   Graphic organizers for writing are used to brainstorm to answer important questions, relate ideas to each other, and develop a logical argument to be presented in the paper. Like text illustrations and charts, graphic organizers are excellent tools for visual learners.

   When introducing the students to graphic organizers, prepare samples and give them to the students prior to a reading or writing task. Model how to use graphic organizers. As students become more adept at using them, encourage students to develop their own organizers.

   Graphic organizers can take many forms: hierarchical charts, decision trees, timelines, mind maps, checklists, or a series of questions to be answered. Their form is generally dependent on the type of information to be covered. Some students prefer one form over another. (See Figures 4-7 and 4-8.)

Student Activity: Reading and Writing

Reading: Write notes about the reading assignment.

	Who or What?	What happened?	Where?	When?	Why?	How?
Title: Author: Date: Pages:						

Reading: Answer questions about the reading assignment, such as:

- What is the reading about?
- What is the main idea?
- When did it take place?
- What other ideas are presented?
- What is the problem?
- What is the significance of the problem?
- What evidence is there?
- What are some examples?
- What solutions are presented?
- What happened as a result of the solution that was tried?

Writing: Use the reading material as a basis for writing an essay. Consider answering such questions as:

- What are the important points presented in this reading?
- How can I incorporate these points into my writing?
- What is my opinion about the topic?
- How does this reading compare with other readings or discussions?
- What ideas does my audience need to know about this topic?
- Do I need additional information about this topic?

Figure 4-6

Graphic Organizers for Complex Reading and Writing Tasks

Directions from the Social Studies portion of a state assessment: "Read the following selection. Write an essay that clearly states your opinion; provides supporting data; includes information you learned in History, Geography, Civics, or Economics; cites a core demographic value; and refutes on opposing viewpoint."

Possible graphic organizers for this task:

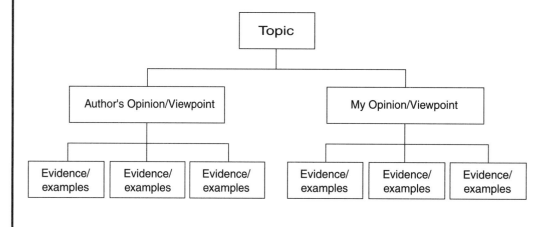

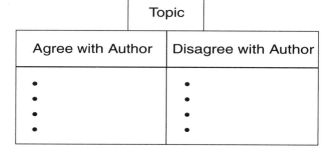

Figure 4-7

Student Checklist for a Complex
Reading and Writing Task

Writing Checklist: Refuting a Viewpoint

Introductory paragraph:
- What is the topic?
- What is the viewpoint I disagree with?
- What is my viewpoint?

Body of essay:
- Why am I taking this position?

    Reason 1:

        Supporting evidence:

        Example(s):

    Reason 2:

        Supporting evidence:

        Example(s):

    Reason 3:

        Supporting evidence:

        Example(s):

- What is the democratic value I will use?
- What information from History, Geography, Civics, or Economics related to the topic/position will I include?

Conclusion:
- Describe topic.
- Explain the author's viewpoint(s).
- Explain a viewpoint I disagree with.
- Provide summary of reasons.
- Present/summarize your viewpoint.

Figure 4-8

10. *Allow students to select alternative assignments based on their interests and strengths.* Students generally read and write more effectively about topics of particular interest to them and topics that are relevant to adolescent life. Provide the student with the alternative assignments from which to choose, or help the student with a particular interest to design an alternative assignment for himself or herself.

You can design alternative assignments that appeal to the wholistic, creative, or intuitive thinker as well as the logical or linear thinker. These assignments can include asking the student to describe how an historical figure might react to a particular situation today, or to write a series of letters from a person in one part of the world to a person in another part of the world comparing their economic or political problems.

ACTIVE READING AND WRITING

It is not enough to teach students with ADHD and/or LD how to do cognitive tasks such as reading or writing. You must also demonstrate the internal thinking and self-management process that comprises reading comprehension and effective writing because the students have no idea what this process entails. (See Figure 4-9.)

Demonstrate how to use self-talk, visualization, and problem-solving strategies with a specific reading or writing assignment. Ask and answer questions such as "What do I know about this topic?" "Am I understanding this? Should I reread it?" "What examples can I use to illustrate this idea?" "Why are these sentences in bold type?" "Does my audience really have to know this?"

Demonstrate self-instruction by saying to yourself, "Pay attention, don't get distracted" at an appropriate time. Demonstrate self-motivation by saying, "Just two more pages and then I can have a snack." Visualize and describe the setting of a particular reading passage or the reader of the paper you're preparing to write.

Demonstrate problem-solving by having a conversation with yourself in front of the class. You might say, "I'm stuck, what should I do? Okay, let's drop this line of thinking and try another approach. If I were the reader, what would I want to know?" or "I'm really having trouble understanding this. Should I go back and reread it for the third time or should I continue reading in hopes that it will become clear? I don't think rereading it for the third time will help. I'll put a question mark here and go on. If I don't understand it by the time I'm finished reading, I'll ask the teacher what it means."

After you model these strategies in front of the whole class, it is important to provide students with guided practice of these new skills. You can also give students checklists of active reading and writing skills, and model the steps in the checklists using a specific reading or writing assignment from your course. These checklists will help students remember the strategies you have taught them. (See Figures 4-10 and 4-11.)

There are many mnemonic devices that have been developed through the years by various authors and researchers which can help students remember reading and writing strategies. Prominent among these are SQ4R, KWL, and COPS:

- SQ4R stands for *Survey, Question, Read, Recite, (w)Rite, Review.* It is a multisensory reading strategy that helps students locate, organize, and remember new material.

Teacher Checklist: Integrating the Teaching of Reading into the Content Area

Pre-Reading Activities

- ☐ Discuss the purpose of the reading assignment.
- ☐ Relate new information to be learned from the text to what students already know about the topic.
- ☐ Survey the text to understand its structure. Show how text structure can assist comprehension.
- ☐ Note reading and study aids included in the text. Note questions at the end of the chapter.
- ☐ Make the topic relevant to student experiences and interests.
- ☐ Introduce critical concepts and vocabulary.
- ☐ Discuss questions using different levels of thinking that might be answered in the text.
- ☐ Locate materials written at a lower reading level.
- ☐ Locate audio tape of the text.

Model Reading Strategies and Provide Guided Practice

- ☐ How to use questions to help with focus and understanding
- ☐ How to activate and monitor attention
- ☐ How to monitor understanding using self-talk
- ☐ How to use checklists and graphic organizers
- ☐ How to paraphrase and summarize
- ☐ How to use reading strategies when taking a test
- ☐ How to develop a plan for completing short- and long-term assignments
- ☐ How to read a section of the text in order to answer questions
- ☐ How to highlight important, interesting, or confusing information (highlighters, sticky notes)

Post-Reading Activities

- ☐ Ask students to review and summarize what was read.
- ☐ Discuss insights and reactions to the reading.
- ☐ Discuss the information provided by illustrations and charts from the text.
- ☐ Compare information from text with information from other sources.

Figure 4-9

Student Checklist: Active Reading

Before Reading

- ☐ Review the reading assignment to identify a purpose for reading.
- ☐ List one to three important questions.
- ☐ Make a plan and set goals (e.g., time allotted, number of questions to answer).
- ☐ Identify what you already know about the topic.
- ☐ Tell yourself the reading strategy you will use (e.g., SQ4R and KWL).
- ☐ Decide if a chart or diagram will help organize the information.
- ☐ Gather materials (e.g., textbook, paper, pencils).
- ☐ Find a pleasant and nondistracting place to work.
- ☐ Schedule a break.

During Reading

- ☐ Pay attention.
- ☐ Search for clues to understanding (e.g., key words, boldface type, illustrations, etc.).
- ☐ Monitor your comprehension. Ask yourself, "Do I understand this?"
- ☐ Try to see a mental picture of the information just read.
- ☐ Reread a section if you don't understand it. Ask the teacher for help, if needed.
- ☐ Write down new vocabulary.
- ☐ Write information on graphic organizers or draw sketches.
- ☐ Relate new information to previously learned information.
- ☐ Take frequent breaks.
- ☐ Talk to yourself to maintain your attention and motivation.

After Reading

- ☐ Think about and summarize what you have read.
- ☐ Create a picture or story in your mind of what you have read.
- ☐ Identify information from other sources that confirms or contradicts what you have just read.
- ☐ Write your opinion.
- ☐ Think about how you can use this information.
- ☐ Recognize your efforts.
- ☐ Reward yourself if you accomplished most of what you set out to do.
- ☐ Set a realistic goal for the next time you read—for instance, answering a certain number of questions.

Adapted with permission. From *Performance Breakthroughs for Adolescents with Learning Disabilities or ADD: How to Help Students Succeed in the Regular Education Classroom* by Geraldine Markel, Ph.D. and Judith Greenbaum, Ph.D. Champaign, IL: Research Press, 1996 (p. 183).

Figure 4-10

Student Checklist: Active Writing

Select a Topic

- ☐ Rephrase the assignment in your own words.
- ☐ Identify the general purpose of the assignment (e.g., compare/contrast, present an argument, solve a problem, describe a sequence of events, etc.).
- ☐ Identify the points the teacher wants you to make.
- ☐ Consider your own interests, strengths, and current knowledge.
- ☐ Identify the audience and the purpose.
- ☐ Think of a topic. Ask yourself, "Do I have enough ideas about this topic?"
- ☐ Try out another topic, if necessary.
- ☐ Plan a topic that is narrow enough to be completed in the time allotted.
- ☐ Check the topic with your teacher.

Make a Plan

- ☐ Identify the length and due date of the assignment.
- ☐ Identify the sources of information you will need to use.
- ☐ List tasks (e.g., select topic, read, use a graphic organizer, make outline, think, discuss, write, edit, etc.).
- ☐ Include time for gathering additional information (reading) in your plan.
- ☐ Develop a schedule or timeline. List all tasks.
- ☐ Make a checklist of all the points or questions your teacher wants you to cover.

Organize the Paper

- ☐ Brainstorm ideas that might be included in the paper.
- ☐ Relate ideas to each other.
- ☐ Focus the topic. Add and delete ideas.
- ☐ Organize ideas. List in a logical sequence.
- ☐ Add examples and supporting evidence.
- ☐ Ask yourself, "What does the audience need to know? What message do I want to communicate?"
- ☐ Ask yourself, "What points or questions does the teacher want covered?"
- ☐ Develop an outline of your paper. Develop a list of questions you will answer. Think of different ways of presenting the information.
- ☐ Ask the teacher for feedback on your outline.

(continued)

Figure 4-11

Write

- [ ] Explain the purpose of the paper in the introductory paragraph.
- [ ] Complete each paragraph by answering one question at a time or making one point at a time.
- [ ] Include examples and supporting evidence for each question or point.
- [ ] Insert transitions between paragraphs.
- [ ] Restate the purpose in the last paragraph; summarize points you have made; include your conclusions, opinions, or recommendations.
- [ ] Ask the teacher for feedback on the first draft.

Revise

- [ ] Check that you have included all the points or questions the teacher wanted covered.
- [ ] Check that information is presented in a logical order.
- [ ] Reorganize, if necessary.
- [ ] Check that there are sections labeled to indicate the introduction, different topics, recommendations, summary, or conclusions.
- [ ] Check that you have included evidence and examples for each point covered.
- [ ] Check that you have correctly used technical vocabulary.

Edit

- [ ] Check that you have included the title, your name, date, and class on the front page.
- [ ] Check that spelling is correct, including technical vocabulary, names, and places.
- [ ] Check the accuracy of facts you cited, including dates, times, locations.
- [ ] Check grammar. Ask yourself, "Is there a capital and period for each sentence?"
- [ ] Check that you have clearly indicated the beginning of a new paragraph.
- [ ] Check that your paper is clean and legible.
- [ ] Check that the references you have included are accurate.

- KWL stands for what you *Know* about a topic, what you *Want* to learn, and what you have *Learned* about the topic. It is a graphic organizer to help students relate new information to what they have already learned, write questions that can help focus their reading, and write down what new information they have learned so that they can remember it.
- COPS is an aid to editing and revising and stands for: Capitalization, Organization, Punctuation, and Spelling.

You can make up your own mnemonics by developing an acronym for a specific strategy or set of strategies that can be easily remembered by your students. Teach several of these to your class and demonstrate their different purposes.

READING AND WRITING ACCOMMODATIONS

All of these reading and writing strategies can help students with ADHD and/or LD. These—as well as other accommodations—can be individualized for students like Mike, Angeliese, and Clyde as needed. (See Figure 4-12.)

A list of additional accommodations can be found in Chapter 7 that deals with IEPs and 504 Plans.

Mike's Accommodations

Mike's writing accommodations in his Language Arts class took the form of a teacher-prepared checklist to help him focus on the topic and organize his thoughts. The teacher consultant helped the classroom teacher design the checklist and—with Mike's input—fine tune it. (See Figure 4-13.)

Although Mike still tended to ramble, his papers were much more coherent when he used the writing checklist the teacher individualized for him.

Angeliese's Accommodations

Since Angeliese had not handed in a paper all semester, her first objective was to write down what she wanted to say and hand it in. The writing accommodation developed for Angeliese allowed her to merely list the points she wanted to make and arrange them in logical order, instead of requiring her to write the complete sentences and paragraphs required by the typical writing assignment, which took up so much of her time. The teacher agreed that he would give Angeliese a passing grade if the points she made were sound and the argument she presented, valid.

For Angeliese's first paper, the teacher used a question-and-answer approach to help Angeliese brainstorm the points she wanted to make and the order in which she wanted to present them. After proudly handing in her first "paper" and getting a B, Angeliese was

Reading and Writing Accommodations for Students with ADHD and/or LD

Reading

- Teach reading strategies.
- Provide audio tape of textbooks.
- Adapt textbooks: highlight main ideas, provide outline of chapters.
- Provide graphic organizers.
- Provide reading material written at a lower grade level.
- Read text and tests to student.
- Give student additional time on tests.
- Limit amount of required reading; give students extra time to complete readings.

Attention, Hyperactivity

- Provide a quiet corner for reading.
- Cue student to get on task and stay on task.
- Provide frequent breaks; allow students to stand and stretch.
- Seat the student near a student role model.
- Allow student to use headphones, per IEP.
- Ignore jiggling, tapping, standing, walking unless it bothers other students.

Writing

- Encourage student to select writing topics in areas of interest.
- Allow student to dictate paper to scribe.
- Provide student with a writing checklist.
- Provide student with checkpoints for topic selection, outline, first draft.
- Allow alternatives to some writing assignments (e.g., oral presentations, projects).
- Do not penalize for poor spelling, punctuation, grammar.
- Provide student with access to computer to take notes in class.
- Arrange for student to get class notes from another student or you provide them.

Homework

- Check accuracy/understanding of reading and writing assignments, and written directions.
- Check that student takes home necessary books and other reading materials.
- Adapt word problems in math.
- Encourage student to select supplemental reading in areas of interest.
- Give student additional time to complete reading and writing assignments.
- Provide a second set of textbooks to keep at home.

Figure 4-12

Mike's Writing Checklist

_____ 1. What does the teacher want you to do: explain, compare, agree/disagree, form an opinion, etc.

_____ 2. Look at the points the teacher wants you to include. Turn these into a checklist. Include an introductory paragraph and conclusion in your checklist.

_____ 3. What will be the main idea of your paper? Select a topic based on your own interest. (Check with the teacher, if necessary.)

_____ 4. Discuss with a friend.

_____ 5. Brainstorm ideas/points you want to make and examples you might use.

_____ 6. Organize the ideas from your brainstorming into logical groupings. Decide specific points to include in your paper. Eliminate nonessential ideas.

_____ 7. Decide on your conclusion or develop your argument _before_ you write the paper.

_____ 8. Write an introductory paragraph. What you are about to tell the audience? What is your paper about? What is your point of view?

_____ 9. Next paragraph: any background information the reader needs in order to understand the points you are making.

_____ 10. Write the next several paragraphs with the points you want to make. Include some facts and examples.

_____ 11. Write a concluding paragraph. State your point of view, summarize.

_____ 12. Go back to your checklist and check that you have included all the points the teacher wanted.

_____ 13. Read the paper out loud to yourself to see if it makes sense. Correct, add, delete sections.

_____ 14. Give the paper to a friend to read. Ask for suggestions.

_____ 15. Use "COPS" to revise: Capitalization, Organization, Punctuation, Spelling.

Figure 4-13

eager to use the same approach for her second paper. This time, after handing it in and getting another B, she asked for additional time to turn each point she had made into a complete sentence. (See Figure 4-14.)

Angeliese told her teacher how much the class discussions of the reading assignments were helping her organize her thoughts and make sense out of what she read.

Angeliese's First Paper for Language Arts

Assignment: Compare and Contrast *The Minister's Black Veil* **and**
The Scarlet Letter

The Minister's Black Veil

- Two principal characters: Hooper and Elizabeth
- Setting: Puritan times (17th century)
- Veil a symbol of secret sins
- Veil seen as horrible, gloomy
- People thought Hooper had committed a great sin and was atoning for it
- Veil separated him from the world
- His bride-to-be, Elizabeth, left him because he refused to remove the veil
- He was unloved and feared
- He became a more effective minister because:
  —the veil added drama to his sermons
  —the people felt he understood them because he was a sinner like themselves

The Scarlet Letter

- Same setting
- Three principle characters: Hester, Dimmesdale, and Chillingworth
- Chillingworth is Hester's husband
- Hester commits adultery with Dimmesdale; Pearl is born
- Dimmesdale hides his sin from community because he thinks his ability to do good as a minister will suffer if he confesses
- Symbol of secret sin: Dimmesdale's self-inflicted scar
- Symbols of evil: Chillingworth's hump
- Scarlet letter A separates Hester from community
- Hester was unloved and feared by community in the beginning

Similarities

- Both by Nathaniel Hawthorne
- Same setting, Puritan times
- Main characters: minister and woman he loves
- Involve idea of secret sin
- Use of symbols of sin: veil, letter A, scar

(continued)

Figure 4-14

- Both alienated from society, great suffering
- Expose intolerance and hypocrisy
- Very little action

Differences

- *The Minister's Black Veil*
  —Characters not well developed
  —We know nothing about why Elizabeth acted as she did
  —We don't know how minister arrived at his decision to wear veil
  —Minister's motivation somewhat unclear
- *The Scarlet Letter*
  —Characters well developed
  —Characters grow and change
  —Motivation of characters clear

Clyde's Accommodations

Due to the nature and severity of Clyde's reading and writing problems, he spent one hour a day in the resource room improving his reading and writing using Project Read, a multisensory approach based on Gillingham & Stillman (1960).

Clyde's resource room teacher consulted with his classroom teachers regarding reading and writing accommodations. One of the most helpful reading accommodations was providing Clyde with audio tapes of his textbooks so that—even though he could not read the texts—he could learn the material. In addition, one of his writing accommodations stated that he would be allowed to dictate his papers to his mother because he had such difficulty with written expression.

Clyde's middle school required all students to take a reading-for-pleasure class to get students in the habit of reading. Among the many books and articles available to the students were several books written for twelve-year-old interests at a third-grade reading level from which Clyde could choose. Clyde enjoyed this class and was essentially immersed in reading a large part of the day.

Clyde's reading and writing improvement program had three components: intensive instruction in a resource room, a reading class open to all students, and reading and writing accommodations in his regular education classes.

A SCHOOLWIDE COMMITMENT

When students with ADHD and/or LD reach middle school and high school, they begin to lag further and further behind their classmates. Other students with poor reading and writing skills also begin to falter as the challenge increases. There needs to be a schoolwide commitment to reading and writing improvement for all students.

Different types of reading and writing improvement programs can be offered by different parts of the school community. A schoolwide committee can oversee the improvement effort:

- Identify student needs in the areas of reading and writing.
- Identify the reading and writing strategies students will be taught.
- Determine who will be responsible for different aspects of the improvement program.
- Use a systems view to align the teaching of reading and writing strategies in all courses at each grade level.
- Arrange for inservice training on how to integrate the teaching of reading and writing in content area courses.

Of course, the responsibility for teaching reading and writing does not fall solely on the shoulders of the classroom teacher. Other school staff—such as special education teacher consultants, remedial reading teachers, tutors, and summer school staff—can be involved in different aspects of the program.

The following ten types of offerings can be considered by your school when designing the new reading and writing improvement program:

1. A required reading and writing course in middle school and high school in which students are taught study skills, note-taking, and test-taking strategies as well as reading and writing strategies

2. A reading-for-pleasure class based on the premise that the more a student reads, regardless of the nature of the reading, the better reader he or she will become

3. Intensive special education instruction for students with ADHD and/or LD in reading, decoding, comprehension, and written expression

4. Reading accommodations in the content area class for students with IEPs and 504 Plans

5. The integration of reading and writing strategies into content area courses such as Social Studies, Science, Language Arts, and Math

6. An analysis of current textbooks to determine their readability and selection of new textbooks to replace those that are poorly written or organized; the location of texts written at a lower reading level that a student can use to learn much the same information the regular text conveys

7. Homework assistance and tutoring after school or on Saturdays to help students with their reading or writing assignments

8. Summer courses to increase reading or writing skills, the benefit being that they are usually small and allow for more individualized instruction

9. Computer-based reading and writing instruction

10. Free SAT and ACT preparatory courses focusing on the critical reading and writing skills required by the tests and an increase in reading speed and comprehension; SATs, ACTs, and statewide assessment exams require an advanced level of reading and writing often not included in the middle or high school classroom (see Figure 4-15)

Student Checklist: Active Reading for SAT/ACT-Type Reading Passages

Survey the questions.

_____ Read the questions. Identify the type of questions you must answer: Main idea? More fact than inference questions? Are there questions about the tone or the author's purpose?

_____ Make a rough guess about the content of the passage.

Survey the passage.

_____ Survey the passage. Identify the topic. Does it relate to Literature? Science? Social Studies?

_____ Read the title, introduction, and summary. What is the passage about? Can I imagine the setting? What do I already know about the topic?

_____ Read the first line or two of each paragraph. What is each paragraph about? What type of passage is it? Explanatory? Cause and effect? Compare and contrast? Sequence of events?

_____ Get an idea where answers to some questions are located.

Read the passage. The goal is to find the answers to the questions.

_____ Read the first paragraph. Circle or write important facts, words, or phrases. Look for the main idea.

_____ Read the next paragraphs. Circle or write important words or phrases. Look for answers to questions.

_____ Visualize the main character(s) and setting. How would I feel and act if I were in this situation: Do I know someone like this?

_____ Reread or say aloud complicated or confusing phrases or sentences.

_____ Use vocabulary skills to make an intelligent guess about words of which you are not sure. Check the prefixes and roots. Look at the context.

_____ What are the important issues discussed in this passage?

_____ Can I relate this information to something I already know?

(continued)

Figure 4–15

_____ Think about the feelings or emotions that are in the passage. Circle words or phrases that indicate a feeling or tone. Are they negative or positive? What feeling(s) do they indicate?

_____ Circle or jot down answers to questions as you go along.

Answer the questions.   The goal is to find the BEST answer.

_____ Read the questions and each possible answer.

_____ Read the choices and select the one that is closest to your choice, crossing out those you feel are incorrect.

_____ Keep referring to the text while you are selecting among the choices and excluding those you feel are incorrect.

_____ Rethink the main idea.

_____ Rethink the type of passage you think it is. Explanatory? Cause and effect? Compare and contrast? Sequence of events?

_____ Look at the amount of evidence that supports your choice for the main idea.

Check your answers.   The goal is to find the BEST answer.

_____ Circle or underline the words, phrases, or other clues in the passage that support the answer to each question.

_____ If you are not sure of an answer, reread portions of the passage.

_____ If you are not sure of an answer, see if you can infer the answer from some portion of the passage.

Notes

_____

_____

_____

_____

_____

_____

A FINAL WORD

The low literacy rate of our adult population and the severity of the problems our students are having with reading and writing serve as a call to arms for all teachers. We are already feeling the pressure from state and federal governments to improve reading and writing for all students. We have already begun to see the new emphasis on literacy in our elementary and middle schools. But is it enough?

The need is clear that academic reading and writing will have to be taught in middle school and high school, and that this is best done in the content area classroom. Admittedly, the retooling required by teachers will at first take time and require some extra work. Once in place, however, integrating the teaching of reading and writing in the content area class will take almost no time away from the teaching of content.

For students with ADHD and/or LD, learning reading and writing strategies in the content areas can mean the difference between failure and success, college entry and a dead-end job. IDEA and Section 504 both consider it "reasonable" to teach reading and writing in the content areas to students with ADHD and/or LD. As long as you are providing these types of accommodations for your students with LD and ADHD, it is easy to provide them for all your students.

We can no longer afford to shift the blame for the country's literacy problems from college to high school to elementary school. Each of us must take responsibility for teaching our students how to read and write.

CHAPTER FIVE

Teaching Homework-Completion Skills

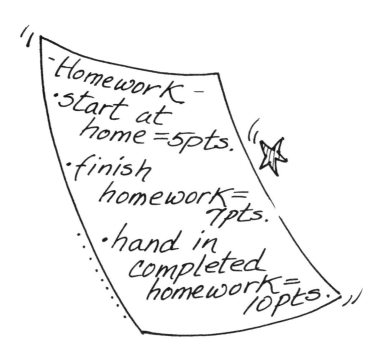

TEACHER:	You're missing seven assignments this month. What's the problem?
BRANDON:	I dunno.
TEACHER:	What happened to your assignment book?
BRANDON:	I lost it.
TEACHER:	Did you have trouble understanding any of the assignments?
BRANDON:	Sorta.
TEACHER:	Why didn't you come to me for help?
BRANDON:	I dunno.
TEACHER:	Couldn't your parents help you?
BRANDON:	They work.
TEACHER:	You know you're in danger of failing this marking period?
BRANDON:	Yeah.
TEACHER:	(Exasperated) Brandon, you're a bright kid, but I don't know what to do with you.

As you might imagine, this is a very frustrating exchange for the teacher. Brandon, a middle school student with ADHD, is quite shaken up also, although he tries to hide it. He has almost stopped working in school.

Homework problems are everyday occurrences in school. Students like Brandon can appear uncaring, disinterested, and lazy.

Variations of this school scenario are also played out in homes across the country every night. However, the hassles at home may enter the realm of high drama.

MOTHER: Haven't you finished your homework yet?
CHRISTINE: No!!! Leave me alone! You don't know how hard this is. You don't understand. You never listen to me. I hate you. I hate school. (Slam!)

Christine and her mother fight constantly over homework. These battles are emotionally draining for both of them. The constant fighting threatens the stability of the family.

Homework problems affect teachers, parents, and students. Many students with ADHD and/or LD become unhappy, frustrated, and angry every time they attempt to do their homework. Even when they are allowed to begin their homework in class, these students often do not understand what is being asked of them. They are also so disorganized at home that they do not know where to begin and feel so defeated that they often do not even try.

Parents and teachers are also angry, frustrated, and unhappy. Parents try to support homework completion but are often met by a barrage of complaints, attacks, and just plain disobedience (Polloway, Foley & Epstein, 1992). Teachers feel as if they are knocking their heads against a stone wall.

HOMEWORK, AN UNHAPPY STATE OF AFFAIRS

The penalty a student paid for not doing an assignment in the 1970s was failing the test or being embarrassed when unable to answer the teacher's questions. The increased emphasis on homework began around 1980. This was largely due to increasing international competition and the resulting higher educational standards adopted by the United States. In the 1990s the penalties for not handing in homework became much more severe.

Teachers—often overwhelmed by the demands for higher student achievement and faced with an increasingly challenging school population—may assign more and more homework. Currently, failing to hand in homework can cost the student 50 percent or more of the course grade, regardless of how well the student does on tests or participates in class discussions.

HOMEWORK PROBLEMS AND THEIR CAUSES

It is important for you to examine some of the factors that can cause homework problems. It is also important for you to understand some of these issues from the perspectives of parents and students. After examining the issues, you may begin to question some of the commonly held assumptions regarding the responsibilities of teacher, parent, and student for homework completion. (See Figure 5-1.)

Homework Problems Reported by Parents of Students with ADHD and/or LD

- Forgets to bring home assignments or materials.
- Fails to copy assignment.
- Copies homework assignment incorrectly.
- Denies having homework assignment.
- Must be constantly reminded to sit down/start homework.
- Procrastinates; puts off doing homework.
- Easily distracted; daydreams.
- Easily frustrated by homework assignment.
- Starts homework but does not finish.
- Takes unusually long time to do homework.
- Argues with parents about homework.
- Hurries through homework and makes careless mistakes.
- Insists on doing homework with television or loud music.
- Puts off doing homework until late at night.
- Misplaces completed homework.

Figure 5-1

Students who have learning or attention problems in school will certainly have problems completing homework at home. These students have great difficulty working independently under unstructured conditions. The teacher in school provides guidance and structure. We cannot expect parents to provide the same level of support at home.

Brandon, who we met at the beginning of this chapter, is a tenth-grader with ADHD. He has problems with distractibility as well as impulsivity and hyperactivity. Brandon often clowns around when he should be working. While he is not considered malicious, Brandon's behavior is often considered noncompliant and disruptive. He rarely completes his class-work and homework. He often arrives late to his classes without books, pencils, or paper. Brandon says that he likes all his classes and his friends, but doesn't like some of his teachers. "They write me up for no reason," he says.

Christine is a seventh-grader who has learning disabilities in writing and some problems with reading. Her reading and writing problems are the cause of her homework problems. She reads very slowly. Her writing is so disorganized that every paper she writes is returned to her covered in red ink. Homework is such a hassle for her that at this point she often just tells her mother that she has no homework.

When students like Brandon and Christine have problems with homework, you will need to identify the particular problems they have. Some homework problems are due primarily to ADHD and/or LD. These students may lack necessary skills, have developed poor habits, or developed secondary emotional problems that interfere with homework completion. Many of these students either don't understand what the assignment is asking them to do or fail to write down these assignments accurately. Homework for these students is usually a "can't do" rather than a "won't do" problem.

To find out more about Brandon's problems with homework, the teacher asked him to fill out a self-evaluation questionnaire (Levine, 1991). His answers were quite revealing. He said that when teachers give him complicated or long directions, he forgets them. He often has trouble remembering what the teacher said just a little while ago. He also said that it is hard for him to keep his mind on his work and it's hard for him to sit still in a classroom. "Sometimes I don't do my work. I'm talking." When asked if he knows how to get teachers to like him, he answers "I don't care."

A checklist can be used by teachers to identify student difficulties and disabilities that interfere with homework completion. (See Figure 5-2.)

Adolescents and their parents are unaware that the pace, difficulty, and importance of homework increases as students move from elementary to middle to high school. The poor study habits that could be ignored previously will now become major barriers to homework completion.

Students with ADHD and/or LD can no longer compensate as they did in earlier grades for reading and writing difficulties. They are faced with learning more advanced skills in reading, writing, math, and self-management, even though they still lack many basic skills.

Adolescence itself often brings negative reactions to homework. This can occur to students who up until this point have been relatively interested in school and compliant. Adolescents want to be independent and they want to be with their peers. They may see homework as interfering with their independence and their friendships.

Another reason a student might have homework problems is that there are differing expectations about parent involvement with homework. For example, teachers generally assume that parents can and should help their children with homework. However, parents often don't know how to or can't help their children with homework. Many parents are working and are often unavailable to help with homework. A large percentage of parents don't have the skills to help with homework. Some parents may not want to help with homework, believing it is not their responsibility.

There are misconceptions about the development of homework skills. Most teachers and parents assume that students will naturally develop good homework habits. However, many students—even those without learning problems—need to be taught how to work without structure and guidance.

Of course, working independently is the goal for all students. However, students will differ in the amount of time it will take them to achieve that goal. Many problems occur when teachers (or parents) assume that a student can work independently when he or she cannot, or assume that because a student can work independently in school he or she can work independently at home.

There are many myths held by teachers, parents, and students that can lead to assumptions and actions that have a negative influence on homework. (See Figure 5-3.)

Some causes of homework problems can be traced to the school and classroom. Texts might be written at too high a reading level. They may be poorly written and boring, and lack critical learning features such as questions at the end of chapters, a glossary, or the use of boldface type and italics for emphasis of important information.

Teacher Checklist: Student Homework Problems

Student _____   Date _____

Directions
- Identify a student who does not hand in homework assignments.
- Check problems that you have observed.
- Discuss difficulties with the student.

Difficulties
- ☐ Low-level reading or writing skills.
- ☐ Slow processing; takes a long time to read or write.
- ☐ Problems with receptive or expressive language.
- ☐ Doesn't know how to begin assignments.
- ☐ Cannot break assignments into steps.
- ☐ Cannot prioritize.
- ☐ Doesn't copy assignments accurately from the chalkboard.
- ☐ Forgets or loses assignments; doesn't bring assignments home.
- ☐ Poor organization.
- ☐ Poor time-management skills, procrastination.
- ☐ Problems with distractibility.
- ☐ Problems activating and maintaining attention.
- ☐ Memory problems—auditory or visual. Forgets what has been memorized; can't remember what was read the night before.
- ☐ Poor fine-motor skills; poor eye–hand coordination. Extremely slow and/or illegible copying from the chalkboard or writing while the teacher is describing the assignment.
- ☐ Difficulty working independently.
- ☐ Procrastination and/or perfectionism.
- ☐ Easily frustrated.
- ☐ Chronic failure, demoralization.
- ☐ Laziness or irresponsibility; lack of motivation.
- ☐ Stress and/or emotional problems.
- ☐ Fatigue (too many activities, illness/allergies, not enough sleep).

Comments:

_____

_____

Figure 5-2

Homework: Myths and Facts

Myths	Facts
Teachers	
• Students could get their homework done if they really wanted to.	• Many students with ADHD and/or LD confront serious barriers when doing their homework. They do not have the required skills.
• Students don't have to be taught homework skills.	• Students do not spontaneously develop time-management, organization, or independent learning skills. They need direct instruction, practice, feedback, and reinforcement.
• If 30 minutes of homework is good, one hour is better.	• A guideline for assigning homework is 20 minutes per course in middle school and 30 minutes per course in high school. With four to five courses, 2½ hours each night is required at the high school level.
Students	
• Homework really doesn't matter. The teacher doesn't even check it—it is not used for our grades.	• Homework matters even if the teacher doesn't check it. In many courses, the material builds on earlier lessons, so students may do poorly on tests because they have not had the practice and review they need.
• Do the homework as fast as you can. All anyone needs to do is copy answers or fill in the blanks.	• Effective completion of homework involves active thinking and practice—not thoughtless "filling in the blanks."
Parents	
• The kids are old enough to work on their own. Besides, I don't have the time.	• Parents have important responsibilities to help students develop independent learning skills and support/recognize efforts.
• Homework is just "busy work."	• Parents need to be informed about the purposes of assignments (e.g., review, practice, problem-solving).

Figure 5-3

Assignments may be unclear or given in a rush at the end of the class hour. Teachers may inadvertently give assignments that are too long and that don't take into account other homework or other responsibilities or interests the student might have (such as extracurricular activities). The optimal total amount of homework to assign is one to two hours per night for middle school and two and a half hours for high school students. Many students with ADHD and/or LD and their parents report spending three to four hours, several nights a week, on homework.

As a result of some of these factors, homework has become the number one academic problem in school for teachers, students, and parents. Grades suffer, self-esteem decreases, and interactions with adults are more strained.

WHY IS HOMEWORK ASSIGNED?

Most students and their parents have no idea why homework is given. They often feel that homework is irrelevant "busy work." Yet there are many educationally sound reasons for assigning homework to students, all of which lead to increased student achievement. (See Figure 5-4.)

Homework is, essentially, the foundation of lifelong learning. Whether we have careers, volunteer in community organizations, go shopping for food, or prepare a birthday party, we have to do our "homework." This means we have to know how to make to-do lists, seek out information, make plans, fulfill our responsibilities, and work independently without anyone telling us what or how to do it. Homework helps to prepare students for their life as adults.

We have all had the experience of attending a class on computers or bicycle repair, for example, and because we did not immediately practice the new skill, we forgot what we had

---

Reasons for Assigning Homework

- Helps students practice newly learned skills.
- Helps students generalize newly learned skills.
- Allows students to work at their own pace.
- Gives students time to complete work they didn't finish in school.
- Prepares students for the next day's lesson.
- Teaches students how to work independently and helps develop good work habits.
- Prepares students for tests.
- Gives students a chance to demonstrate mastery.
- Engages students in active learning.

Figure 5-4

been taught. Practice is an important part of the learning process. Homework provides the practice students require to learn new material.

HOMEWORK RESPONSIBILITIES OF THE TEACHER, PARENT, AND STUDENT

Teachers, parents, and students all share in the responsibility for homework completion, although parents and teachers often think that students bear the entire responsibility themselves.

The Teacher's Responsibilities

Your goals when assigning homework are to give students the chance to practice newly learned skills, to expand student knowledge and skills, and to increase student responsibility for learning. In order to do this, you have to make sure your assignments are well thought out, interesting, not too long, and at the appropriate level of difficulty for the students in your class. (See Figure 5-5.)

Teacher Checklist: Responsibilities for Homework

- ☐ Clearly communicate homework assignment to students.
- ☐ Base homework on skills and content already learned in class.
- ☐ Relate assignments to classwork.
- ☐ Carefully assess the amount of homework that you give.
- ☐ Coordinate your assignments with those of other teachers.
- ☐ Maintain accurate and current records about the number of assignments completed by each student, the dates they were turned in, and the grade.
- ☐ Give students timely and specific feedback about their homework.
- ☐ Give parents timely feedback about any homework-related problems the student might have.
- ☐ Provide remedial help for the student or refer the student for help.
- ☐ Provide homework accommodations for students with ADHD and/or LD.
- ☐ Don't give assignments when you are rushed.
- ☐ Don't use homework for learning new material.
- ☐ Don't expect parents to be teachers.

Figure 5-5

For students with ADHD and/or LD who need more intensive help with homework, the special education teacher can be a valuable resource. (See Figure 5-6.)

You and the teacher consultant or resource room teacher need to be in close contact to coordinate homework completion. The special education teacher can suggest homework completion strategies to you (and the parent). You can ask the special education teacher to help a student with ADHD and/or LD with a specific homework skill.

You and the special education teacher can refer to the student's psychological evaluation to understand the student's problems and how they can affect homework completion.

The Parent's Responsibilities

Parents should not be required to teach the student or offer substantive help to the student, since many parents cannot do this. Students whose parents provide such help have an unfair advantage over students whose parents cannot help them academically. In fact, students prefer to be given homework that they can do themselves without parental help.

Parents *can* help their children by providing a supportive environment in which to do their homework.

Like teachers, parents have several responsibilities for helping their child complete their homework. (See Figure 5-7.)

Special Education Teacher Checklist:
Responsibilities for Homework

- ☐ Check that the student has copied the assignment correctly.
- ☐ Help the student to understand the assignment.
- ☐ Help the student break down a long-term assignment into steps and schedule the steps on a calendar.
- ☐ Help the student begin the assignment.
- ☐ Remind the student to bring home assignments and materials.
- ☐ Develop a checklist of steps needed to complete homework assignments, based on the student's special needs.
- ☐ Check with classroom teachers about any missed or late homework assignments.
- ☐ Read or help the student to read the assigned text portions.
- ☐ Highlight main ideas in the textbook; prepare an outline of the material.
- ☐ Create or use graphic organizers to help the student read, learn the material, or write reports.
- ☐ Reteach content that the student has trouble learning.

Figure 5-6

Parent Checklist: Responsibilities for Homework

- ☐ Arrange a quiet, nondistracting place where the student can work.
- ☐ Provide supplies such as paper, pencils, book bag, calendar, timer, or clock.
- ☐ Encourage the student to do some homework every night.
- ☐ Be available to support or help the student solve problems.
- ☐ Assist in understanding directions.
- ☐ Help the student develop a homework plan.
- ☐ Encourage a realistic study schedule.
- ☐ Check on the student occasionally.
- ☐ Talk to the teacher about any homework difficulties the student is having.
- ☐ Praise the student for working on homework.

Figure 5-7

Student Checklist: Responsibilities for Homework

- ☐ Copy assignments accurately into an assignment book.
- ☐ Make sure that directions for assignments are understood before leaving class or school.
- ☐ Highlight due dates.
- ☐ Bring home necessary books, materials, etc.
- ☐ Develop a daily homework plan with the help of the teacher consultant or parent.
- ☐ Plan to do a certain amount of homework every day.
- ☐ Decide when and where to do homework; limit distractions.
- ☐ Work on homework without constant reminders from parents.
- ☐ Complete homework to the best of your ability in a timely fashion.
- ☐ Check over homework for mistakes and readability.
- ☐ Hand in homework to the teacher on time.
- ☐ Ask for help when needed from parent or teacher.

Figure 5-8

Send home information to parents about your homework policy, types of student assignments, and how parents can help the student.

The Student's Responsibilities

Of course the student's responsibility is to do the homework and hand it in. The student must use many self-management and thinking strategies in order to do this (see Chapter 6). There are many intermediary self-management tasks the student must accomplish if homework is to be completed. (See Figure 5-8.)

PREVENTING HOMEWORK PROBLEMS

Many homework problems of students with ADHD and/or LD are predictable. In fact, if you have taught for several years, you will find that the homework problems of all students are predictable. If we can predict homework problems, we can be proactive and integrate into the curriculum ways of preventing those problems that are avoidable.

A preventive thrust for homework problems includes the rethinking of:

- The purpose of homework
- How much homework is optimal
- What percent of the course grade should be allotted to homework
- What are common homework problems
- How we can solve or prevent homework problems

Homework should be viewed as an important learning experience for students. A schoolwide homework policy should be developed with the proviso that homework-completion skills be taught to all students. (See Figure 5-9.)

Teaching Homework-Completion Skills

Many homework problems can be prevented by integrating the teaching of homework-completion skills whenever assignments are given during the first month or so of the school year. In order to teach homework-completion skills, use authentic assignments and model each step using self-talk. Then ask the students to do the same with another assignment. Provide the students with guided practice of homework-completion skills for several weeks whenever an assignment is given. (See Figure 5-10.)

It is important for you to go over homework in class, explaining why certain answers are correct. Tell students to put corrected homework back into their notebooks so that they can use the homework to prepare for tests.

All skills cannot be taught at one time. It may be necessary to reteach some skills during the semester, depending upon feedback you obtain from student homework and student

---

Skills Students Need to Complete Homework

- Have reading and writing skills close to grade level (with accommodations as needed).
- Remember to bring home assignment, books, other materials.
- Break down long-term assignments into steps.
- Schedule assignments and due dates on a calendar.
- Correctly estimate the amount of time needed to complete each assignment.
- Prioritize tasks and activities.
- Organize backpack, notebooks, assignment sheets, completed homework.
- Work independently in an *unstructured* environment.
- Carefully plan when to do homework.
- Design workspace to eliminate distractions.
- Know when to take breaks.
- Stay on-task until assignment is completed.
- Check homework for mistakes.
- Ask for help when needed.
- Hand in homework when due.
- Manage frustration.
- Self-motivate.

Figure 5-9

report. Homework provides a natural opportunity for students to use and learn self-management: goal-setting, self-monitoring, self-motivation, etc.

The checklist given in Figure 5-11 covers the entire homework-completion process. Only part of the checklist can be taught at one time. The checklist may need to be reworded and modified depending on student needs. Be sure each item is clear, short, and easy to read when rewriting the checklist. Parts of the checklist can be given to each student as the homework-completion process is being taught. A copy of the checklist can also be given to the parents during parent–teacher conferences. (See Figure 5-11.)

You should have sample aids available for students, including a sample "To Do" list, daily schedule, and contract/plan. (See Figures 5-12, 5-13, and 5-14.)

Occasionally, after an assignment is handed in, you should ask the students how long it took them to complete the assignment and what difficulties they encountered. In this way you can create assignments that are reasonable, interesting, and more likely to be completed by the students. (See Figure 5-15.)

Teacher Checklist: Ten Steps for Teaching Homework Completion

1. Set the stage.
   - ☐ Explain the purpose of homework in general.
   - ☐ Explain the relationship between homework, tests, and grades.
   - ☐ Explain the purpose of a particular assignment and its relation to what has been already learned in the course.
   - ☐ Activate what students already know about the topic.

2. Provide structure and classroom routines.
   - ☐ Always write assignments in the same place on the chalkboard.
   - ☐ Tell students to copy assignments from the board.
   - ☐ Give students a copy of the assignment.
   - ☐ Tell students to place the assignment in their notebook.
   - ☐ Remind students to bring home their notebook, textbooks, and other materials at the end of class.
   - ☐ Check that every student understands the assignment.
   - ☐ Check that students have copied assignments accurately.
   - ☐ Provide homework checklist for students.

3. Teach step-by-step homework-completion strategies.
   - ☐ Circle key words in assignments.
   - ☐ Help students break down each assignment into steps.
   - ☐ Help students list books and materials needed to complete assignments.
   - ☐ Provide graphic organizers for reading and writing assignments to help students with low-level reading and writing skills learn and organize new information.

4. Provide guided practice in class of homework-completion strategies.

5. Individualize homework assignments.
   - ☐ Allow optional assignments based on student's interest.
   - ☐ Modify assignments for students with disabilities, per IEP or 504 Plan.

(continued)

Figure 5-10

6. Request and collect homework on time.

7. Give immediate, specific feedback and positive reinforcement after homework completion.
   - ☐ Return corrected homework as soon as possible.
   - ☐ Give students specific suggestions on how to improve the homework.
   - ☐ Give positive feedback about accuracy, completeness, legibility, creativity, etc.

8. Get feedback from students.
   - ☐ Ask students what difficulties they encountered when completing assignments.
   - ☐ Ask students for their suggestions regarding homework.
   - ☐ Ask students how long it took them to complete assignments.

9. Provide checkpoints for long-term assignments.
   - ☐ Help students break down long-term assignments into steps.
   - ☐ Ask students for homework on the due date or at the checkpoint.
   - ☐ Help students estimate amount of time needed for each step.
   - ☐ Teach students to schedule assignments and steps on a calendar.
   - ☐ Schedule checkpoints for long-term assignments.

10. Consider accepting late homework with minor penalties.
    - ☐ Focus first on having students hand in homework.
    - ☐ Focus next on handing in homework on time.
    - ☐ Give some credit to students who hand in homework late.

Student Checklist: Homework Completion

At School

☐ Place each assignment in a notebook to be brought home.
☐ Read the homework assignment aloud and circle key words.
☐ Ask the teacher for help to break down the assignment into small steps.
☐ Ask the teacher for help understanding the assignment.
☐ Locate materials and resources.
☐ Bring home assignments, textbooks, and other necessary materials.

At Home

☐ Select a time and place to do homework.
☐ Read the assignment carefully, repeating each direction.
☐ Make a daily homework plan based on all assignments.
☐ Set the day's homework goals.
☐ Schedule reading, thinking, and writing activities for the number of minutes and at the times of the day when you are most alert.
☐ Employ the reading and writing skills needed to complete the homework.
☐ Recognize your efforts by making positive statements.
☐ Keep on track by checking off tasks as they are completed.
☐ Decide when the homework is done by reviewing the assignment and any checklists you used.
☐ Check work for accuracy, completeness, legibility, and neatness.
☐ Place completed homework in the front of your notebook, ready to return to school.
☐ Praise yourself for your efforts and discuss your positive progress with a friend or family member.

Back at School

☐ Bring homework back to school and give it to your teacher(s.)
☐ Bring textbooks, materials, and resources back to school.
☐ Revise and correct homework based on feedback from your teacher(s.)
☐ Review and record whether you met your goal or stayed with your schedule.
☐ Save all completed homework in your notebook.
☐ Make a list and discuss with others your own "best homework tips."

Reprinted with permission. From *Performance Breakthroughs for Adolescents with Learning Disabilities or ADD: How to Help Students Succeed in the Regular Education Classroom* by Geraldine Markel, Ph.D. and Judith Greenbaum, Ph.D. Champaign, IL: Research Press, 1996 (p. 269).

Figure 5-11

Student Checklist: My "To Do" List

Name _____ Date _____

My "To Do" List

Directions:

- **Brainstorm.** Jot down all the things you want and need to do today.
- **Prioritize.** Number each one from the most important to the least important.
- **Star.** Put a star next to the things that must be done today.

_____

_____

_____

_____

_____

_____

_____

_____

_____

_____

_____

_____

_____

_____

_____

_____

Figure 5-12

Sample Daily Schedule

Name _____ Date _____

My Daily Schedule

Directions:
- Look at the starred items on your "To Do" list.
- Estimate the amount of time it will take you to do each task.
- Using the schedule, write in the tasks that you starred.
- Write in your after-school activities and responsibilities.
- Check off each task as you finish it.
- Place check marks on the tasks that are not completed.

1 P.M. _____

2 P.M. _____

3 P.M. _____

4 P.M. _____

5 P.M. _____

6 P.M. _____

7 P.M. _____

8 P.M. _____

9 P.M. _____

10 P.M. _____

Figure 5-13

Sample Homework Contract/Plan

Name _____ Date _____

Course _____

Homework Contract/Plan

Before doing homework, fill in/discuss with teacher:

- What assignments do I have to make up? When do I have to turn them in?

  Assignment: _____ When? _____

  Assignment: _____ When? _____

  Assignment: _____ When? _____

  Assignment: _____ When? _____

- Which assignments will the teacher excuse?

  Assignment: _____

  _____

  Assignment: _____

  _____

- What books or resources do I need? Do I have them or can I get them? _____

  _____

- The teacher will help me with: _____

  _____

- A tutor will help me with: _____

  _____

- I will keep track of my progress by checking off assignments on this form.

If I complete this contract, the teacher will not remove homework credit from my course grade.

Figure 5-14

Student Survey: What Do You Think About Homework?

Class _____ Teacher _____ Date _____

What Do You Think About This Week's Assignment?

Directions:

- Read each item.
- Check "yes" or "no" for questions 1–6.
- Write your answers for questions 7–10.

		Yes	No
1.	Assignments are interesting.	___	___
2.	My homework is too hard.	___	___
3.	I have trouble reading or understanding the textbook.	___	___
4.	I didn't understand what I was supposed to do.	___	___
5.	The assignment was boring.	___	___
6.	There are too many problems or too much to read.	___	___

7. The types of assignments I like best are: _____

_____

8. The worst kinds of assignments are: _____

_____

9. It took me about _____ minutes to complete each problem, answer each question, or read each page/section.

10. It took me _____ minutes/hours to complete my homework for this class.

Figure 5-15

PROVIDING SUPPORT FOR
HOMEWORK COMPLETION

Our challenge as teachers is to ensure that assignments are explained in terms of their relevance to classroom learning, to provide assignments that have some fun or humor built in, to integrate the teaching of homework-completion skills into the content area, and—most of all—teach students how to learn and review the material. Too many students don't know how to read and comprehend the textbook, how to effectively learn and memorize material, and how to effectively review material for a test. (See Chapter 4 on reading and writing strategies.)

Collaborating with Other Teachers

Grade-level teachers can prevent homework problems by collaborating on homework-related activities such as homework routines, the teaching of homework-completion strategies, and the amount of homework given.

They can share information about homework policies and expectations, addressing questions such as:

- How often is homework assigned in each class?
- How much time will students spend on homework per night?
- How does homework influence grades?
- Are there ever alternative assignments or extra-credit assignments?

It is easier for students to write down and understand the assignments if they are in the same place on the chalkboard of every classroom and every teacher uses the same words in the directions. (See Figure 5-16.)

Having Students Support Students

Students should discuss and develop homework plans in class. Although many teachers do allow students to start their homework in class, few encourage the students to work in small groups. Learning with peers can be a useful way of learning homework skills, however, especially if this is modeled in class. Some students with ADHD and/or LD learn best by talking and interacting with others. We sometimes forget the usefulness of working with others when the task is important but repetitive, boring, or unrelated to the students' lives. Working with others can make the time spent more interesting and provide encouragement.

Students often need to read and talk to friends about an assignment, especially if it is a longer project or paper or is relatively complex. Working in small groups is a good way to learn a foreign language or study for the SAT or the ACT.

Students can also help each other with homework. Bright students can serve as peer tutors. They can answer questions, demonstrate strategies, and help solve problems. They can explain what the assignment requires and help plan how to go about doing it. They can sit

Teacher Checklist: Collaboration Strategies

☐ Write assignments in the same place on the chalkboard every day.
☐ Use the same key and signal words for assignments and test directions.
☐ Give the same assignment book to all the students and teach them how to use it.
☐ Teach and reinforce the same homework-completion skills.
☐ Use a large class calendar to note all assignments and class and school activities. This serves as a model for students as they schedule their assignments in their own assignment book.
☐ Check the amount of homework other teachers are giving to prevent homework overload.
☐ Share homework accommodations with other teachers.
☐ Institute a homework hotline for students who have missed or forgotten their assignments.
☐ Consider instituting an after-school homework tutorial for all grade-level students.
☐ Send home the same homework materials to all grade-level parents.

Figure 5-16

Parent Checklist: How to Teach Your Teenager

☐ Involve the teenager in the entire process.
☐ Ask the teenager questions to stimulate thought.
☐ Keep teaching sessions short and provide frequent breaks.
☐ Communicate optimism (e.g., "We can solve this problem.")
☐ Be clear and give short explanations.
☐ Use examples your teenager can understand and relate to.
☐ Don't do the homework for your teenager.
☐ Be patient.
☐ Be creative and have fun.
☐ Reinforce progress and effort.
☐ Change your strategy if the plan is not working.
☐ Maintain loving, respectful communication with your teenager.
☐ Make time for family relaxation and fun.
☐ If one parent works better with the teenager than the other, that parent should do the teaching.

Figure 5-17

with the student and answer questions as they arise. This can be especially helpful for students with ADHD and/or LD, as well as other students with homework problems.

Helping Parents Help Students with Homework

You can help the student by helping the parent help the student. Most parents would welcome information from the school on how to help their teenagers with homework and how to deal with the inevitable impasses that occur. Provide information to parents by sending home occasional handouts or having handouts available at parent–teacher conferences. The PTA can schedule occasional parent workshops on the topic of homework.

Parents need information. Generally speaking, teachers should tell parents that they should not try to teach their teenager new material or material that the student has learned imperfectly—that is the teacher's responsibility. However, speaking realistically, parents cannot stand idly by when the teenager is going to fail because he or she does not understand the material. Parents and tutors may need to teach at some times. Handouts can provide tips for effective teaching and tutoring. (See Figures 5-17 and 5-18.)

Parent Tips: How to Help Students with Homework

- Help with reading. Read the assignment or read portions of the text to the student.
- Ask the school for audio tapes of the text that the student can listen to.
- Help with writing. Act as a secretary; type or write exactly what your teenager dictates and no more.
- Help with proofreading. Identify items that need to be revised or corrected.
- Help the student understand the assignment.
- Help the student organize time and materials.
- Cue the student to move to the next task.
- Provide encouragement and motivation.
- Correct homework only if the student asks.
- Help the student with his or her daily homework plan.
- Look for warning signs signaling when to contact the teacher:
  —Neither you nor the student understand the assignment.
  —The student hasn't learned skills covered in the assignment.
  —The student is spending more than one to two hours a night on homework.
  —The student fails to bring home assignments.
  —There are frequent arguments about homework.

Figure 5-18

PROVIDING HOMEWORK ACCOMMODATIONS

In addition to being taught the homework-completion process, students with ADHD and/or LD may also need to have assignments modified. Homework accommodations must take into account individual student needs while not compromising course objectives. This might mean that an assignment can be shortened for an individual student by removing duplicate problems, lower level problems, or problems that would be "nice" for the student to solve but not truly necessary. Special education staff can help the regular classroom teacher design "reasonable" homework accommodations. (See Figure 5-19.)

Christine's Homework Accommodations

When Christine's mother finally told the teacher how much she and Christine had been battling, the teacher said, "Why don't we arrange for Christine to do her homework in school? Then you can relax and Christine can have someone else help her, maybe another student. I think we should talk to Christine and look at her work. It's possible she needs more support from the teacher consultant. She probably needs additional accommodations in class." (See Figure 5-20.)

Accommodations for Homework

For reading disabilities:

- A second set of books to keep at home.
- A grade-level textbook in which the main ideas are highlighted.
- An outline of the text.
- Audio tapes of the textbook and other required reading.
- A shortened assignment so there is less reading.
- Additional time to complete an assignment.
- Graphic organizers.

For writing disabilities:

- Shorten the assignment so there is less writing.
- Allow student to dictate responses instead of writing them.
- Check that student has copied the assignment correctly.
- Give student additional time to complete an assignment.
- Allow student to use a word processor for writing.
- Provide a checklist for writing a paper.
- Don't remove points for poor spelling, capitalization, punctuation.
- Don't require student to copy math problems from board or text.

Figure 5-19

Christine's Homework Accommodations

Name: _Christine, Grade 7_

Eligibility: _LD in writing_

Strengths and interests: _acting, singing, psychology_

Weaknesses: _slow reading rate, some problems with reading comprehension, poor organizational skills, poor spelling_

Homework Accommodations:

Reading:
- Audio tape all required reading material.
- Give her graphic organizers to help with reading comprehension.

Organizational skills:
- Develop checklists for homework completion.
- Develop checklists for book reports and other writing assignments.

Writing:
- Don't require her to copy from chalkboard or textbook.
- Teach her to use word processor for written assignments.
- Allow her to dictate written homework to a scribe.
- Allow her to use calculator for math.
- Allow alternatives to written assignments.
- Check to see she has written assignment correctly.

Figure 5-20

SOLVING HOMEWORK PROBLEMS

Teachers need to help solve homework problems as well as teach homework-completion skills. Even with systematic teaching and effective classroom management, however, there can be some slippage, unforeseen circumstance, or deeper vulnerability than was anticipated. Although prevention goes a long way, homework problems can develop that must be solved.

Sometimes homework problems are the first signs of undiagnosed learning or attention problems that can no longer be managed by the student. Homework problems can be a sign that the needs of the student with ADHD and/or LD are not being met. Teachers may need to consider homework difficulties as a student's cry for help rather than as a behavior problem.

There are a number of strategies that you can employ when homework problems occur. Some of these are:

- Check the level of challenge of the assignments for the student.
- Increase or modify accommodations.
- Talk to the student and his or her parents for their suggestions.
- Check the student's multidisciplinary evaluation for clues and/or refer the student for additional testing.
- Arrange for study buddies for the student according to common interests.
- Establish some time for study sessions within class or after school.
- Develop a behavioral support plan for the student that includes all components of behavior change: a goal (e.g., homework completion), a reinforcement system, student commitment, parent involvement, and teacher support.
- Divide homework completion into steps. Reinforce the student for achieving the individual steps.
- Make a *realistic* plan for catching up on past homework. Consider not requiring the student to make up all missed homework.
- Make a progress chart for the student.

It can be useful to make a weekly homework report form for students and parents. This is a concrete way of showing the student which work he or she has missed and enables the student to make up work before he or she gets too far behind. It also gives the parents information that enables them to help the student in a timely fashion. (See Figure 5-21.)

You should consider accepting late homework with little penalty. Although the ultimate goal is for students to complete their homework and hand it in when due, the first emphasis should be on homework completion itself. Some students need longer to complete assignments for a variety of reasons, but the fact that they *do* the work needs reinforcement. If students receive no credit for completing the assignment and handing it in late, there is no incentive for them to complete the assignment.

Brandon's Homework Support Plan

When talking to Brandon, his teacher discovered—among other things—that Brandon wanted to be on the basketball team. Using that as an incentive, the teacher told Brandon how he could increase his grades just by doing his homework. She convinced Brandon to give it a try. The social worker talked to Brandon about how ADHD affected his schoolwork and told him that he could do better if his ADHD was brought under control. She also talked to Brandon's mother about the possibility of medication, suggesting that his mother talk to Brandon's doctor.

Brandon and his teacher developed a homework reinforcement system that gave Brandon a certain number of points for each specific homework activity he

Sample Form: Weekly Homework Report
Form for Student and Parents

Student: _____   Subject: _____

Teacher: _____   Dates: _____

Date	On Time?	All Homework Complete?	Comments:
Mon. _____	Yes ____ Excused ____ No ____	Yes ____ No ____ None Assigned ____	
Tues. _____	Yes ____ Excused ____ No ____	Yes ____ No ____ None Assigned ____	
Wed. _____	Yes ____ Excused ____ No ____	Yes ____ No ____ None Assigned ____	
Thurs. _____	Yes ____ Excused ____ No ____	Yes ____ No ____ None Assigned ____	
Fri. _____	Yes ____ Excused ____ No ____	Yes ____ No ____ None Assigned ____	

Figure 5-21

completed. His teacher also modified some of her instructional strategies to accommodate Brandon's stated learning needs.

A FINAL WORD

It is time for teachers and schools to put homework on the agenda. Teachers need to take a good look at the reasons for giving homework, the amount of homework given, and the relationship between homework and course grades. Teachers also need to reconsider their expectations of parents and students in the process.

Students and parents should be part of a dialogue that seeks to uncover student problems with homework and discusses possible solutions.

The emphasis should be placed on preventing homework problems rather than on "mopping up" after problems occur. In order to do this, it is important to understand the skills students need to complete homework and the difficulties many students have completing homework assignments. Modifying the learning environment is the first line of attack. Teaching homework skills to the whole class can prevent problems for *all* students—not just students with ADHD and/or LD. Adding appropriate educational accommodations for students with ADHD and/or LD can help prevent homework problems for these students.

Homework can positively affect student achievement. However, in order to maximize these effects, homework should be appropriate in length and difficulty, interesting to the students, based on material learned in class, and requiring skills the students have been taught as part of the curriculum. *That* is the challenge.

CHAPTER SIX

Teaching Adolescents to Use Self-Management

Maria's struggle with undiagnosed ADHD and frequent school failure convinced her that she was stupid. She was finally diagnosed with ADHD in her senior year of high school. Maria suffered great anxiety before taking tests and often "shut down" due to extreme worry that she would fail. Because of this Maria did not even dream of going to college, despite the fact that she was a bright student and knew the work.

Ophelia, a high school senior with LD in math, recently took the SAT in order to get into college. She received a 578 on the Verbal portion of the SAT and a 270 on the Math portion. When asked if she had enough time to finish the math section, she responded that she had plenty of time. In fact, she said, she finished the math test early. She said that, because she always did so badly on math tests (after all she had a learning disability in math), she didn't bother going over her answers.

Each of these students has problems related to test taking. Maria needs to learn how to self-manage her test anxiety so that she can show what she knows on her tests. Ophelia needs to learn test-taking strategies from which she can select those that will maximize her performance. Test taking is but one area in which students with ADHD and/or LD have problems with self-management.

IMPORTANCE OF SELF-MANAGEMENT SKILLS

We tend to think that the lack of self-management skills results primarily in disruptive behavior on the part of the student. Poor behavior such as interrupting, arguing, or defiance is only part of the problem. Poor time management, poor organization, and difficulty maintaining attention are also part of the problem as are difficulty in getting to class on time, test anxiety, and "shut down" due to fear of failure. The lack of self-management skills can have devastating affects on academic performance.

No matter how smart a student is, the lack of self-management skills can prevent the student from learning, remembering, expressing, and applying new information. The student who has great difficulty paying attention will not be able to focus on new information long enough to make it a part of his or her working memory. This type of student will have difficulty with all aspects of learning. The student who has difficulty with time management will not be able to hand in homework on time or get to class on time. The student with organizational difficulties will have difficulty with remembering what he or she has read and difficulty writing a satisfactory paper. (See Figure 6-1.)

As teachers, we see students like this every day. As we think about these students, we say to ourselves "if only . . . ." We often think that these unruly, disorganized students are their own worst enemies.

Self-Management Difficulties of Students with ADHD and/or LD

- Distractibility, impulsivity, hyperactivity
- Problems focusing and maintaining attention
- Tendency to be passive learners
- Discouragement; low self-esteem
- Fear of failure; perfectionism
- Learned helplessness
- Easily frustrated; angered
- Poor time management and organization
- Procrastination
- Poor study skills
- Poor planning
- Poor listening skills
- Loses important papers
- Late to class
- Denial

Figure 6-1

Self-management is a universal and lifetime goal. No matter how old we are, most of us would like to become better organized. Many of us have little quirks we would like to eliminate, such as being late to appointments or constantly losing our keys. These self-management problems are relatively common. But it is amazing how much even these small things can interfere with our lives and increase our stress.

As we have grown older, we have developed many self-management strategies on our own through trial and error, or by observing someone else complete a task efficiently. Students with ADHD and/or LD, however, rarely develop these strategies on their own. In fact, often these students develop bad habits and ways of coping that interfere with learning.

Although all of these students have the intellectual potential to succeed in school, they often do quite poorly. Poor self-management or self-regulation skills go hand in hand with ADHD and/or LD and are now considered to be part of their definitions.

Definition of Self-Management

Self-management refers to the student's ability to plan, carry out, monitor, and adjust his or her thinking and actions in order to complete a task—without the constant supervision or reinforcement of teachers and parents. Self-management brings learning, behavior, and performance under the student's control. These abilities are all considered part of "executive functioning." (See Chapter 1.)

Benefits of Self-Management for Students with ADHD and/or LD

Current research indicates that self-management strategies can be taught to students. When students with ADHD and/or LD use these strategies, they have a greater chance of optimizing their performance in and out of school. Self-managed students can:

- Use their strengths and interests.
- Circumvent their weaknesses.
- Work with others.
- Attend to instructions.
- Focus on work.
- Study efficiently.
- Remember what they have read.
- Perform optimally on tests.
- Complete homework in a timely fashion.
- Cope with uncertainty, failure, and stress.
- Manage anger and frustration.
- Plan ahead for difficult situations.
- Maintain motivation until an activity is completed.

In short, self-management can greatly enhance student achievement, behavior, and self-esteem.

Many teachers feel that the teaching of self-management skills is not their responsibility and that, by the time the student arrives in middle school or high school, the student should have developed these strategies on his or her own. But should educators leave the development of these important skills to chance? Isn't it our obligation to systematically develop each student's potential for thinking and learning?

Of course some students will need more intensive instruction and/or more practice time. For students with more severe problems, it is the teacher consultant, school social worker, or social psychologist who may bear the responsibility for teaching self-management skills. Of course, parents can play an important role in the development and maintenance of self-management skills.

Benefits of Student Self-Management for Teachers

Student self-management provides benefits to teachers as well as students. In addition to higher achievement, students who are self-managed are less disruptive and take up much less of your time and patience. Classroom management becomes easier, there is more time for teaching, and your teaching satisfaction increases.

Instructional Methods that Enhance Self-Management

In a sense, this entire book is about teaching students self-management strategies. All the strategies that are included in this book lead to self-management of academic behavior. (Examples are Figures 4-10 and 4-11 in Chapter 4.)

In this chapter we will focus on ways to help students:

- Manage attention.
- Manage impulsivity.
- Manage anger and frustration.
- Self motivate.
- Cope with failure.
- Manage test anxiety.
- Solve problems.

These self-management strategies can be used by students in every class they take and for every task and activity they face.

It is important to note that self-management strategies should never be taught in a vacuum. These strategies should always be integrated in the content area along with other skills and strategies described in this book.

The following five techniques can be used to enhance self-management for *all* students in your class, not just those with ADHD and/or LD.

1. Provide a learning environment conducive to self-management. (See Chapter 3.) More specifically, you can:

- Provide structure and predictability.
- Grade students for effort and progress.
- Organize the physical environment to remove distractions.
- Teach learning and thinking strategies.

2. Teach and model cognitive behavioral strategies such as self-talk and visualization to help students with self-management.

3. Teach and model self-monitoring and self-management. Students need specific instruction on what strategies to use and how and when to apply them. Many students with ADHD and/or LD cannot learn self-management skills unless classroom teachers provide explicit instruction and practice regarding how to be on time, how to organize materials, or how to use self-talk.

You will need to model how to self-monitor and how to use the feedback you collect to adjust your activities. This provides a powerful lesson to students on how adults manage their own responsibilities. Teachers and parents of adolescent youth cannot afford to say, "Do as I say, not as I do." Adults need to model the behaviors they want students to develop.

4. Use behavior-management techniques such as reinforcement and contracting. (See Chapter 8.) Like any other new behavior to be learned, students are reinforced consistently at first and then intermittently, as they become more competent in and confident of their self-management skills.

Although functional assessment and the development of behavioral support plans are required for many students with ADHD and/or LD, quick, informal plans can be developed for other students in the class, if needed.

5. Include self-management skills and strategies in everything you teach. If you want to foster student independence and self-management, then you must provide students with ample practice in using such skills.

SELF-TALK

Most of us are aware of talking to ourselves at one time or another. Young children talk to themselves aloud as they are developing speech and language. You hear them say such things as "No, no, mustn't touch" or "Hot" as they remind themselves of a parent's admonitions. They say "Good boy!" "Good girl!" when they have done something of which they are proud. As children grow older, speech becomes internalized. In fact, we are encouraged to internalize speech. But as adults, many of us have found that it is very helpful to talk aloud to ourselves as we solve problems, "think things through," or remind ourselves of obligations and responsibilities. Essentially, self-talk helps us understand the world around us through the use of words.

We can use self-talk to:

- Tell ourselves how to do something.
- Help us remember new information.

Student Checklist: Managing Behavior with Self-Talk

Behavior	Self-Talk

Behavior

Self-Talk

- Manage Attention
  - "Pay attention."
  - "Am I paying attention?"
  - "It's too noisy here. Move to a quieter place."
  - "Do I remember what the teacher just said? I'd better pay attention."
  - "Am I tired? Do I need a break?"
  - "When I get to class I will sit down right away and begin working."

- Manage Anger
  - "Stop. Think."
  - "What is happening here?"
  - "Why is this person acting the way he is?"
  - "I can control my feelings."
  - "I'd better take a deep breath and try to relax."
  - "I'm getting tense. Relax."
  - "Take it easy. Stay cool."
  - "When I see _____, I will just ignore her and walk on."
  - "Be careful. If I lose my cool one more time, I will be suspended."

- Manage Impulsivity
  - "Stop, think."
  - "Slow down."
  - "What strategy should I use?"
  - "Read the directions slowly and carefully."

(continued)

Figure 6–2

- Self-Motivate
  - "I will feel so good when I finish this task."
  - "When I'm finished with this, I can leave for the movies."
  - "This is a challenge but I bet I can do it."
  - "This will only take me fifteen minutes if I work hard."
  - "I will answer two more questions and then I will take a break."

- Cope with Failure
  - "I can handle this."
  - "Failing one test doesn't mean I'm stupid."
  - "What can I learn from this?"
  - "I'll try again tomorrow."
  - "So I'm not good at everything. Big deal."
  - "I won't give up. I'm going to keep trying."

- Solve Problems
  - "What strategies should I use?"
  - "What would happen if I did this?"
  - "What are the problems I need to solve in order to get to my goal?"
  - "What exactly is the problem?"
  - "I can solve this if I go slowly and systematically."
  - "Would it help if I used a flowchart or map?"
  - "I'd better write down all the things I will need to do in order to solve this problem."

- Help us remember rules and routines.
- Ask and answer questions of ourselves in order to solve problems.
- Argue ourselves out of impulsive responses, irrational beliefs, or self-defeating thoughts or behavior.
- Maintain our motivation in order to finish a task.
- Remind ourselves to pay attention, think, or relax.
- Cope with disappointment or failure.
- Compliment ourselves on a job well done.
- Manage stress.

We often hear students using negative self-talk, such as: "I just know I'm going to fail!" or "I will make a fool of myself." *Negative self-talk* is discouraging and defeating. It can become a self-fulfilling prophecy. *Positive self-talk,* however, is encouraging and motivating. It can help students overcome hesitancy, fear, and anxiety. Even though they frequently use negative self-talk, many students do not know when and how to use positive self-talk.

Suggest to your students to pretend they are talking to their best friend who has just failed a test or who has just been teased. Ask your students what they would say to their best friend in such a situation to help him or her cope. Encourage the students to say the same words to themselves in similar situations.

When you hear a student say such things as "I just can't take tests. I always fail," you can suggest the student ask himself or herself, "Is that really true? Didn't I get a B on my math test last week and a B– on my history test? That's not failing. In fact, I've only gotten one failing grade. Most of the time I do well on tests." (See Figure 6-2.)

Self-talk and self-questioning can help students remember new information, remember what the teacher has said, remember what they have read, and locate lost objects such as books and homework. Self-instruction can help students remember the steps needed to complete a task or manage a difficult situation.

VISUALIZATION

Visualization means creating an image in one's mind of a remembered situation, or a new situation in which one is performing efficiently and effectively. When teaching visualization techniques we often ask students to imagine or see themselves successfully performing tasks they thought they couldn't accomplish. We encourage them to accompany their visualizations with emotions, feelings, and physical sensations.

Imagery and visualization are greatly underutilized in learning. Many people learn better visually than verbally. Athletes, for example, have long used visualization to learn new movement sequences. Visualization can be used by students as a rehearsal of a chosen action. Athletes are encouraged to feel their muscles responding during visualization. When students visualize a relaxing situation or visualize themselves appearing calm and competent, you can encourage them to not only see themselves but feel relaxed.

Students can use visualization to:

- Pay attention.
- Remember where they have put something.

- Motivate themselves to do a difficult task.
- Learn ways of performing tasks efficiently and effectively.
- Practice performing tasks efficiently and effectively.
- Experience satisfaction for a job well done.
- Solve problems.
- See the big picture.
- Relax.
- Manage stress.
- Overcome fear.
- Remember new information.

Students can imagine themselves listening alertly, sitting straight, looking at the speaker, and taking occasional notes. When students are learning new material, they can visualize hanging the new information on a hook in their brain where they have placed similar information, thus relating new information to information already learned. In order to understand self-monitoring, students can visualize a copy of themselves looking over their own shoulder and watching themselves working. Students can visualize themselves working steadily on a test with smiles on their faces and feeling competent.

MANAGING ANGER

Use the following script to help students use visualization to manage anger:

"Visualize yourself in a recent angry confrontation you had with another student. What did you say? How did you say it? How did you look? How did you feel? What did the other person say? Did you feel successful?

"Now visualize yourself in a situation that generally makes you angry. See yourself looking and feeling under control. Hear yourself speaking calmly and firmly."

Everyone gets angry sometimes. It is part of the human condition. However, angry thoughts are one thing, angry actions are another. The goal of anger-management training is to teach students how to express their anger appropriately. Anger management for students with ADHD and/or LD is usually taught by a teacher consultant, school social worker, or school psychologist. Students who seem to be angry all the time should be referred to private therapists. Sometimes middle schools and high schools offer elective anger-management/ conflict-resolution classes for all students. You may want to integrate anger management into the regular education curriculum.

One anger-management strategy is the Triple A Strategy, developed by H. M. Walker and described in *The Walker Social Skills Curriculum* (Austin, TX: Pro-Ed, 1988). Triple A stands for "Assess," "Amend," "Act." It tells a student to stop and assess the situation as to what is happening and why. Then the student is to amend or edit his or her angry response by first telling the other person how the situation is making him or her feel and then asking

---

Student Checklist: Strategies for Managing Anger

- Stop what you're doing, take a deep breath, and let it out slowly.
- Use self-talk.
- Visualize yourself in a peaceful or enjoyable place.
- Write notes to yourself.
- Remove yourself from the situation.
- Tell the person, "I feel angry when you say that."
- Understand the other person's feelings.
- Use humor.
- Listen to relaxing music.
- Engage in physical activity.
- Work on another activity.
- Avoid situations and people you know make you angry.
- Tell a friend what happened and how you felt.
- Write a note about how you feel to the other person even if you don't send it.
- Practice stating a concern or giving your opinion in a direct and respectful way.

Figure 6-3

the other person how he or she is feeling. The student self-instructs regarding an appropriate response and then acts accordingly. (See Figure 6-3.)

Anger management includes managing nonverbal as well as verbal behaviors. The following are several appropriate nonverbal behaviors:

- Look directly at the other person.
- Relax your arms and hands.
- Ensure nonverbal behavior is consistent with verbal message.
- Use nonthreatening gestures.
- Use nonprovoking facial expressions.

MANAGING ATTENTION

To begin managing their attention, students must first become aware of when they are and are not on task. Use the following simple exercise to help students become more aware: During a student activity ring a buzzer or small bell at 5-minute intervals and ask the students if they were on-task or off-task. The same thing can be done at home as well. This exercise increases on-task behavior by making students more aware of how frequently their thoughts are far away from the task at hand.

When students understand the extent of their attention problems, they can use self-talk and visualization strategies to help them get on track and stay on track.

MANAGING TEST ANXIETY

Test anxiety can be caused by a variety factors, such as:

- Poor understanding of subject matter
- Lack of awareness of what to study
- Lack of test preparation (e.g., students don't study, don't study enough, don't study effectively)
- Poor test-taking skills
- Past failures and low self-esteem

In a conference with the student, uncover the problems the student has by going over how the student prepared for the test and by going over the student's answers to the test questions.

Test stress or anxiety is common in students with ADHD and/or LD, as they rarely know how to approach studying, have great difficulty concentrating, or have a history of test failure.

Test stress and anxiety can be addressed when you:

- Provide tutoring in the subject matter.
- Encourage students to study for tests.
- Teach students how to study for tests.
- Provide students with practice tests or pretests.
- Teach students test-taking skills.
- Teach students self-management skills such as positive self-talk and visualization.

Self-management checklists provide a way for a student like Maria to exert greater control over her test-related anxiety. Maria's checklist listed specific strategies to use before, during, and after a test. In some classes Maria experienced greater nervousness before the exam, while in other classes she experienced stress only when she couldn't complete a particular problem. A checklist can be used by many students if it is individualized according to the student's particular needs. (See Figure 6-4.)

SELF-MONITORING

You can respond in several different ways when a student displays negative behavior—such as not working in class, frequently late to class, or easily frustrated or angered. You can

Student Checklist: Managing Test Anxiety

Review the list of steps. Star those that you intend to use. Check off each one as you complete it.

Before entering the room

____ Arrive a few minutes early. Avoid feeling rushed.

____ Check that accommodations you requested are available.

____ Check that you have necessary materials or equipment.

____ Avoid anxiety-provoking talk with others (e.g., "How much did you study?").

Before beginning the test

____ Avoid anxiety-provoking self-talk (e.g., "I know I'll fail").

____ Think positive thoughts (e.g., "I know how to keep myself on track").

____ Establish a warm-up routine. Shift your focus from your tension to reading the directions aloud or writing helpful hints to yourself.

____ Become aware of your feelings (e.g., "I'm feeling tense—this is a good time to stretch").

____ Create positive images (e.g., "I can see myself working efficiently").

____ Rehearse visually (e.g., "I can see myself walk in, arrange materials, take a deep breath, and begin to work").

____ Breathe deeply and relax muscles.

During the test

____ Think positive thoughts (e.g., "I'm using my test-taking strategies").

____ Be prepared to confront problems (e.g., "If I come to questions that I can't answer, I'll skip them and do the ones I can").

____ Create positive images (e.g., "I can see myself working steadily and staying calm").

____ Use visual imagery (e.g., "I can see several possible solutions to this").

____ Relax. Flex and stretch some muscles a few times during the test.

Reprinted with permission. From *Performance Breakthroughs for Adolescents with Learning Disabilities or ADD: How to Help Students Succeed in the Regular Education Classroom* by Geraldine Markel, Ph.D. and Judith Greenbaum, Ph.D. Champaign, IL: Research Press, 1996 (p. 220).

Figure 6-4

reprimand the student each time he or she exhibits the negative behavior. You can lower the student's grade after a certain number of infractions. You can cue the student to act appropriately. You can reinforce the student for the useful behaviors he or she is demonstrating while shaping further positive behavior. In each of these cases it is you, the teacher, who observes, monitors, and provides the consequences.

You can also teach the student how to monitor his or her own behavior in order to self-manage or control negative behavior and increase positive behavior.

Christopher, who you will meet in Chapter 9, was late to school and late to class more often than not. Christopher was taught how to self-monitor the time he arrived in each class for a week. (See Figure 6-5.) He was astounded when he saw the results. He realized for the first time how often he was late to class and how late he actually was. Now he understood what his teachers had been talking about when they reprimanded him for being late so often!

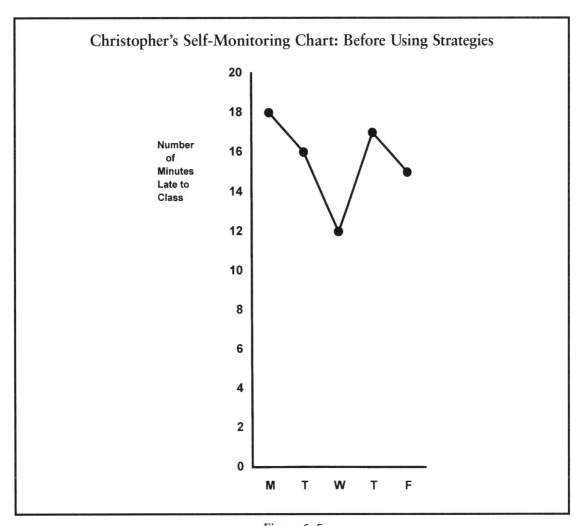

Figure 6-5

The first step of self-monitoring is to show the student how to monitor the occurrence of a particular negative behavior in order to see the frequency of the behavior and the situations in which it occurs. This provides the student with concrete evidence of the problems. The student can then decide if, when, and how to improve.

The student is ready to set behavioral goals after he or she understands the extent of the problem. Self-monitoring strategies—coupled with student self-awareness—helps lead the student to goals that make sense to him or her.

The second step of self-monitoring is to track the positive behaviors the student is trying to maximize. The student compares his or her current performance with the goal he or she has selected. The student then tracks the positive behavior specified by the goal. Utilizing feedback from self-monitoring, the student can change or modify the strategies he or she is using to achieve the goal if progress is not occurring or is too slow. (See Figure 6-6.)

Self-monitoring is the first action to take toward becoming responsible for one's learning and behavior. It introduces the idea that students, even those in early adolescence, can exert control over their behavior as they move toward greater autonomy.

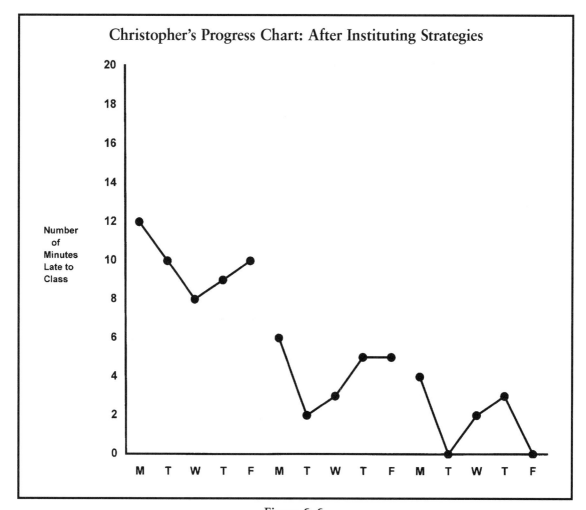

Figure 6-6

SETTING GOALS

The goal-setting process, while important in and of itself, can also increase student motivation if the student sets his or her own goals. Students set personal goals, develop a plan to achieve their goals, and self-monitor progress as they work toward the attainment of their goals. This is an excellent activity for the whole class.

Goal setting can begin after the results of the initial self-monitoring have been analyzed and the students are aware of the extent of their problem. Goal setting can also begin without the initial self-monitoring if the student is relatively self-aware and motivated.

You can teach/model the goal-setting process using academic, behavioral, and/or social goals. Despite the fact that you may have some goals in mind for particular students, goals must be set by the student if they are to be effective learning tools.

There will need to be several intermediary objectives for each goal. Each goal and objective must be specific and measurable. Goals referring to the frequency of a specific behavior are measurable. Goals that refer to a person's feelings and goals that are undefined generalizations are unmeasurable. Describing a behavior as "appropriate" or "respectful" is not sufficient. Examples of appropriate or respectful behaviors must be discussed and written.

Help students select one or two realistic, attainable goals. The goals must be compelling for the students. Help students convert these goals into concrete targets with specific timelines. Ask students to list the types of resources and support they will need from you, other adults, and their classmates in order to attain goals. Help students develop a reinforcement system that includes self-reinforcement.

Students are to self-monitor their progress. Teach students how to adapt and modify their goals based on feedback from their progress charts, self-observation, and teacher observation.

Teacher Checklist: Goal Setting

Directions: Check that each goal is:

____ Specific.

____ Written.

____ Achievable. Can the student accomplish the goal during the time allotted? Have intermediary goals been developed?

____ Relevant. Is the goal important to the student?

____ Measurable. Can the goal be quantified?

____ Reinforced. Are the teacher and parent supports in place?

____ Monitored. Has a checklist or progress chart been developed to track progress?

____ Reviewed. Have time(s) been set by student and teacher to review and discuss progress?

Figure 6-7

In order to move from talk to action you may need to persuade, encourage, and/or help some students take the first steps toward their goals. (See Figure 6-7.)

You and the student decide on the type of support you will provide in order to help the student modify behavior. The student fills out the progress chart at agreed-upon intervals to see if the frequency of the negative behavior has lessened and the positive behavior has increased. Students use feedback from the progress chart to make decisions regarding the effectiveness of the strategies they are using. Some strategies may need to be changed. Student self-management strategies (and teacher-support strategies) are continued or modified until positive behavior replaces negative behavior most of the time.

This, of course, presupposes that the positive behavior is already in the student's repertoire—even though not strictly under the student's control at this time. If the student does not have the skill in his or her repertoire, the teacher consultant or school social worker will need to teach the student the particular behavior.

Student Worksheet: Getting to School on Time

Answer the following questions:

What time do you have to be in your first class? _____

(If appropriate) What time does the bus pick you up? _____

Time yourself:

If you walk, ride your bike, or drive a car to school, how much time does it take you? _____

How much time does it take you to make and eat breakfast? _____

How much time does it take you to choose your clothes and get dressed? _____

How much time does it take you to brush your teeth, do your hair, and wash or shower? _____

How much time does it take you to get up after the alarm rings? _____

What other things do you have to do before you go to school, and how much time does it take you to do them? _____

_____

_____

What is the total amount of time it takes you to do all of these things? _____

What time do you need to get up in order to get to school on time? _____

Figure 6-8

Student Schedule: Getting to School on Time

Make a morning schedule and fill in the time it takes to complete it.

Time   Task

_____   What time do you have to be at school in order to arrive on time to your first class?

_____   What time does the bus come or the time you have to leave in order to get to school on time?

_____   What time do you have to start making and eating breakfast in order to be ready to leave on time?

_____   What time do you have to start choosing your clothes and getting dressed in order to eat breakfast on time?

_____   What time do you have to start your bathroom routine in order to get dressed on time?

_____   What time do you have to get up in order to do these things?

_____   What time do you need to complete other activities?

Figure 6-9

For example, Christopher had to be taught how to get to school on time. The school social worker developed a worksheet and schedule to help him get to school on time. This worksheet and schedule can be used for the many students who have the same difficulty. (See Figure 6-8.)

This worksheet can be turned into a self monitoring device. (See Figure 6-9.)

SELF-MOTIVATION

Many students with ADHD and/or LD appear unmotivated. They may rarely finish their schoolwork or they may not begin the work at all. It is hard for a student with ADHD and/or LD to maintain motivation for school-related activities in the face of constant criticism or failure to attain teacher standards. In addition, these students may have great difficulty maintaining motivation. Motivation is the driving force behind student achievement. Without it, even the brightest student will not be successful in school.

Motivation can be either *extrinsic,* meaning that the teacher and the school provide it to the students, or *intrinsic* to the task, such as an interesting book or an all-consuming project. Successfully overcoming barriers or completing challenging tasks can be very motivating to students. However, students who are capable of seeing a project through to its conclusion do so largely by using self-motivation. In particular, self-motivation is necessary for a student to begin and complete a task when that task is boring or uninteresting.

In order to self-motivate, students can:

- Use positive self-talk to encourage themselves to begin or continue.
- Use visualization to see themselves completing the task.
- Reinforce their own progress by using self-selected rewards.
- Take pride in their efforts and accomplishments.
- Limit negative self-talk.
- Set goals and keep a self-monitoring chart.

STEPS FOR INTEGRATING THE TEACHING OF SELF-MANAGEMENT STRATEGIES IN CONTENT AREA CLASSES

All students, including those with ADHD and/or LD, can increase their self-management skills through direct instruction. Self-management strategies can be combined with other cognitive strategies and integrated into the teaching of subject matter.

1. *Explain how the use of self-management strategies can help students learn and remember new material, pass tests, complete homework, manage attention, and manage anger.* Students will be more apt to use new skills and strategies if they know their efforts will pay off. It is important to tell about others' successes with these strategies since it contributes to improved expectancies of personal power. The conviction that a student can succeed improves the chances that positive outcomes will occur.

2. *Observe current self-management strategies students are using and the tasks and activities in which they use the strategies.* You can understand how and if students are using self-management strategies when you observe students as they work. This is done by giving students a task to complete or a problem to solve. Try to discover if students:

- Know how or when to use self-management strategies to understand, remember, or use new information.
- Know the strategies but do not use them.
- Use strategies but do not use them effectively, at the right time, or for long enough.

More specifically, you look for:

- how students begin the task
- what they do when they appear to be encountering problems
- what strategies they appear to be using, and
- what they do after they have completed the task

In addition, you can ask students questions before they begin work and after they finish. Before students begin to work, ask: "How difficult does this appear? How much time do you think it will take to complete? How will you go about doing it?"

When students are finished working, ask: "Did you need to visualize anything? What was it? Did you talk to yourself? What did you say? Did this take longer to do than you expected? Why? What did you do if the strategies that you were using weren't helpful? What was the most useful thing you did to help yourself?"

3. *Teach/model self-management strategies for managing attention, impulsivity, anger, and disappointment.* Model the use of self-talk and visualization in different situations relevant to the students. Describe each strategy and list the steps needed to perform the strategy. You should begin with simple tasks and move gradually to more complex tasks. Be prepared to help students target a specific behavior or situation on which to work.

4. *Teach/model self-management strategies for academic tasks.* You can select a few self-management skills to work on and integrate the teaching of these skills in various projects throughout the year (e.g., how do students give themselves a "pep talk" while they are studying and while they are taking a test).

5. *Provide students with aids to self-management.* Checklists can help students remember self-management strategies you have taught them and the steps leading to such things as homework completion, problem solving, test taking, and the management of attention and impulsivity. Graphic organizers can greatly enhance organization and problem solving. Posters, with lists of rules or steps, and cue cards can help support self-management.

6. *Teach students how to use and develop checklists and graphic organizers.* Although you, the teacher, provide students with these supports, they will need to be able to personalize them based on their own needs and learning styles. Eventually, they will need to develop their own checklists and graphic organizers without teacher supervision. You will need to provide direct instruction on how to personalize these supports for specific tasks and how to develop one's own checklists.

7. *Provide opportunities for guided practice.* Arrange for on-going practice in using self-management skills. Just explaining or demonstrating a task does not mean that a student will learn how to use it or use it effectively, especially under unstructured, stressful, or timed conditions. Students with ADHD and/or LD will often need more practice than other students in the class.

8. *Coordinate the teaching of self-management with other grade-level teachers.* Students will have more practice of newly learned self-management strategies if all the grade-level teachers teach the same strategies at the same time. You and the other teachers can select the same few strategies to be taught each month. One of the benefits of this collaborative effort is that each teacher will be able to spend less time teaching and modeling the strategies because every teacher is teaching, modeling, and providing guided practice.

9. *Discuss the effectiveness of the strategies and problems encountered.* Without reflection on how helpful the strategies were to them and the difficulties they encountered when using the strategies, students cannot truly understand how to use self-management strategies to their best advantage. You will need to encourage students to modify strategies or develop new ones to replace strategies that didn't work. Discuss problems they encountered when using the strategies at home in an unstructured or more independent setting.

10. *Facilitate maintenance and generalization.* Extend, practice, and reinforce the use of the strategies in new situations and tasks throughout the year.

Ten Steps for Integrating Self-Management
Strategies into Content Area Classes

1. Explain how the use of self-management strategies can help students learn and remember.
2. Observe the current self-management strategies students are using and the tasks and activities in which they use the strategies.
3. Teach model self-management strategies, including self-reinforcement strategies.
4. Provide direct instruction of self-management skills and strategies for academic tasks.
5. Provide students with aids to self-management.
6. Teach students how to use and develop checklists and graphic organizers.
7. Provide opportunities for guided practice.
8. Coordinate the teaching of self-management with other grade-level teachers.
9. Discuss the effectiveness of the strategies and examples of problems encountered.
10. Provide reinforcement and facilitate maintenance and generalization.

Figure 6-10

Your goal is to get to the point where the behaviors students acquire under one set of conditions are likely to be used under another set of conditions. If we want maintenance and generalization of the skills and strategies we teach, we need to plan for it and monitor the students' use of newly acquired strategies. Once a new behavior is learned, the degree to which it is maintained or carried over to another situation depends on whether it is reinforced by the teacher, the school, parents, and the general public. (See Figure 6-10.)

Students with ADHD and/or LD may need to be taught explicitly how to use the same skills and strategies (e.g., on-time behavior) in several different contexts. They may also need more time to practice newly acquired skills. This may be done either in the context of the content area class or in the Resource Room. Ideally, Special Education staff should collaborate with classroom teachers in the teaching of self-management skills and strategies.

A FINAL WORD

The teaching of self-management skills can help students—regardless of disabilities—focus on and understand what they are reading, write a well-organized paper, hand in homework on time, and manage their attention, impulsivity and anger.

Maria was able to do quite well on tests when she learned and practiced positive self-talk and relaxation techniques before and during a test. The teacher's encouragement gave a necessary boost to Maria's self-esteem.

Ophelia's Checklist for Math Tests

Review the list of steps. Star those that you intend to use. Check off each one as you complete it.

Previewing the test

____ Preview the entire test to identify the different types of questions.

____ Review the point system.

____ Determine whether or not to guess. (Guess if there is no penalty for guessing and if guessing does not take time away from answering questions you are sure about.)

Answering the questions

____ Ask the teacher for help if you do not understand directions for a particular question.

____ Answer the easy questions first.

____ Skip the questions you don't know or are unsure about.

____ Use a symbol (e.g., stars or question marks) to indicate the degree of difficulty of the questions you skip.

____ After completing questions you know, go back and work on questions at the next level of difficulty.

____ When answering questions you are unsure about, cross out those alternatives you know are wrong and make an educated guess from among the other answers.

____ Be sure to answer those sections or questions that have the most points.

____ Don't rush. Stop to give yourself time to think.

Checking your answers

____ Do not change an answer unless you remember a fact that provides a reason for the change.

____ Check for careless mistakes (e.g., symbols used inaccurately, decimals placed inaccurately).

____ Check all directions to see that you have followed them correctly.

____ Check that you have answered all the questions that you are sure about.

____ Go back and try to answer those questions you have skipped.

____ Reread or say each word to yourself to see if your answer makes sense.

____ See if you can estimate the answers to difficult questions.

Adapted with permission. From *Performance Breakthroughs for Adolescents with Learning Disabilities or ADD: How to Help Students Succeed in the Regular Education Classroom* by Geraldine Markel, Ph.D. and Judith Greenbaum, Ph.D. Champaign, IL: Research Press, 1996 (p. 218).

Figure 6-11

Even though she had a severe learning disability, Ophelia did much better on the Math section when she retook the SAT. The test-taking strategies she learned in the classroom enabled her to use her time wisely, check her answers, and make educated guesses on many test questions she was unsure. (See Figure 6-11.)

Once Frank (the angry, impulsive student you'll meet in Chapter 8) became more aware of his strengths and weaknesses, he benefited a great deal from being taught self-management strategies. These include self-talk and self-monitoring to understand and manage his anger more effectively.

Christopher's self-management of on-time behavior required much support from his mother as well as his teachers. Christopher had to change many bad habits, such as going to sleep after midnight and sleeping through the alarm clock in the morning. Consequently, it took him much longer to meet his goal.

All of these students had gotten poor grades, but not because of their specific reading or writing disabilities. They got poor grades because of their lack of self-management skills.

Most self-management strategies can be taught in the content area class to all students. You can teach a few of these strategies to individual students during student conferences. More in-depth teaching is the responsibility of the teacher consultant, school social worker, or psychologist.

Self-managed students are engaged and productive. They feel good about themselves and generally like school. The time it will take you to teach self-management skills is more than offset by the time you will save in classroom management. When students are able to self-manage their behavior, everybody benefits.

CHAPTER SEVEN

Developing IEPs and Section 504 Plans

Things are not working well for Monte this year. He received two D's on his last report card. This highly articulate young man has both LD and ADHD. Although he is a frequent contributor to class discussions and works well with the other students, he is slowly losing confidence in himself.

Monte is in ninth grade. His IQ scores are in the average range with his Verbal Score higher than his Performance Score. He has learning disabilities in mathematical calculation and writing. He writes very slowly, struggling to form his letters and numbers. In fact, he is generally a slow moving person. His strengths are his reading comprehension and fund of information. His ADHD is reflected in his difficulty staying on task and his poor organizational skills. He forgets to copy down his assignments. He loses his assignments. He loses his textbooks.

Monte's first IEP (Individualized Education Plan) was written when he was nine years old and determined to have LD and ADHD. At that time he had some balance problems and some visual–motor deficits as well as writing problems, and received occupational therapy services in addition to teacher consultant services. He is still rather clumsy and bumps into walls occasionally, but no longer receives the services of an occupational therapist.

Subsequent IEPs provided Monte with Teacher Consultant (TC) services three times per week to help him with written expression and math. In middle school Monte was placed in a special education academic support class one period a day to help him with homework completion as well as writing and math. He often forgot to bring his assignments to class and usually told the academic support teacher that he had no homework.

Monte stopped taking Ritalin® when he was in seventh grade because, he says, he felt ashamed and embarrassed in front of the other kids. At that time he also said that he did not want any help in school. He felt he was doing okay.

Due to the increased challenge of high school, Monte will need additional support. But first of all, he will need to confront his ADHD and LD and acknowledge that he does indeed need help in school and that it is not anything to be ashamed of. He also needs to reconsider medication as he admits that it did help him in the past.

Monte's mother requested a new IEP at the end of December because of his poor grades. The IEP Team met to reconsider Monte's program. Everyone agreed that he needed additional support.

Monte's IEP Team decided that he needed a teacher consultant to help him learn organizational skills and how to manage his ADHD. The IEP Team also decided that he should take a keyboarding class so that he could eventually do all his writing on a computer. This should speed up his writing. His new IEP states that he will also need supplemental aids and services (accommodations) in the regular education classroom. According to the IEP, Monte's regular education teachers are to:

- Communicate daily with Monte's mother in order to be sure his homework assignments reach home and his completed homework is turned in.
- Reduce the amount of writing for Monte and allow him to fulfill some writing assignments orally, such as presenting oral reports in school or tape recording his reports.
- Provide note-taking assistance for Monte in class since he writes so slowly that he cannot keep up with the teacher.
- Check at the end of class to see that Monte has copied the assignment accurately.
- Help Monte break down the long-term assignments into steps and schedule checkpoints for him so the teacher can check on his progress.
- Help him get started on assignments in class. Although he is capable of doing the work, he really does not know how to begin.
- Allow him to take untimed tests.
- Develop a system for reinforcing Monte for homework completion.
- Reinforce Monte's effort and progress and reduce negative feedback.

Monte's self-esteem is rather shaky, although he appears self-confident, and his teachers were asked to give him all the encouragement they could.

Several of Monte's teachers feel his problems stem from the fact that he seems to prefer socializing with the other students rather than working. They believe he could do his homework if he wanted to. Although most of these accommodations are relatively simple, his teachers see them as time consuming, especially in light of the needs of the other 28 students in their classes. His teachers feel that Monte's accommodations will take up time they could best use elsewhere.

Many classroom teachers perceive special education laws as unwelcome intruders in their classrooms. Instead of being able to rely on their own professional judgment, teachers may feel that the laws are dictating how and what they should teach. Regular education teachers sometimes feel they are slighting their other students by having to plan and individualize for students with ADHD and/or LD.

In addition, these teachers may not agree that a particular student has a disability, or they may disagree with the type of disability the team has decided the student has. You may see many students in your classes with the same problems as Monte who are not considered as having a disability. You probably feel these students need your help as much as or more than Monte.

Monte is lucky. When Monte was nine years old and having both behavioral and academic difficulties in class, Monte's mother asked the school to evaluate Monte for learning problems. Many parents, especially poorly educated parents, don't realize that their children are having problems in school and also don't realize that the school can provide additional services to a student who is having difficulties.

Many teachers don't realize that they too can refer a student for evaluation (after discussion with the parent and securing parent permission). Some elementary teachers, expecting that some learning problems will resolve themselves as the student matures, do not refer young students for evaluation. This is why you see students in middle school or high school who do not have IEPs or Section 504 Plans but who really need them.

A written IEP or Section 504 Plan serves several purposes. It is, first of all, a written commitment by the school to provide services and supports for the particular student with a disability. It also represents school and parent agreement on the provision of these services and supports. It spells out the responsibilities of special education personnel and classroom teachers and how student progress towards specified goals will be evaluated.

Many teachers ask, aside from legal requirements, why an IEP or Section 504 Plan needs to be written, when they are already providing the accommodations specified in the plans. The IEP or Section 504 Plan is a blueprint that shows classroom teachers the way to help these students learn. It is a systematic compilation of information about the student that helps teachers focus on the learning goals and objectives for that student. Written IEPs and 504 Plans also help next year's teachers understand a student's needs and how to work with him or her.

A TEAM APPROACH TO THE DEVELOPMENT OF IEPS AND SECTION 504 PLANS

Eligible students under both IDEA and Section 504 are to be provided with a free, appropriate, and individualized education program that meets their educational needs and helps them progress in the general education curriculum.

The IEP and Section 504 Plan are developed in a three-stage process:

- Determine student eligibility.
- Develop the Individualized Education Program (IEP) or Section 504 Plan.
- Decide on educational placement.

Student eligibility and placement decisions and the development of the IEP or Section 504 Plan are all done by either the IEP Team or 504 Planning Committee. Section 504 does not specify the members of the planning committee, except to say that they must know the student. IDEA, on the other hand, requires the following IEP team members:

- The parents of the student with a disability
- At least one regular education teacher who knows the student or who will likely have the student in class
- At least one special education teacher who knows the student
- A representative of the local education agency who is qualified to provide or supervise the provision of special education services
- An individual who can interpret psychological evaluations
- Related services staff and others who know the student, invited by the parent or school
- The student, where appropriate

Related services staff are invited depending on individual student need. This means that if the student is currently receiving occupational therapy services or if it is anticipated that the student might need occupational therapy, the occupational therapist is invited to attend the meeting. The same holds true for the physical therapist and the speech and language pathologist. Related services staff can include:

- A school psychologist
- A school social worker
- An occupational therapist
- A physical therapist
- A speech and language pathologist
- An audiologist

Transportation to and from school is also considered a related service. Others who may be invited by the parents are:

- An outside psychologist, social worker, and/or educator
- A physician
- A tutor
- An advocate
- A friend

Many school staff members are afraid of advocates. When the parent tells the school that he or she is bringing an advocate to an IEP or 504 meeting, it is often like waving a red flag. Parents don't generally bring advocates to meetings unless the student has been having problems in school that the parents feel have not been addressed. Often there have been problems between the parents and school staff as well.

Advocates are at an IEP meeting to protect the rights of the student and parents, just as union stewards protect the rights of teachers during disputes. It is true that advocates can be quite assertive—this is their job. Unless an advocate is insulting or disruptive, he or she should be seen as an asset in helping to solve problems.

Generally, at a Section 504 planning committee meeting, you will find:

- The parent
- One or more classroom teachers
- The principal of the school (or his or her designee)
- Others as invited by the school or parent

By requiring a team approach that includes the parents, the laws hope to ensure that the student will have the benefit of several good minds working together on solving his or her problems.

In order to determine student eligibility for services, the student must be evaluated by the school using a variety of assessment tools and strategies from a variety of sources. (See Chapter 1.) Parental consent must be obtained before beginning the evaluation process. The student is assessed in all areas of suspected disability. Any independent evaluation of the student by an outside psychologist must also be considered by the team.

The results of the multidisciplinary assessment are then compared with the eligibility criteria under IDEA or Section 504. The IEP team or 504 committee decides whether the student has met the criteria and—if he or she has—begins to develop the IEP or 504 Plan.

When to Call an IEP Team Meeting

- Initial meeting to determine eligibility
- Annual review/revision of plan
- Three-year redetermination of eligibility
- Transition planning for post-secondary options
- Change of level (elementary to middle, middle to high school, high school graduation)
- Change in program or service:
  - —Add or delete a special education program or service
  - —Change special education service delivery: number of minutes or times per week/month
  - —Change regular education program
  - —Ten-day suspension, expulsion
- No longer eligible for Special Education
- Transfer to or from another district
- Program inappropriate
- Results of new evaluations
- Request for additional or new evaluation by parent or school

---

Figure 7-1

IEP team and 504 planning meetings are usually held once a year to review the student's program and his or her progress towards the goals and objectives and to determine special education services and accommodations for the coming year. However, these team meetings can also be called for a variety of other purposes. (See Figure 7-1.)

Although IDEA spells out when the school must call a new IEP, 504 does not. However, 504 meetings are usually called for the same reasons as IEP team meetings, and 504 Plans should be reviewed annually as are IEPs.

ELEMENTS OF THE IEP AND SECTION 504 PLAN

A well-designed IEP or 504 Plan can anticipate and prevent problems while teaching the student new skills. IEPs and 504 Plans are based on student needs as ascertained by the multidisciplinary team. The purpose of these plans is to help the student progress in the regular education curriculum and to help correct any other educational weaknesses the student might have.

The school psychologist reevaluated Monte before the IEP team meeting in January. The evaluation indicated that Monte had the following problems:

- A slow processing speed that affects test taking and assignment completion.
- Poor visual–motor integration abilities that affect his writing. He has great difficulty forming his letters correctly, which greatly slows his writing.
- Distractibility that affects everything from listening to test taking.
- Poor organization skills.
- Difficulty analyzing whole to part relationships.

Special education services and accommodations in regular education classes written into Monte's IEP will help prevent many of these problems. Teaching Monte organization skills and how to manage his ADHD will greatly reduce other problems.

It is important that the student be part of the IEP or 504 process. Unfortunately many students do not want to participate in the IEP team or 504 committee meeting for several reasons. They may feel overwhelmed by the number of people present. They may not feel free to express their opinions, especially if they disagree with what someone is saying. Often when students do attend these meetings, they do not say anything and just nod their heads when asked if they agree with the plan.

This is not student participation. Students need to prepare themselves to be active participants—and this active participation needs to be welcomed and respected by parents and staff. (See Figure 7-2.)

School staff and parents may develop what they consider an excellent program, but if the student doesn't agree with certain elements, the plan will not work.

In Monte's case, the school and Monte's parents thought that Monte should sit up front in each class, close to the teacher, to help him focus. Monte vetoed that idea. He wanted to sit with his friends like everyone else did. The team decided that this wasn't that

Student Checklist: How to Participate in IEP or Section 504 Meetings

Prepare

_____ List the courses in which you do best.

_____ List your strengths.

_____ List courses you liked the most this year. Why?

_____ List courses you didn't like this year. Why?

_____ List things with which you need help.

_____ What could teachers do to help you in each course?

_____ List after-school activities in which you are involved.

_____ Discuss your psychological evaluation results with the psychologist or your parents.

_____ List your questions or concerns.

Plan

_____ Read your current IEP or 504 Plan.

_____ What courses would you like to take next year?

_____ What course(s) do you think you will have difficulty with?

_____ What kind of help will you need to pass the difficult course(s)?

Participate

_____ Find out when the meeting is to be held.

_____ Find out what will be discussed.

_____ Decide if you want to attend all or part of the meeting.

_____ Listen actively; stay alert; take notes.

_____ Speak up about your questions and concerns.

_____ If you don't want to attend the meeting, discuss your questions and concerns with your parents.

_____ Make sure what is being planned and why.

Figure 7-2

important and acquiesced. Monte also disagreed about having another student take notes for him. He didn't want to be singled out in this way. This time the team disagreed with him; they felt that Monte needed the class notes. However, they were willing to explore with Monte other ways in which he could get the class notes.

IDEA spells out what must be included in the IEP. Some IEPs are quite extensive; others include the bare minimum required by law. States have developed IEP forms to be used by local districts which include all the required elements. These forms generally allow a minimum amount of space for specifics. If there is not enough space on the IEP form, additional pages may be attached to the IEP.

IEPs should communicate important information to the student's teachers as well as fulfill the letter of the law. To state that a student has ADHD or LD and not include how these disabilities affect student functioning does not give the teacher enough information. It is also important to state other problems that the student might have, such as depression or poor organizational skills, that can also affect school functioning. (See Figure 7-3.)

Content of the IEP According to IDEA

- Statement of student's present level of performance
- How the student's disability affects progress in general education curriculum
- Parent and student concerns
- Strengths of student
- Least Restrictive Environment (LRE) considerations: placements considered, placement chosen, statement of amount of time student will spend in general education classes
- Special education and related services to be provided; number of times per week, month; number of minutes per session
- Measurable annual goals and short-term objectives meeting the student's educational needs, and how, by whom, and with what frequency the objectives will be measured
- Supplementary aids and services to be provided in the regular education classroom (accommodations); supports for classroom teacher
- Student participation in statewide testing; testing accommodations
- Frequency and type of communication with parents
- Transition services beginning age 14
- Date of initiation of services
- Parent consent
- Placement of student
- Signature of administrator responsible (e.g., school district superintendent)

Figure 7-3

Some students also require a positive behavior support plan which is attached to their IEP. (See Chapter 8.)

As Section 504 does not specify the elements of a 504 Plan, you will find that individual school districts use different formats for writing the plan. Some 504 Plans are as elaborate as IEPs, but most are short and simple. The bottom line is that these plans should also be able to serve as a blueprint for how to help the particular student with ADHD and/or LD learn.

Although none are required, many of the elements of the IEP should be included in the 504 Plan. (See Figure 7-4.) Even though Figure 7-4 does not include goals and objectives, these would be a good addition to a 504 Plan.

When developing the 504 plan, it is important to remember that Section 504 affects the provision of special education services as well as regular education services. Many teachers and school administrators are not aware that a student may receive special education services, such as Teacher Consultant services, under Section 504.

Recommended Content of the Section 504 Plan

- Student demographic information
- Date and place of meeting
- Signatures of participants and their titles
- Summary of evaluations and reports
- Eligibility under Section 504
- Specific student disability, weaknesses
- Student strengths
- Specific accommodations needed:
  —Name courses in which specific accommodations are needed
  —List any teacher consultation needed, any additional resources
- Assistive technology
- Other services to be provided, including special education services
- Case manager to:
  —Monitor plan
  —Ensure implementation
  —Locate resources for student or teachers
  —Contact parents with any problems
- Beginning and ending dates of plan
- Parent agreement or disagreement with plan
- How parents can appeal decisions of 504 committee

Figure 7-4

Tiffany's Section 504 Plan

Mayfair High School/Helber Public Schools

Section 504 General Education Accommodations

Student: *Tiffany Williams* **Date:** *September, 2001*
504 Committee: *Dickson, Albert, Copeland, Mrs. Williams*

STUDENT STUDY TEAM SUMMARY:

Tiffany was a special education student through fifth grade after being diagnosed with dyslexia. Her parents also indicate she has been diagnosed as having Attention Deficit Disorder in the past. She has worn special lenses to assist with reading and depth perception. She learns best with a multisensory approach. She is a hard worker but continues to have difficulty with reading, spelling, and test-taking. Tiffany becomes very anxious because she wants to be successful at school and becomes frustrated that it is so difficult for her. She is slow to process information and has difficulty understanding whole to part concepts. Her parents state that she is an auditory learner.

CLASSROOM AND SCHOOL ACCOMMODATIONS:

1. Teachers will accept papers with spelling and other writing mechanics mistakes, giving additional time, if needed, for corrections.
2. Tiffany may need additional time on tests. If scantron sheets must be used, she may choose to use a ruler to keep her place on the answer sheet. She may need to ask for breaks since the intensive visual concentration required is stressful for her. The use of colored paper may also help.
3. Sitting near a window with natural lighting for working and reading makes it easier and more comfortable for Tiffany to learn.
4. Tiffany may use a tape recorder in her classes if needed.
5. Tiffany will be encouraged to use a calculator in her math class for calculating basic math facts.
6. The school will provide audio tapes of all her textbooks. The reading consultant will meet with classroom teachers to help develop reading accommodations.

SPECIAL EDUCATION SERVICES:

- Teacher Consultant: Three times per week for 40 minutes.
- Social Worker: Once every two weeks for 20 minutes.
- Case Manager: Ninth-grade counselor

(continued)

Figure 7-5

STUDENT RESPONSIBILITIES:

1. Tiffany will ask for assistance and accommodations when she needs help. If she knows she will need additional time on tests, she will arrange this with the teacher ahead of time.

2. Tiffany will plan ahead to allow time for corrections on written assignments before the due date. She will ask for additional time as needed on written in-class work.

PARENT RESPONSIBILITIES:

Parents will monitor Tiffany's progress and continue teacher and counselor contact as needed.

_____ _____   _____

Agree   Disagree   Parent

                                            _____

                                            Foster La Grant, Principal

This plan runs from 9/2001 through 6/10/2002.

This might occur when a student no longer meets the definition of LD under IDEA but the team decides the student needs some special education support as he or she transitions from an IEP to a 504 Plan. The special education support is then listed on the 504 Plan.

Tiffany is one such student. She had been diagnosed with dyslexia in the past and had received special education services through sixth grade. At the end of sixth grade it was determined that she no longer met the eligibility of LD under IDEA because there was not a severe discrepancy between her ability and her achievement. Since she did meet the criteria of a person with a disability under Section 504, a 504 Plan was written for her. In addition to her core courses, she was to take a reading course that was open to all students in seventh grade who were reading below grade level. She had some accommodations in her Language Arts class, including extra time on tests and shortened reading assignments.

Tiffany managed to get through junior high school with a C+ average because she is such a hard worker. However, now that she is in ninth grade and the amount of reading has increased, Tiffany is really struggling. Her mother tried to get her recertified as LD under IDEA but she still didn't meet the criteria.

A new 504 meeting was called and it was decided that Tiffany would have a teacher consultant to help her learn some reading strategies. In addition, the reading consultant would help the classroom teachers design reading accommodations for Tiffany. Tiffany would also see the school social worker once every two weeks to help her with her test-related anxiety. (See Figure 7-5.)

RESPONSIBILITIES OF THE CLASSROOM TEACHER

The IEP or 504 Plan spells out the responsibilities each team member has for a particular student. The classroom teacher is arguably the most important member of the team. You, as the classroom teacher, may have a variety of responsibilities. (See Figure 7-6.)

Most IEPs and 504 plans have to be fine-tuned by the classroom teacher. You may find that some suggested accommodations don't work for the student. You may discover other accommodations that do work aren't listed in the IEP or 504 Plan. You are certainly allowed to make decisions about what works best for the student, as long as you bear the intent of the plan in your mind.

In order to be a successful teacher of a student with ADHD and/or LD, you will need to be knowledgeable, accepting, and flexible. Teaching these students can be quite a challenge, as you know. You must always remember that there are special education and related services staff who can help you. Regular education staff—such as the counselor, the principal, or other classroom teachers—can also be of help. Under IDEA you may also ask for an instructional aide if you feel you need one, and additional training or information about how to teach students with ADHD and/or LD.

Responsibilities of the Classroom Teacher at IEP or Section 504 Meetings

- Contribute information about the student to the IEP team.
- Help determine special education services that the student needs.
- Help develop accommodations in the regular education class.
- Help develop goals and objectives.
- Help determine student placement and select courses.
- Translate evaluation results into instructional strategies you will use.
- Help develop reinforcement system, if required.
- Ask for help, when needed, to carry out plan.
- Communicate with parents to help prevent problems from escalating and inform parents of progress.
- Implement the student's educational plan in the classroom.

Figure 7-6

RESPONSIBILITIES OF THE
TEACHER CONSULTANT
AND RESOURCE ROOM TEACHER

The teacher consultant or resource room teacher shares many of your responsibilities and has specific responsibilities for more involved students. (See Figure 7-7.)

Since most students with ADHD and/or LD have problems with homework, the teacher consultant and resource room teacher often find themselves helping students with overdue homework rather than teaching new skills. Peer or volunteer tutors can help students with homework, but only a trained special education teacher can help students learn new skills. As the adage says, "Give me a fish and I eat for a day. Teach me *to* fish and I eat for a lifetime." Students with ADHD and/or LD must learn new skills and strategies if they are to function independently.

Responsibilities of the Teacher Consultant
and Resource Room Teacher

- Help the student with homework completion.
  - —Check that the student has copied assignments accurately.
  - —Help student get started on homework.
  - —Check that the student is taking the necessary materials home.
  - —Check with classroom teachers regarding missing assignments.
- Teach subject matter: math, language arts, science, social studies.
- Help the student prepare for tests.
- Help the student acquire new skills in time management, organization, problem-solving, self-management.
- Team teach with the classroom teacher to provide additional help in class to students who are having difficulty.
- Reteach concepts the student does not understand.
- Suggest teaching strategies to classroom teacher to help particular students and locate resources for the teacher.
- Monitor the IEP.
- Help develop behavioral support plan, reinforcement system.
- Communicate with parents.

Figure 7-7

RESPONSIBILITIES OF THE SCHOOL SOCIAL WORKER AND SCHOOL PSYCHOLOGIST

Many students with ADHD and/or LD do not need services from a school social worker or psychologist. Some do. (See Figure 7-8.)

Monte received the services of a teacher consultant and a social worker. The IEP team decided that Monte would continue in the Academic Support class taught by the teacher consultant for help with homework completion. He would also elect a regular education study skills class taught the first four weeks of the semester and a regular education keyboarding class for the next eight weeks. The social worker would include Monte in a small group of students with ADHD that would focus on self-management. This group was to meet once a week throughout the semester.

These support services—plus the accommodations in the regular education classes—should help Monte pass most of his courses. Monte, however, must do his part.

GOALS AND OBJECTIVES

In order to measure a student's progress, yearly goals and objectives are written for the student by the IEP team and student progress is measured at specified intervals. Three to five goals with about three objectives each are the optimal amount. The educational program becomes too chaotic if there are more goals.

Responsibilities of the School Social Worker and School Psychologist

- Observe or evaluate the student as needed.
- Provide small-group instruction in conflict management, social skills, and/or self-management.
- Defuse confrontations between students or between teacher and student.
- Consult with classroom teacher on how to work with the student.
- Help develop behavioral support plan.
- Help develop reinforcement system.
- Provide individual therapy, student consultation: self-esteem, self-awareness, anxiety, depression.
- Evaluate the student.

Figure 7–8

Monte's IEP Goals and Objectives

PRESENT LEVEL OF PERFORMANCE:
Monte has great difficulty writing. His writing is slow, messy, and incomplete.

ANNUAL GOAL:
Monte will improve his writing.

Short-Term Instructional Objectives	Assessment Procedures	Performance Criteria	Schedule for Evaluation
1. Using computer software, Monte will brainstorm ideas to be included in his papers. 2. Monte will organize these ideas into an outline. 3. Monte will write the first paragraph of his papers using the computer. 4. Monte will write an entire paper using the computer.	Teacher observation	75% of the time	Once a month

PRESENT LEVEL OF PERFORMANCE:
Monte rarely hands in his homework.

ANNUAL GOAL:
Monte will hand in his homework on time.

Short-Term Instructional Objectives	Assessment Procedures	Performance Criteria	Schedule for Evaluation
1. Monte will bring his assignment book to class every day. 2. Monte will record all assignments in his assignment book and ask teachers to check them. 3. Monte will bring his assignment book home every day and ask his mother to check it. 4. Monte will complete his homework, place it in his course folder, and place the folder in his backpack.	Teacher observation Monte will use a self-monitoring checklist	75% of the time	Monte will review checklist with teacher and parent each week.

Figure 7-9

Teacher Checklist: How to Develop Goals and Objectives

- ☐ Describe the student's present level of performance and compare it with the previous year's goals and objectives. Check:
  - ☐ Did the student make progress?
  - ☐ Does the student still need some work on a particular goal?
- ☐ Determine new annual goals based on student's current performance. Check:
  - ☐ Are goals appropriate?
  - ☐ Are goals important?
  - ☐ Are goals achievable in one year?
  - ☐ Do goals include input from student and parent?
  - ☐ Do goals include both academic and nonacademic goals?
  - ☐ Are the number of goals limited to five or fewer?
- ☐ Develop short-term instructional objectives (e.g, the two to five intermediary steps leading to a goal). Check:
  - ☐ Are objectives measurable?
  - ☐ Are objectives specific?
  - ☐ Are objectives relevant?
- ☐ Select ways to measure student progress. Consider:
  - ☐ Tests
  - ☐ Homework
  - ☐ Portfolios
  - ☐ Projects
  - ☐ Observations by teacher or parent
  - ☐ Student self-report
  - ☐ Reports from nonschool activities
- ☐ Decide on assessment procedures.
- ☐ Decide how frequently checks will be made on student progress.

Figure 7-10

Goals help move the student in a systematic way, from where he is now to where we want him to be. Objectives describe how the student is going to get there. Measuring progress allows us to fine-tune the strategies we are using to help the student achieve the goals and objectives. Each goal must include a description of the student's current level of achievement in the target area as well as a description of the goal. Objectives must always be measurable.

Use a phrase like "The student will demonstrate . . ." rather than "The student will learn . . . " or "The student will understand . . . ." Phrases such as "The student will write a paragraph containing . . . ." or "The student will correctly answer . . ." are also measurable. (See Figure 7-9.)

The IEP team should give much thought to the development of goals and objectives. Unfortunately, the teams spend little time on developing goals and objectives at most 504 and IEP meetings. These are usually written at the end of the meeting when everyone is rushed. In fact, goals and objectives often seem to be an afterthought.

Each person who has worked with the student during the current semester should give thought to the development of goals and objectives for the student. (See Figure 7-10.)

Remember, you are developing goals and objectives for the student based on your course requirements. These goals and objectives will need to be integrated into the curriculum.

ACCOMMODATIONS OR SUPPLEMENTAL AIDS AND SERVICES IN THE REGULAR EDUCATION CLASSROOM

The purpose of classroom accommodations is to help level the playing field for students with ADHD and/or LD, just as eyeglasses do for a person who is farsighted and crutches do for a person who has a broken leg. Schools and teachers are not required by law to do anything that is considered unreasonable or that would cause them "undue hardship." The tests for accommodations tend to be: How much does it cost? and How much time will it take?

The accommodations listed in Figure 7-11 are generally considered "reasonable." (See Figure 7-11.) Accommodations, based on student needs, can prevent many problems from arising in the first place. They can also help students overcome the barriers to learning that their disabilities cause.

PREPARING FOR THE IEP OR SECTION 504 MEETING

Everyone needs to prepare for IEP and 504 meetings. Reports need to be read and information needs to be collected. It is important to gather your thoughts before the meeting and write yourself notes regarding your recommendations and concerns. (See Figure 7-12.)

Types of Accommodations

Presentation of new material

- Oral
- Written
- Demonstration
- Combination
- Clearly reproduced worksheets/handouts
- Key concepts written on the board
- Use of visual aids and graphics

Testing alternatives

- Read to student or tape test directions or test items.
- Allow student to answer orally.
- Provide alternative ways for student to demonstrate mastery.
- Give students additional time on tests.
- Provide a nondistractable environment.
- Provide an alternative form of test (e.g., multiple choice vs. essay).
- Do not penalize for spelling, grammar, and punctuation errors if due to disability.
- Allow student to dictate, record, or type answers and use a calculator.
- Break instructions into smaller sections.
- For scantron tests:
  —Allow student to write answers in test booklet.
  —Enlarge size of preprinted/bubble answer sheet.
- Provide frequent breaks.
- Have teacher consultant or resource room teacher supervise test-taking.

Reinforcement/grading system

- Develop point system.
- Provide certificates, notes home.
- Display work.
- Grade for effort and progress in addition to finished product.
- Create progress charts for student.
- Provide frequent reinforcement.
- Limit negatives.

School/parent communication system

- Meet once a week, every two weeks, once a month.
- Provide progress reports (weekly or monthly).
- Provide weekly written and/or telephone communication.
- Contact promptly, when problem occurs.

Writing

- Limit amount.
- Use computer for papers, reports, etc.

(continued)

Figure 7-11

- Allow student to dictate to a scribe.
- Allow oral reports and answers.
- Allow student to draw maps and graphics in place of writing.
- Provide student with copies of lecture notes.

Teach student

- Organization skills
- Time-management skills
- Keyboarding
- Reading strategies
- Test-taking strategies
- How to break down large tasks into small steps

Rules and discipline policy

- Provide clear, simple, written rules.
- Communicate clear consequences.
- Establish a progression of consequences.
- Discuss rules in class; post them on the board.
- Give more chances per infraction than discipline code allows.
- Don't penalize behavior not currently under the student's control.

Slow processing

- Don't call on student in class unless he/she raises hand.
- Give extra time to read and write.
- Give extra time to formulate answers to questions.
- Summarize frequently.

Reading/textbooks

- Provide a second set at home.
- Tape textbooks and required reading.
- Highlight textbooks: main points, vocabulary, etc.
- Locate easier textbooks.
- Provide videotapes or movies of novels.

Preferential seating

- Sit near teacher.
- Sit away from distractions.
- Sit near student role model.

Homework system

- Give student assignment in writing.
- Give student assignments two to four weeks in advance.
- Use special assignment notebook.
- Allow alternative assignments.

(continued)

- Shorten assignments or give extra time to complete.
- Check for accuracy, understanding.
- Help student begin assignment in class.
- Give assignments to teacher consultant.
- Give copies of assignments to parents.
- Notify parents as soon as possible if homework is missing.
- Allow student to give oral/taped presentations instead of written assignments.
- Break down long-term assignments into steps.

Math

- Use calculator for basics.
- Don't require student to copy problems.
- Allow student to write answers on the test rather than on answer sheet.
- Base grading on correct procedures used as well as correct answers.

Note-taking system

- Give a copy of another student's notes.
- Provide teacher-made notes or outlines.
- Allow student to use a tape recorder.
- Write key concepts on chalkboard.
- Summarize frequently.
- Review student's notes.

Attention, impulsivity, hyperactivity

- Help student begin task.
- Cue/signal student to focus on task.
- Limit distractions.
- Dispense medication: remind student, inform parents.
- Ignore jiggling, tapping, etc.
- Provide opportunities for physical activity.
- Provide organizational aids and checklists.
- Help student with self-management.
- Develop routines for student.
- Develop Behavioral Support Plan to help prevent problems.

Self-esteem

- Provide frequent encouragement and positive reinforcement.
- Help student with self-awareness of strengths.
- Support student interests and strengths.
- Arrange for student to help another student; give responsibilities.
- Provide success experiences.

Memory

- Provide student with checklists, graphic organizers, and other organizational aids.
- Provide student with written directions and instructions.
- Repeat directions and instructions, if necessary.
- Give student vocabulary words in context.

Teacher Checklist: How to Prepare for an IEP or Section 504 Meeting

1. Review the student's current classroom performance.
   - ☐ Review the student's school work and performance in school.
   - ☐ Observe the student's social interactions in and out of class.
   - ☐ Ask the student about his or her performance and learning problems (e.g., what was helpful and what was not).
   - ☐ Collect samples of student work.
   - ☐ Review student attendance, timeliness.
   - ☐ List student strengths, interests, and weaknesses.
   - ☐ Review results of statewide testing.
   - ☐ Review current IEP or 504 Plan, services, goals and objectives.

2. Compare current performance with expectations and past performance.
   - ☐ Have IEP goals been met?
   - ☐ Has the student made progress? Why? In what areas? Are you disappointed with the student's progress? Why?
   - ☐ Review previous reports and records.
   - ☐ Identify positive or negative changes in the student.
   - ☐ Analyze classroom tests and look for patterns in specific areas.
   - ☐ List strategies that have worked and those that have not.
   - ☐ Identify any questions or concerns you may have.

3. List your recommendations for the coming year.
   - ☐ List student's strengths to build upon.
   - ☐ Generate suggestions on how to work with the student.
   - ☐ List your goals and objectives.
   - ☐ Specify a preferred placement.
   - ☐ Identify special education services.

(continued)

Figure 7-12

☐ Specify teacher preference.

☐ Identify contents of the educational program.

4. Review policies, if necessary.

☐ Review school and district policies and state requirements.

☐ Review your legal rights and responsibilities and the student's rights.

5. Arrange materials and prepare yourself psychologically.

☐ Collect materials such as student work samples, test results, your recommendations for next year.

☐ List your questions and concerns to bring to the meeting.

☐ Outline possible strategies to cope with nervousness, frustration, anger.

☐ Predict what others may say and how you can respond.

Notes

_____

_____

_____

_____

_____

_____

_____

_____

After you have thought about your recommendations and concerns, try to predict what the parent's reaction to them will be. Put yourself in the parent's place and ask yourself the following questions:

- Will the parent agree or disagree with my recommendations?
- Why will the parent disagree?
- What are the parent's recommendations and concerns? Why?
- Will anything I say offend the parent or make him/her angry? What specifically?
- Is there some way I can prevent this?
- What will be the disagreements between us?
- Are there some compromises that would be acceptable to both the parents and me?
- Are there some assurances I can give the parent about monitoring the student's program and communicating with the parent about problems and progress?
- Can we try out either my or the parent's recommendations for four weeks or so and then reevaluate how the student is doing?

Often you can solve parent–teacher disagreements before the IEP or 504 meeting by reconsidering your recommendations or your method of presentation. As you think about the parent's point of view and feelings, you may modify your recommendations or you may come up with better ways of persuading the parent to try your recommendations. (See Chapter 11 on diversity and parent involvement.)

THE WELL-RUN MEETING

Many of us approach an IEP team meeting with a certain amount of trepidation under the best of circumstances: We feel this way even though the evidence is such that most of these meetings proceed quickly and peacefully.

There should be few surprises if you have prepared yourself for the meeting. Disagreements will occur at times but they often can be solved with compromise. Although it is understandable that a school might want to limit the meeting to one hour or less, if it is known that parents disagree with what the school is proposing, more time will be needed. A well-run meeting of sufficient length can help generate compromise and prevent hard feelings. (See Figure 7-13.)

It is important to make sure that parents understand what is being said and to what they are agreeing. You can do this by checking with the parents frequently to be sure their opinions and concerns are expressed.

A FINAL WORD

A well-written IEP or 504 Plan can mean the difference between success and failure, and satisfaction and discouragement for a student with ADHD and/or LD. Wendy, a tenth-grade student with ADHD and Learning Disabilities in Math can attest to that.

How to Run a Difficult Meeting

- Use a chalkboard or flip chart to list all questions and concerns, regardless of whether or not they will be addressed at the meeting.
- Clarify the purpose of the meeting and the decisions to be made.
- Accept all concerns and opinions without comment.
- Ask all participants to refrain from personal attacks.
- Agree on an agenda and schedule time for listing concerns, problem-solving, and decision-making.
- Ensure that parents get to voice their concerns and opinions.
- Clarify areas of agreement and disagreement.
- Discuss compromises.
- Encourage creative thinking.
- Solicit agreement from all participants.
- Schedule another meeting if this one was not conclusive. This provides people more time to think of solutions to problems.

Figure 7-13

"I had a great English teacher last semester. We had to do a research project. We had about 1-½ months to complete it. I picked the Triangle Shirtwaist Company fire in New York City because my great-grandfather and great great-grandfather worked in the garment industry. My great-grandfather actually saw the building right after it burned down with all the women in it.

"We had to describe the background, what happened, and what change it brought. We kept notes on notecards with the author, page number, and the information. We learned to do this in the study skills course all ninth graders were required to take. We had to check with the teacher once a week so she could see how we were doing and help us if we needed help. She gave us checklists so that we could remember what she expected us to do, things like free of spelling errors, clear and consecutive sentences.

"The teacher thought is was a really interesting project and she gave me an A.

"I didn't have a great teacher for Math. I couldn't understand what he was saying—even when I asked for help. The resource teacher had to help me a lot with my math. I got a B the first marking period. The math teacher said everything was fine so I thought I was doing fine. But he gave me a D in the final marking period. I know I have trouble taking tests—but I knew the work!

"The resource teacher helped me with any homework I had problems with. She made sure I understood my math, which is really hard for me. The teacher consultant helps anyone who needs her and helps keep chaos at bay. She talked to my regular classroom teachers so she could stay on top of any problems I'm having. Actually, (Wendy laughs) the teacher consultant kept me from going insane.

"What I really liked about this year's resource teacher was that she used to say things like 'according to this teacher report you're not doing so well. Let's see what we can do.' And she really helped me!"

Wendy is still an eager learner in tenth grade, largely because of her classroom and resource room teachers and the IEPs they helped develop over the years.

Before we had the laws that required IEPs and Section 504 Plans for students with ADHD and/or LD, students like Wendy failed course after course, became increasingly discouraged, and eventually dropped out of school. With the laws came educational programs that changed these students' lives.

We teachers are an integral part of that change. Without us these students cannot reach their potential. Yes, writing IEPs and 504 Plans takes time—but the benefits to the students are beyond price.

CHAPTER EIGHT

Behavioral Interventions

Frank is busy finishing his art project. He draws in one last quick stroke and, holding up the poster he has made, says "Ta da." He seems very pleased with himself. As he hands his poster to the teacher, he looks over at another student's work. "Man, you can't draw," he says laughing.

When the bell rings, Frank goes to his homeroom. He asks the teacher if his desk has been moved. She tells him that it has—to make way for a new student in the class. He tells the teacher that is not fair. It's his place. He is angry and slams his desktop up and down several times, making comments about where his desk belongs. He says he hates the new student (who he knows) and says, "He has a hollow head—know what I mean?" (He points to his head, circles his index finger around his ear, and rolls his eyes.) "I don't want him sitting next to me." He glares at the new student menacingly. He is really simmering.

The teacher loudly tells Frank to stop and walks over to stand in front of him with her arms folded. She threatens to send Frank to the Principal's office if he doesn't sit down. He sits down but jumps up immediately. He starts to walk backward around the room. When he gets to the chalkboard, he turns and begins to erase the chalkboard with his face. Calling across the room, the teacher tells him to stop acting silly and to sit down. He turns away, makes a stern face, smacks his hands together, and walks back to his seat. He starts to sit down just as the bell rings. He rises triumphantly.

Frank slowly saunters into his Resource Room and loudly drops his bookbag on his desk. The teacher catches his eye and points to the chalkboard. On it is written: "Language arts. Finish your paper. Hand it in. Read." Frank sits down and looks around the room. The teacher catches his eye again and points to the board. Frank gets his paper from his folder on the teacher's desk, sits down, and starts to write. He works steadily until he is finished. He then takes out a book and reads raptly until the bell rings. The teacher collects all the papers at the door as the students leave.

Frank walks into gym class with a smile on his face. The students start playing a game of dodgeball while they wait for the teacher. Frank is clearly having fun.

As class begins the teacher lowers the volleyball net and challenges the students to get over the net without anyone touching the net. At first, thinking it is quite simple, everyone tries to step over the net. Some make it, some don't. Frank quickly grasps that the smaller students have to be lifted over the net by the taller students. After several tries and near misses, they make it—with Frank's encouragement. Everyone cheers. Frank raises his hands in a self-congratulatory handshake.

Math class is a disaster. Frank has forgotten his book. His teacher sends him back to his locker to get it. When he returns 10 minutes later, the teacher asks him where he has been and sends him to the office to get a pass. When he returns, the teacher tells him to sit down and start working on page 112. Frank opens his book and starts to read. He frowns and turns back a few pages, then a few pages more. "We never learned this s—t," he says while slamming his book shut. The teacher says, "Frank, I warned you if you ever said that again in my class, you're out. Go to the office and tell them I said you're suspended."

Frank has been suspended from school many times. He has a terrible temper and can go from 32 to 212 degrees in seconds. He has thrown books and erasers at his teachers. He gets into fights with the other students. He is often verbally abusive. Some teachers refuse to have him in their classes. If his behavior escalates, he will be in danger of being expelled from school. If he hurts a teacher or another student, he could be sent to jail.

Frank's behavioral problems place him squarely in the Emotionally Impaired category. This has been exacerbated by his chaotic home life. He lives with his grandmother because his mother died from an overdose when he was 18 months old and his father is always in and out of jail.

But is emotional impairment (EI) the whole story?

Frank presents many paradoxes. Despite his absences and suspensions, he is doing "A" work in Language Arts and "B" work in Social Studies. His teachers say he is very bright but inconsistent. He can be very likable and helpful one day, then very irritable and angry the next. Because Frank was about to enter middle school, it was decided that he should have a comprehensive psychoeducational evaluation. The evaluation uncovered some interesting facts: Frank has a high-average IQ with superior Verbal scores and problem-solving ability. He has severe ADHD with impulsivity and hyperactivity. He has some problems with auditory processing which may be caused by his attention problems. The discrepancy between his ability and his achievement in Math is quite severe. These results—coupled with classroom observations—suggest that at least some of Frank's behavior problems can be traced to his ADHD and LD.

There are many students like Frank in the school system who are both EI and ADHD/LD; in fact, over 50 percent of students with EI have ADHD or LD. They may appear emotionally disturbed, but their primary disability is ADHD and/or LD. Few of these students receive an appropriate educational program, one that addresses their learning and attention problems as well as their emotional impairment.

PAST EMPHASIS: PUNISHMENT

Before IDEA 1997, behavior management plans for Frank and students like him focused largely on punishment for misbehavior. In previous years, if Frank violated classroom rules or school disciplinary policy, he was removed from class, forbidden to participate in school sports or performances, and suspended from school for longer and longer periods of time.

Behavior management often included school social work services such as group and individual therapy. In Frank's case the social worker placed him in a conflict-resolution group and, in individual sessions, tried to make him aware of the psychological origins of his anger. She also told Frank's grandmother that she let him walk all over her, that her parenting skills were weak, and that she must be firmer with him at home and punish him for misbehavior.

Punishment is used to stop harmful and dangerous behavior, and behavior that prevents the teacher from teaching. It serves to remove a disturbing element from the classroom. Unfortunately, it is often used in anger by a teacher whose patience has been sorely tried and, in some cases, is used for relatively minor offenses.

Punishment assumes that the responsibility for negative behavior resides primarily within the student and results from a negative home situation. Punishment also assumes that negative or positive behavior is totally under the student's control and that the student has the ability and skills to behave in a more positive manner. For students like Frank, punishment doesn't work and may eventually cause the student to give up on school altogether.

A NEW DIRECTION: PREVENTION

IDEA 1997 takes a different approach. It moves from punishing a behavior after it occurs to the prevention of negative behavior. It focuses on changing or modifying the student's learning environment and by teaching the student positive skills and behaviors to replace problematic ones.

In order to do this, IDEA 1997 mandates the development of a Behavioral Support Plan that includes positive interventions, strategies, and supports for the student. IDEA describes the behavior to be covered by a Plan as behavior that impedes the student's learning or the learning of others. This does not refer only to severe behavior such as fighting; it also can mean "milder" behavior such as impulsivity, not paying attention, and not following directions.

Some of the "disruptive" behavior of a student with ADHD and/or LD reflects the nature of the disability. Some of the disruptive behavior arises as secondary to ADHD or LD (e.g., a severe reading problem can lead to frustration that can lead to class disruption). Behavioral Support Plans can target both primary and secondary behavioral problems. Psychosocial behavior problems can also be addressed.

BEHAVIORAL SUPPORT PLANS

The following assumptions underlie the development of Behavioral Support Plans:

- Most students want to be successful in school.
- Many students don't know how to succeed or how to overcome their weaknesses.
- Students deal with their difficulties the best way they know how.
- Students often develop bad habits or ineffective ways of dealing with problems.
- Students can learn new positive behaviors to replace negative, inappropriate behaviors.
- The learning environment strongly affects student learning and behavior.
- The learning environment can be modified to prevent some negative behaviors from occurring and to ameliorate others.

For example, we know that students with ADHD learn best in a structured, predictable environment. We know that the learning environment for these students can be manipulated to encourage on-task behavior by increasing structure, increasing the interest of the task, cueing the student to remain on task, etc. We know we can prevent off-task behavior by decreasing the visual and auditory distractions in the environment. We can also increase on-task behavior by teaching the student new learning and self-management skills. (See Chapter 6 on teaching self-management.)

Behavioral Support Plans are tied into IEP goals and objectives. Whenever behavioral goals are part of the IEP, a Behavioral Support Plan should be developed to help the student attain these goals. As progress toward goals and objectives are monitored, the plan can be modified if progress does not occur. (See Figure 8-1.)

In order to develop the Behavioral Support Plan, the IEP team is required to conduct a functional assessment of the student's behavior in the classroom.

Functional Assessment

Functional assessment takes place in the classroom and challenges you to discover why a particular behavior occurs at a particular time. In other words, you ask questions such as, "Is the student trying to escape from a task because it is too difficult?" "Does the student crave attention from the teacher or from the other students?" "Is the student lacking some skills?" "Is the student's disability interfering with following teacher directions or understanding what is being said?" "Is the student bored?" "Is the problem behavior being reinforced in some way?"

In this context, it is important to fully understand the effect of the student's disability on classroom functioning. During the functional assessment process, you may decide that

---

Teacher Checklist: Writing Behavioral Support Plans

- Describe the targeted negative behavior(s) and its severity.
- Describe the function of the targeted behavior or why the student is behaving in that manner.
- Clearly describe the desired positive behavior.
- Specifically identify how the environment can be changed to eliminate the negative behavior.
- Identify the positive behaviors and skills to be taught to the student.
- Identify reinforcers to increase or maintain positive behavior.
- Describe the method(s) of monitoring the behavioral plan and who will be responsible for monitoring the plan.

Figure 8-1

the student needs additional psychoeducational evaluation in order to help explain student functioning.

Interviews with parents, teachers, and the student can also produce important information on student functioning.

During our observations of the classroom, we look for the ecological conditions that immediately precede the behavior in question. For example, analyzing the observations we made of Frank in the classroom setting, we can see that he demonstrates positive behavior in both Gym and Resource Room Language Arts, but for different reasons. We hypothesize that Frank works well with the structure and predictability of the Resource Room. In addition, Frank seems to work well on tasks he enjoys and/or in which he is interested. He also seems to like challenge and is capable of high-level problem solving. We hypothesize that the time of day has little effect on his behavior.

Frank had some difficulty with attention in the Resource Room, but—whenever he seemed off task—the teacher would catch his eye or touch his shoulder to get him back on task.

Frank demonstrated his impulsivity and lack of self-control in homeroom and Math. His impulsivity was evident when he blurted out comments in Art, Math, and the Resource Room about the other students without regard for their feelings. His avoidance behavior, defiance, and disruption in Math might stem from the fact that he is having great difficulty understanding what is being taught and is quite frustrated. (See Figure 8-2.)

Avoidance and escape are the primary functions of negative behavior. Students may be trying to avoid or escape from a difficult task or a demand by the teacher. Students may be trying to avoid the humiliation of not being able to perform as either they or the teacher would wish. Another function of negative behavior can be to protest a perceived unfairness by the teacher or school, as evidenced by Frank's negative behavior in homeroom. Attention from the teacher or the other students may also be a function of the negative behavior.

Observation Form for Functional Assessment

Course _____ Teacher _____ Date _____ Time _____

Targeted Behaviors: _____

  Points gained for: _____

  Points lost for: _____

Examples of Behavior

Setting: What is the activity?

          What is the teacher doing?

          What are other students doing?

          What is the student doing?

Behavior	Time	What Happened Just Before	What Happened Immediately After	Possible Functions

Figure 8-2

Analyzing Antecedents

In order to prevent negative behavior from occurring, you must discover and analyze the antecedents of that behavior as well as the functions of the behavior. In this way you hypothesize a causal relationship between specifics in the learning environment and the negative behavior.

Antecedents are events (social, emotional, and/or environmental) that occur just prior to the targeted behavior which can trigger the negative behavior. Antecedents can be specific physical or instructional arrangements, classroom rules and structure, teaching style, the demands of a specific task or activity, the emotional climate of the classroom, the level of noise or other distractions, or interaction with another student or students.

In Frank's case the specific antecedents of his negative behavior seem to be the fact that his desk was moved without notice, he does not know how to control his anger, and the math work is too difficult for him. (See Figure 8-3.)

After a functional assessment is completed and correlated with psychoeducational data, the IEP team can discuss positive interventions, strategies, and supports that will be used to achieve the behavioral goals of the IEP. Here's how to do this:

- Modify the conditions immediately preceding the problem behavior in a way that will help prevent the behavior from occurring.
- Teach the student positive behavioral strategies to replace problematic ones.
- Develop a reinforcement system to increase and maintain positive replacement behaviors.

Frank's Functional Assessment Chart		
Antecedent (What Happened Just Before)	Behavior	Possible Function of Behavior
Desk moved without notice (Homeroom)	—Disruptions —Defiance —Silliness	—Protest —Gain attention
Math work	—Forgot book —Late return to class —Disruption	—Avoid work
Problem-solving (Gym class)	—Thinking —Planning —Leadership	—Challenge himself —Increase pride —Increase self-esteem —Gain attention

Figure 8-3

It is important to remember that the relatively quick functional assessment that takes place in the classroom results in hypotheses that need to be tested, not in "facts" discerned by scientific method. As hypotheses are tested, modified, and tested again, they can become effective blueprints for modifying student behavior.

Modifying Behavior

Increasing Frank's self-awareness of his strengths and weaknesses and discussing the results of the functional assessment with him is a necessary first step to teaching him replacement behaviors. Specific positive behaviors that contribute to academic success should be identified for him. Since he is already capable of gaining the other students' attention and respect in a positive way (e.g., in Gym class), we do not need to teach him a "new" behavior to replace silliness and disruption as an attention-getting device. We need to reinforce him for using the positive behavior in other settings.

A highly verbal student like Frank can greatly benefit from being taught to use self-talk and self-instruction to gain some control over both his anger and his impulsivity. He will also benefit from learning some relaxation skills to help him manage his anger. (See Chapter 6 on teaching self-management skills.)

The school social worker must first help Frank become aware of his negative behavior and the situations that trigger it. Although the school social worker is the person responsible for teaching Frank the replacement behaviors, *all* his teachers need to be responsible for reinforcing him for using the replacement behaviors. Frank can also be taught how to self-monitor his behavior using a checklist. (See Figure 8-4.)

Frank: Modifying the Learning Environment

Frank needs structure and predictability in all his classes. It is clear that he does not adjust easily to change. If changes in Frank's learning environment do occur, they need to be discussed with Frank before the change occurs and/or he needs to be prepared as much as possible for the change. (See Chapters 3, 6, and 7.)

Setting up routines in all his classes (e.g., writing a list of activities on the chalkboard, as in the Resource Room, that students are to begin as soon as they enter the room) would greatly help Frank to get on task. Nonverbal cues to help him get on task should be discussed by Frank and his teachers. Clear, short verbal directions and written checklists will also aid him in understanding what he is expected to do at a given moment.

Frank needs to be intellectually challenged and would both enjoy and do well with high-level tasks and tests that include analysis, application, and synthesis. He needs these opportunities to utilize his problem-solving skills.

It is important to analyze the difficulties Frank is having with math. Since it has been discovered that he has a learning disability in math, he will need teacher consultant services to help him learn some concepts he does not understand and some help with basic math skills. In addition, the possibility of placing Frank in a lower-level math class should be explored.

Student Checklist: Self-Monitoring

Student: _____   Date: _____   Teacher: _____

Directions: Use this form to keep track of your feelings and behavior.

I felt angry with the teacher.

Describe situation.	What did the teacher say or do?	What did you say or do?	Why were you angry?

I argued with the teacher.

Describe situation.	What did the teacher say or do?	What did you say or do?	Why were you arguing?

I felt angry with another student.

Describe situation.	What did the student say or do?	What did you say or do?	Why were you angry?
			(continued)

Figure 8-4

I argued with another student.			
Describe situation.	What did the student say or do?	What did you say or do?	Why were you angry?

Other:			
Describe situation.	What did the other person say or do?	What did you say or do?	What were your feelings and why?

The following strategies were included in Frank's Behavioral Support Plan:

- Teach Frank basic math skills.
- Allow him to use a calculator.
- Involve Frank in decisions and changes that affect him.
- Provide him with cues to get on task and checklists of tasks to be completed.
- Develop opportunities for Frank to utilize his problem-solving abilities.
- Design tasks with an appropriate level of challenge for him.
- Teach Frank to become aware of situations in which he gets angry.
- Teach him ways to manage his anger.
- Reward Frank for managing his anger.
- Help Frank set long- and short-term goals.

Special Education Services

Frank spent 40 minutes a day in the Resource Room and 20 minutes, twice a week, with the school social worker. Both worked on teaching him new behaviors. They also helped Frank's teachers modify the learning environment. Frank's seat was changed in homeroom, after a careful discussion with Frank. He decided that he would rather sit in a corner of the room so that the other students wouldn't "bother" him.

The teacher consultant helped the classroom teachers develop checklists of steps needed to complete specific tasks. The laminated checklists were given to Frank at the start of a task and retrieved afterward. These same checklists were used by the teacher to help several other students complete their work.

Frank's Math class was changed to a less demanding one, and he was given intensive math help in the Resource Room.

In addition to providing direct services to Frank, the teacher consultant and school social worker helped the classroom teacher develop a reinforcement plan for Frank.

REINFORCEMENT

Reinforcement is the *sine qua non* for modifying student behavior: Unless a change of behavior is reinforced or rewarded in some way, it will not be maintained. Reinforcement is necessary to learn, maintain, increase, and generalize positive behavior. A student can be reinforced for progress toward, effort involved, and achievement of behavioral goals.

There are two types of reinforcement: intrinsic and extrinsic. Intrinsic reinforcement comes from within the student and relates to a particular task. Such things as curiosity, interest, pride, the satisfaction of completing a task, and the avoidance of pain or failure are all internal reinforcers of positive behavior.

Extrinsic reinforcers exist outside the person or task and can be used by teachers to help the student learn, maintain, or increase positive behaviors. Extrinsic reinforcers are needed when the behaviors to be learned are difficult, frustrating, time consuming, or uninteresting. These types of reinforcers can be concrete (e.g., points, progress charts) or social (e.g., praise), as shown in Figure 8-5.

Specific reinforcers should be discussed by you and the student to determine which reinforcers will work best. Reinforcers such as privileges can either be *given* when positive behavior occurs or *taken away* when positive behavior doesn't occur or the student exhibits negative behavior.

For praise and other verbal reinforcement to be effective, they should be:

- *specific and accurate:* "You included two examples. That's great!"
- *accepting:* "You came up with a different solution. Good for you!"
- *appreciative:* "You raised your hand today. Thanks!"
- *respectful:* "I can see that you tried. You and I can work on it some more tomorrow."
- *acknowledging:* "I know this is hard for you, but you *are* making progress. Keep up the good work."

Sample Reinforcers for Secondary Students

Concrete	Social

• Points, stars for positive behavior (aggregated for larger awards)
• Progress charts
• Written messages of appreciation to student or parent
• Certificates and awards
• Specific activities including
  —free time
  —additional access to computer
	• Teacher attention
	• Praise, applause
	• Teacher or principal recognition of effort, progress, achievement
	• Time to talk to teacher
	• Go to lunch with teacher
	• Give student responsibility for classroom or school jobs
	• Privileges

Figure 8-5

If the student does not respond to verbal or social reinforcers at first, then you can pair concrete reinforcers—such as points with social reinforcers—until social reinforcers alone are enough to maintain the positive behavior. As progress and change occur, the student will begin to develop an internal reward system and need less frequent external rewards.

PLANNED IGNORING AND EXTINCTION

Not all negative behaviors are replaced by positive ones. Some are simply ignored. Ignoring is the absence of reinforcement of any kind. When a behavior is ignored, it eventually disappears. Needless to say many types of behavior cannot be ignored, but some can. Planned ignoring can be used for negative behavior that is:

- minor, such as sneering
- irrelevant, such as saying "I can't do it" or "It's too hard"
- not under the student's control, such as jiggling

It is important that everyone in the classroom ignore the behavior in question. This means that you must explain to the other students which behavior to ignore, preferably without reference to the particular student.

By ignoring such behaviors, you can focus on one or two major behaviors that need changing.

RESPONSE COST

Response cost refers to the removal of such things as preferred activities or privileges from the student when a behavioral infraction occurs. Sometimes response cost is paired with reinforcement so that the student receives points for positive behavior and loses points for negative behavior. Sometimes response cost is used only for relatively major infractions and can include such things as the removal of computer privileges. Suspension from class can be considered the ultimate response cost for unacceptable behavior.

The negative behaviors penalized by response cost must be carefully spelled out. The "costs" can be determined by you and the student. The cost must be clearly and specifically stated and should include the number of minutes of penalty.

Response cost should not be used alone or as the primary technique. The teaching and support of positive replacement behaviors should always be the focus of any behavioral plan.

Frank's Reinforcement System

While Frank's Behavioral Support Plan was being put into effect, a point system was developed for him by the teacher consultant, school social worker, and his classroom teacher. Frank was to gain or lose points for following the teacher's directions without comment, stopping a particular behavior when requested to do so, staying on task, and controlling his anger (e.g., no outbursts in a 10-minute period). The teacher consultant designed two simple charts that were taped to Frank's desk: one for gaining points and one for losing points.

As the classroom teacher moved about the room, a felt-tipped pen in her hand, she would place a mark on Frank's chart at approximately 10- to 15-minute intervals if his behavior was positive. The teacher would also keep track of the instances of negative behavior on a different chart. (See Figure 8-6.)

The pluses and minuses were added at the end of the day and Frank was given a total score. When he earned a certain number of points, he was rewarded by a reinforcer he had chosen.

The teacher gave Frank a lot of praise and verbal reinforcement when he successfully completed a task. The teacher also used verbal cueing and encouragement if she saw him beginning to lose control, telling him that he could maintain control, that he "could do it."

The teacher consultant helped his teachers locate intellectually challenging activities, such as riddles and mazes, that Frank could do after his work was done. It was discovered that Frank loved mysteries, so several books were located that he could read after task completion. These activities proved to be very effective reinforcers for positive behaviors.

Frank did not have points subtracted from his score if he grimaced, mumbled to himself, or made gestures. Although the goal was to extinguish these negative behaviors, at this time only "outbursts" were penalized. As outbursts came under his control, the other negative behaviors would be targeted. The point system was helping to "shape" Frank's behavior.

Points Chart

TEACHER'S NOTES

Course _____ Teacher _____ Date _____

Student _____

Targeted Behaviors:

This student earns points when he or she: _____

This student loses points when he or she: _____

Directions: Place a mark every 10 to 15 minutes to give or take away points on the appropriate index card.

ON STUDENT'S DESK

Points Gained	Points Lost

Figure 8-6

Teacher Checklist: 10 Steps for Shaping Behavior

1. Explain the process to the student.
2. Identify the target behavior.
3. Describe the student's current behavior.
4. Break the targeted behavior into small steps.
5. Describe the first step of the behavioral goal.
6. Identify what reinforcement to use and when.
7. Teach or demonstrate the step.
8. Reward the step.
9. Repeat the process with each behavioral step.
10. Shift from providing reinforcement every time to only once in awhile.

Figure 8-7

SHAPING BEHAVIOR AND CHAINING

Shaping refers to the systematic reinforcement of successive approximations of the desired behavior until the desired behavior itself is reached. Shaping can be thought of as a fine-tuning process. It begins by reinforcing the student for taking the first step in the behavior-change process. The criterion for reinforcing behavior is then gradually shifted in order to move the student closer to the targeted positive behavior. The key to success is the use of successive approximations that are small enough so that there is an easy transition from one step to the next. (See Figure 8-7.)

Chaining several behaviors together helps to build complex behaviors from simple behaviors. You begin by reinforcing combinations of behavior already in the student's repertoire.

CONTRACTING

A contract is a written agreement between the student and the teacher. It is *quid pro quo:* If the student will meet specific behavioral goals, then the teacher will give specific rewards to the student when the goals are attained. Contracts usually include a timeline, supports the student will need, and criteria for measuring progress. Both parties, after discussion and negotiation, develop and sign the contract. (See Figure 8-8.)

The process of contracting can be as important as the results. When implemented appropriately, contracting provides an opportunity for you to help the student set long- and short-term behavioral and academic goals. Contracts can help clarify expectations, responsibilities, and ways the student can help himself or herself.

Sample Contract

Background Notes

Targeted behaviors to replace during lectures
- Getting out of seat
- Making noise (interrupting teacher or other students)

Replacement behaviors (1 point for each)
- Sitting in seat
- Being quiet
- Listening
- Not disturbing others
- Taking notes

Contract

Student: _____

Teacher: _____

Date: _____   Course: _____

- I will sit in my seat during lecture time.

- I will be quiet and not disturb others.

- I will listen to the lecture and take notes.

- The teacher will signal me to be quiet and listen if I forget.

- Each day the teacher will write the number of points I earn on my desk chart.

- I will review my progress with my teacher at the end of every week.

- If I earn at least 20 points, I get a pass for an extra session in the computer lab (for use with a GAME of my choice!)

- The teacher will assign me extra-credit points for:

_____

_____

Signed Student: _____

Signed Teacher: _____

Figure 8–8

Generally, a contract should focus on behavior that is already under the student's control to some extent. When behavior that is not currently under the student's control is the focus, a series of behavioral steps must be delineated, beginning with behavior that is currently under the student's control. This type of contract is more complicated because it must include what you, the teacher, will do for the student for each behavioral step.

It is important not to use teacher-written contracts. A contract written by a student is more motivating than one written by you. In fact, a contract written without strong student input has little chance of success—students will either ignore it or stonewall it. It is also important that the contract not be punitive. Punishment has no place in a contract and can be counterproductive. The well-written contract assumes success.

INTEGRATING BEHAVIORAL SUPPORT PLANS FOR SEVERAL STUDENTS

Behavioral Support Plans should be developed by a team that includes both special education and general education staff. You, the classroom teacher, have strong input into all Behavioral Support Plans written for students in your class. This means that although these plans are individualized, they must be reasonable as far as your time and effort are concerned. Most students have similar needs and their plans can dovetail nicely with other classroom-management strategies. If a student's plan requires an inordinate amount of your time, you can ask for an aide to help carry out the plan.

STOPPING ESCALATION OF NEGATIVE BEHAVIOR

Teachers need a repertoire of strategies to deal with negative behavior. Mild negative behavior can often be ignored. Students can be redirected to a more positive behavior. You can change a student's seat to remove him or her from negative interactions with another student. You can state a rule and ask the student to take care of the problem, or give the student some options of acceptable behavior from which to choose. Consequences can be restated.

It is important to recognize incipient student frustration or agitation and stop it before it escalates. Asking the student what the problem seems to be is the first step. Moving near the student and communicating your concern can help the student regain composure, as can changing the task in which the student is engaged. Asking the student to help you in some way may also help prevent a downward spiral.

If there is an immediate, serious threat to the health or safety of others, or an immediate and serious threat to property, you must be prepared to quickly and appropriately intervene. School staff should develop a crisis-intervention plan that can be easily activated in an emergency. The first step is to stop the threat of violence by physically isolating the student.

After the crisis is over, the school should be prepared to discuss the problem with all concerned—teacher(s), student, other students, parents—with the purpose of reevaluating the student's IEP or 504 Plan and preventing a similar incident in the future.

Teachers who work with students with behavioral difficulties need a strong understanding of behavioral principles. They also need patience, understanding, flexibility, and a sense of humor.

VIOLATING DISCIPLINARY RULES OR CODE OF CONDUCT

Students bringing weapons to school has been an increasing concern of both school and community. Rumors abound regarding the suspension or expulsion of students with disabilities who bring guns to school. The safety of the students and staff is weighed against the rights of the individual student to an education. Students with disabilities who bring weapons to school can be removed from school as long as they are provided an alternative education.

Special Education law (IDEA) does require that specific procedures be used when a disciplinary action results in a change of placement of more than ten days for a student with a disability. This includes extended suspensions and expulsions for weapons and other serious offenses.

The student's IEP must be reviewed to determine whether the behavior in question was a manifestation of the student's disability, whether the student's IEP was appropriate, and whether the student was provided with the support services spelled out in the IEP. If it is determined that the behavior is not a manifestation of the student's disability, the disciplinary procedures used are the same as those for students without disabilities. If it is decided that the behavior is a manifestation of the student's disability, a new IEP is written for the student, which spells out the appropriate support services and placement for the student.

If the student is not yet eligible for special education services, but there is reason to believe the student has a disability, the procedures are the same as those for a student with a disability.

In cases when the student is in possession of a weapon, an illegal drug or a (controlled) substance, or the student's behavior is likely to result in injury to self or others, the student with a disability may be moved to an alternative setting where he or she can receive educational services, or is provided with educational services in his or her home. If a crime is committed (e.g., weapons or illegal drugs), the school is to report it to the authorities.

Regardless of the outcome of either school or judicial hearings, IDEA wants to ensure that the student is provided with appropriate educational services.

A FINAL WORD

Behavioral Support Plans represent major shifts in thinking about the education of students with disabilities whose behavior is inappropriate and unacceptable. The new legislation tells us to focus on preventing negative behaviors by teaching positive behavior and self-management to students whose behavior interferes with learning.

It is important to remember that change will take a long time and that progress will ebb and flow. Behavioral Support Plans will probably need modification as feedback on progress is collected. Goals and reinforcers may need to be modified and replacement behaviors may need to be reconsidered. If all this is understood by both teacher and student in advance, neither will be too discouraged by setbacks. When progress is made toward goals, the motivation of the student and the teacher will carry the process toward successful behavior change.

CHAPTER NINE

Understanding the Role of Medication

Sensational headlines such as, "Medication used by schools to control kids" and "Ritalin® overprescribed" can frighten parents into refusing to even consider the idea of medication for their children.

Cruz, on the other hand, a middle school student with ADHD, credits Ritalin® with "saving" his life. "You know, all these great ideas that keep flitting through my head all the time. Ritalin® gives me a chance to catch one. I guess what is so great about it is that it seems to give me an extra couple of seconds before I react to someone jumping on me for something."

Medication is but one of the tools we can use to help improve the symptoms of ADHD. Medication by itself can improve concentration and behavior, but medication alone cannot improve time management, organization, homework completion, or other academic problems a student might have (NIMH, 2000). Education, positive behavioral support, counseling, and classroom accommodations need to be incorporated into a comprehensive plan in addition to medication in order to make a significant difference in the student's functioning.

Medication can make a student "available" for learning. For example, when you teach students homework-completion skills, medication can help students with ADHD pay attention and remain focused on what you are saying. By helping the student stay focused, medication can also provide the student with the opportunity to utilize the skills he or she has been taught.

Not all students benefit from medication for ADHD and some students report uncomfortable side effects from particular medication, but this occurs infrequently. Generally speaking, the benefits of taking medication for ADHD far outweigh any problems.

THE TEACHER'S ROLE

Although you may believe that medication can be of great help to a particular student, you can only recommend that a parent seek medical advice about medication and its use. You are not qualified to give advice on medication to parents. You can only provide the parents with information about ADHD and medication from a reputable source such as CH.A.D.D. It is the parents' decision whether or not their child should take medication for ADHD, and the parents' decision must be respected.

The question of whether or not a student with ADHD should take medication is a difficult one for parents and teachers to answer. Are we looking for a "quick fix" for a difficult or disturbing student, or are we trying to develop strategies to help the student to learn?

You have a professional responsibility to consider all the possible solutions, remedies, and alternative methods that can help the student to improve. You cannot "push" medication, but you can inform yourself about the effects of various medications on student behavior.

BELIEFS AND ATTITUDES
ABOUT MEDICATION

There are many reasons why parents, teachers, and students may refuse to try medication for ADHD. These include religious beliefs that preclude medication, negative attitudes toward medication of all kinds, a belief that there is nothing "wrong" with the student, and myths about Ritalin®.

Students who refuse to try medication usually say, "I want to be like the other kids" or "I don't need it." Other students, in their rush for independence, see medication as a symbol of parent control and refuse to take it. Still other students who refuse to take medication may do so because they enjoy the "high" they get from the many ideas that constantly flow through their minds. They are afraid that Ritalin® will make their lives dull and boring or will negatively effect their intelligence.

Parents who refuse medication for their children may say things like: "I've gotten by all these years without it. My child can get by without it too" or "Medication will just turn my child into a zombie."

Both teachers and parents may believe that the student is just "lazy." "He doesn't need medication," they say, "he just needs to get down to work." Or the adults may blame each other and say, "She (teacher or parent) is letting the student get away with murder. If she would just provide more discipline, the child wouldn't need medication."

On the other hand, medication is sometimes overprescribed. There might be a "push" toward medication by the schools and/or the parents because both may think of medication as a magic potion for an adolescent who has severe behavioral or academic problems. Teachers and parents may ask for medication merely to help them with an uncooperative, defiant adolescent. Sometimes both teachers and parents are too quick to think that all or most of a student's problems are caused by ADHD. Physicians may sometimes prescribe medication for a student without careful evaluation and monitoring of the student.

COUNTERING MYTHS

These types of beliefs, myths, and behaviors can interfere with the appropriate use of medication to help a particular student manage his or her ADHD. To overcome these barriers takes patience, empathy, information about medications and their effects on ADHD, and understanding of strategies that can help allay fears. Attitudes will begin to change as soon as the student begins to make progress.

There is strong evidence to counter these myths and misconceptions. The American Medical Association, in reviewing research studies from 1975 through 1997, reported there is little evidence of widespread overdiagnosis or misdiagnosis of ADHD or of widespread overprescriptions of Ritalin®. (See Figure 9-1.)

There is also strong evidence supporting the benefits of medication for ADHD. One hundred seventy studies of over 6,000 children with ADHD found that 90 percent are noticeably less hyperactive or more attentive when taking a stimulant medication. You can be a source of information for parents about medication, and you can discuss the arguments for and against medication with parents. In this way, you may be able to address some of their concerns. (See Figure 9-2.)

However, if a parent of a student with carefully diagnosed ADHD still refuses to place the teen on medication after presented with additional information, then you must accept this and begin appropriate educational planning.

The following are some strategies you can use to help parents consider medication for their child:

- *Provide a reality check*. Discuss the facts of the classroom situation with the parents and present possible solutions and their ramifications.
- *Provide information*. Present the family with reputable information regarding the use of medication for ADHD. This information can be obtained from your local or state education agencies or from CH.A.D.D. (**Note**: Some of the information on the Internet is excellent, while some of it is false and misleading, so use with caution.)

Medication: Myths and Facts

Myths	Facts
• Ritalin® is addictive and can lead to drug abuse.	• Research shows that Ritalin® is not addictive and does not lead to drug addiction.
• All you have to do is give a student with ADHD some medication and he/she will be all right.	• Medication is only one part of the puzzle. The teacher needs to provide accommodations for the student and teach the student cognitive and self-management strategies.
• Ritalin® is the only treatment for ADHD.	• Other medications are available, some of which also alleviate the symptoms of other problems such as anxiety or depression.
• Ritalin® turns teenagers into zombies.	• If the parent observes or the student reports the medication is having negative effects, the medication will be stopped by the physician.
• The use of Ritalin® is skyrocketing.	• Research indicates that the rate of new prescriptions of Ritalin® has not increased. The total number of people taking Ritalin® has increased because we add the people newly prescribed to those who are already taking Ritalin® for diagnosed ADHD.
• Ritalin® will solve all the student's ADHD-related problems.	• An effective treatment plan includes effective teaching, behavior modification, and counseling in addition to medication.

Figure 9-1

Dealing with Negative Parent Attitudes toward Medication

Parent Attitude	Teacher Response
• "I never take drugs. I don't believe in taking drugs and I certainly don't want my child taking drugs."	• "We are lucky to be living in a world where science has advanced so far that medications recently discovered can cure many types of cancer. Scientists have also developed medications for diabetes, migraine headaches, and ADHD. Of course, no parent wants his/her child 'on drugs.' But if your child had diabetes, you would get medication for him or her."
• "I don't want to give my son (daughter) the impression that drugs are all right. You know, something goes wrong and you take a pill to make it all better."	• "Your son (daughter) has a chronic problem that interferes with learning. Medication has been shown to help some types of ADHD."
• "You (teacher) just want to control my child."	• "When I see a student having a problem, I want to help that student. My job is to alert the parent when problems occur."
• "If you (teacher) did your job, there wouldn't be any problem."	• "I have been working very hard to help your child. But your child is still struggling."
• "My son (daughter) doesn't act like that at home." (Therefore, the teacher is doing something wrong.)	• "Students like your son (daughter) often do not have much of a problem at home, except for homework. Problems do occur, however, when the student is in a class with 25 or more others or when he (she) has to work independently."
• "My child just needs to try harder. He (She) can do better."	• "He (She) is already working hard. If someone needed glasses, would you say 'If you just tried harder, you could see?'"

Figure 9-2

- *Encourage participation in parent groups.* Parents can discuss the pros and cons of medication with other parents. The parent can meet with other parents of students with ADHD to see how medication affects those students.

- *Discuss safeguards.* Discuss how the medication will be carefully monitored by the teacher, parent, and student. Recommend that the family go to a physician who specializes in ADHD and has a strong knowledge of the various medications that can help relieve symptoms. Discuss how the physician will also help monitor the medication.

- *Suggest a trial.* Propose that medication be tried for a brief time so that the effects can be assessed and discussed. Help the parent arrange for a Ritalin® Challenge Test in which a neuropsychologist evaluates the student with and without Ritalin® using the T.O.V.A., to determine if Ritalin® can help the student focus or not react impulsively.

- *Involve the student.* It is very important to involve the student in making the decision to try medication and in monitoring the efficacy and side effects of the medication.

- *Discuss possible reasons for past failures.* Explain that medication might not have worked in the past for the student because the dosage was incorrect or the medication was not the right one. There are new medications for ADHD that have proved effective.

- *Design workshops.* Provide training for teachers, students, and parents about ADHD and how it affects a student's learning and behavior.

MEDICATION CHOICES

It is interesting that both parents and teachers (and the general public) usually refer only to Ritalin®. There are, however, other medications that a pediatrician, family physician, or psychiatrist can prescribe depending upon the individual student's needs. Parents and students need to discuss the advantages and disadvantages among various medications with their physician. (See Figure 9-3.)

The physician usually begins with the mildest medication and the smallest dosage and then makes modifications as needed. It can take several months to arrive at the "best" medication and dosage. The physician must be careful of the interaction of medications with each other, with over-the-counter medications, and with certain foods (e.g., grapefruit juice).

One important difference among the medications is how much time it takes them to begin working and how long they are effective. The stimulants, such as Ritalin®, work much like aspirin. They begin to work at the first dose and wear off in about four hours. The antidepressants, mood stabilizers, and Serotonin Reuptake Inhibitors (SRIs) need to build up in the body to a therapeutic level before they begin working. This may take as much as six weeks. Similarly, they remain in the body for as much as two weeks after the last dose has been taken. The antihypertensives and the beta blockers need to be taken regularly without missing a dose; both of these medications help regulate blood pressure and pose a danger to health if a dose is skipped.

Physicians often suggest that the student take medication only during school hours because those are the hours the student needs to be most alert and focused. They also

Medication: Types, Uses, and Possible Side Effects

Type/Name	Used For	Possible Side Effects*
• *Stimulants* Ritalin® Dexadrine® Adderall® Cylert®	Attention, focus, impulsivity, hyperactivity, aggression, emotional lability, memory, organization, task completion, self control	Decreased appetite, tics, sleep disturbances, irritability, mood disturbances, increased heart rate and blood pressure, rebound
• *Antidepressants* Wellbutrin® Tofranil® Prozac® Zoloft® Paxil® Effexor® Desyrel® Norpramine®	Depression, irritability, anxiety, emotional lability, impulsivity, hyperactivity, sleep and mood disturbances, aggression, poor attention span	Slower heart rate, increased risk of seizures, dry mouth, constipation
• *Antihypertensives* Clonidine® Tenex® Inderal®	Hyperactivity, impulsivity, opposition/aggression, socialization, overarousal, sleep disturbances, attention problems, obsessive–compulsive disorder	Sedation, tiredness, mild depression, drop in heart rate and blood pressure, nausea, diarrhea, fatigue, skin rash, fever, congestive heart failure, colitis
• *Mood Stabilizers* Tegretol®	ADHD and seizure disorders, mood disturbances	Dizziness, drowsiness, nausea, blood/skin/cardiovascular disturbances

*For all drugs, there may be minor side effects. If they occur, they are usually short-term and not severe.

Figure 9-3

suggest this because the stimulants have a tendency to cause mild insomnia. On the other hand, many students find they need medication in the late afternoon in order to study. These students may combine the 8-hour time-released medication taken at 7 or 8 A.M. with a 4-hour dose at 4 P.M.

Some students forget or refuse to take medication in school because they don't want the other students to know they have ADHD. These students can take time-released Ritalin® in order to preclude the necessity of taking medication in school. The other types of medication are taken once or twice a day and need not be taken during school hours. There are as many possible regimens as there are students. It is only with careful monitoring that the optimal plan can evolve.

Often students with ADHD become depressed and anxious due to chronic school failure. Physicians can prescribe medication that serves to both alleviate the depression or anxiety and increase attention or decrease impulsivity. Many of the antidepressants can be used for both depression or anxiety and ADHD.

WARNING SIGNS OF SIDE EFFECTS

About 60 percent of students taking medication for ADHD report some mild side effects such as insomnia or decreased appetite. In general, possible negative side effects of medication include:

- *Stimulants:* tics, minimal suppression of growth, anxiety
- *Antidepressants:* dry mouth, constipation, dizziness, confusion
- *Antihypertensives:* sedation

More serious warning signs include changes in skin and eye color due to jaundice. These signal the need to terminate the medication as soon as possible.

It is important to understand that antidepressants and antihypertensives must be phased out slowly, according to the physician's directives.

Parents should be notified in a timely fashion when warning signs appear, if the student refuses to take a dose in school as prescribed, and if the medication runs out. All warning signs indicate that medication should be checked by the parent and physician. (See Figure 9-4.)

It may not be necessary to discontinue medication if the student has a relatively mild side effect such as insomnia. If the stimulant medication is otherwise benefiting the student, the physician may indicate that the student not take the stimulant after 4 P.M. or may add a mild sedative to be taken at bedtime. Developing a relaxing sleep routine is a must.

Medication: Warning Signs

- Sleepiness
- Insomnia or sleep disturbances
- Listlessness
- Irritability
- Overexcitement
- Sadness
- Withdrawal
- Confusion
- Loss of appetite
- Rapid weight loss
- Tics
- Increased anxiety
- Nervousness
- Dizziness
- Fatigue

Figure 9-4

STUDENT NONCOMPLIANCE

Although many students with ADHD may have taken their medication faithfully for several years, that might change when the students reach adolescence. The students may refuse to take medication in school because they don't want to appear "different" or because they don't want to think of themselves as "sick." They may also see medication as a symbol of adult control.

> Ronnie, an adolescent in full rebellion mode, appeared to be taking his Ritalin® every morning. His mother, however, discovered almost 20 pills Ronnie had tossed behind the sofa, instead of taking them. When questioned by his mother, Ronnie claimed that medication didn't help him anyway.

Parents and teachers must carefully monitor student compliance with medical directives, since abrupt termination of some medications can have serious consequences.

Approximately 25 percent of students do not respond to medication. When a student complains that the medication is not helping her or him, it is important to either adjust the dosage or change the medication. Although it is true that medication might not help some students with ADHD, it is often the case that the particular dose or type of medication is at fault.

Schools may be able to forestall noncompliance by bringing medication out of the closet, so to speak. Students with ADHD tend to think they are the only ones in the school taking medication. If medication is openly discussed, not just for ADHD but for juvenile diabetes as well, for example, students might come to realize that a sizable number of people take medication for a variety of reasons. Taking medication can be compared to wearing glasses if a person is nearsighted or using crutches if someone has a broken leg. **Note:** It is imperative that the school emphasize distinctions between taking medications for health reasons and using drugs and alcohol for recreation.

THE IMPORTANCE OF MONITORING

It is often difficult to find the right dosage of medication for an adolescent. If the dosage is too low, there is little or no benefit. If the dosage is too high, the student may suffer side effects. If it is the wrong medication for that particular student, the behavior may worsen. There is a huge variation among individuals and how they respond to a particular medication or dosage. That is why monitoring is so important (NIMH, 2000).

You can use the checklists described here to monitor the use of medication and determine its effectiveness. It is important to use these checklists before medication is begun in order to get a baseline, and then several times after medication is initiated to determine its effect and whether there is a need for adjustment.

Observations should be made by teachers, parents, and students. Students' self-reporting of both academic behavior and feelings or sensations before and after taking medication is particularly important. (See Figure 9-5.)

Medication: Possible Reactions and Feelings

Student _____ Teacher _____ Date _____

Negative Responses	Positive Responses
___ Sleepy	___ Alert
___ Fatigued	___ On-target
___ Stressed	___ Calm
___ Anxious	___ "Getting more done"
___ Irritable	___ Focused
___ Depressed	___ Can tune out noise
___ Angry	___ "Feel smart"
___ "Zoned out"	___ In control
___ "Not myself"	___ Ready to work
___ Rushed	
___ Unable to focus	
___ "Feel dumb"	
___ Dizzy	
___ "On a roller coaster"	

Other: _____ Other: _____

Comments: _____ Comments: _____

_____ _____

_____ _____

Figure 9-5

Checklists must be individualized for a particular student's needs. Use a behavioral checklist, such as the following, to determine specific problem behaviors:

- Stephen Carney's Attention Deficit Disorders Evaluation Scale
- Connor's Rating Scale
- Levine's Answer System Parent Questionnaire (some sections)
- Levine's School Questionnaire
- Levine's Student Self-Administered Profile
- Barclay's checklists included in *Attention-Deficit Hyperactivity Disorder: A Clinical Workbook*

You, the student, and the parents can use the checklist shown in Figure 9-6 to identify more specific problem behaviors. After checking the problem behaviors, you and the

Observation Form: Problem Behaviors

Student: _____ Date: _____

	Number of Times per Week	Comments
At School ☐ Absent ☐ Late to school ☐ Late to class ☐ Inappropriate behavior: in hallway, between classes, in study hall, in lunch room (e.g., yelling, tripping)		
With the Teacher ☐ Interrupts ☐ Argues		
In Class ☐ Late ☐ Unprepared ☐ Slow to start work ☐ Sleeps ☐ Gets out of seat ☐ Talks out of turn ☐ Uses obscenities, gestures ☐ Doesn't work, is off task ☐ Doesn't finish work ☐ Very distractible ☐ Leaves without permission		
With Other Students ☐ Bothers others (e.g., makes noise, grabs things, pokes) ☐ Teases or bullies ☐ Interrupts ☐ Fights		
Homework ☐ Doesn't turn in at all ☐ Doesn't turn in on time ☐ Doesn't complete ☐ Incorrect ☐ Doesn't start homework in class		
Other: _____		

Figure 9-6

Behavioral Goals

Student: _____ Date: _____

	Description of behavioral goal including number of times per day or week, percent of time, specific class.

• At School
   ☐ In class
   ☐ On time
   ☐ Appropriate behavior: in hallway, between classes, in study hall, in lunch room (e.g., walks quietly)
• With the Teacher
   ☐ Listens
   ☐ Acts respectfully
• In Class
   ☐ On time
   ☐ Prepared
   ☐ Starts promptly
   ☐ Maintains alertness
   ☐ Stays in seat
   ☐ Takes turn
   ☐ No obscenities
   ☐ Works, on task
   ☐ Finishes work
   ☐ Less distractible (describe)
   ☐ Stays in class
• With Other Students
   ☐ Leaves others alone
   ☐ Does not bully or tease
   ☐ Does not interrupt
   ☐ Does not fight
• Homework
   ☐ Turns in homework
   ☐ Turns in homework on time
   ☐ Completes assignment
   ☐ Does accurate homework
   ☐ Begins homework in class
• Other: _____
_____	

Figure 9-7

student can target a specific behavior, such as "out of seat" or "off task" and monitor it at 5- or 10-minute intervals.

Goals should be set around the target behavior, either for increasing a desired behavior or decreasing an undesirable behavior. You and the student must agree on the goals. It is usually more advantageous to select a behavior already in the student's repertoire to be increased so that teachers and students get to see positive progress on the checklist. (See Figure 9-7.)

A progress chart should be developed that can be used before medication is started, daily the first week after medication has been started, and at weekly intervals for a month. The charts should be discussed with students and parents to determine progress. With or without the teaching of self-management strategies, the first benefit that will occur is an improvement in focusing and maintaining attention and/or a reduction in hyperactivity, depending on the medication.

Another way of determining the efficacy of Ritalin® or another stimulant might be for the physician to give the student a placebo for several weeks and alternate it with the medication. Comparing the behavior of the student while on medication with behavior while on the placebo provides a lot of information regarding that particular medication and its dosage.

It will take a long time before course grades, interim reports, and results of standardized testing will reflect a positive change in academic behavior and can be used to measure progress. The student's motivation to continue to improve will depend on his or her success with short-term goals such as being on task, copying the assignment correctly, and, later on, completing homework.

CHRISTOPHER, ONE STUDENT'S STORY

Christopher is one of the many students with ADHD who refuse to take medication. Christopher is a former substance abuser who has made a difficult two-year journey to recovery. He has refused to take medication for his ADHD because he is afraid that taking medication on a daily basis will cause him to slip back into dependency. He is very adamant about this.

There is a strong correlation between ADHD and substance abuse. Many people with undiagnosed ADHD self-medicate with alcohol or drugs, trying to calm down and feel less anxious. In reality drugs and alcohol have little benefit and pose many serious dangers for the individual.

Christopher wants to finish high school so that he can join the Marines, since only high school graduates can enlist in the Marines. Christopher's persistence and willingness to work hard, which he developed in the substance abuse program—coupled with his strong motivation to graduate—can help him overcome some of the problems presented by his severe ADHD. The other strengths he will call on are his high-average IQ score, good verbal ability, and good reading comprehension.

Christopher feels accepted in his new school, something he never felt before in school. He feels he is doing a lot better at this school than he did in other schools he attended. Christopher's teachers report that they like him, think he is very capable, and want to help him.

Christopher's problems involve poor attendance, tardiness, and not working in class. He rarely turns in homework. He falls asleep in class. These problems are largely caused by his ADHD. A checklist was used to identify specific problems Christopher was experiencing in school. (See Figure 9-8.)

We developed a plan for Christopher, which included suggestions for designing an effective learning environment in the school and at home, providing structure, using frequent recognition and reward for increasing desired behaviors, and teaching him to self-monitor his behavior. (See Figure 9-9.)

The first step was to make Christopher aware of how often he was late and absent from school. It always came as a great surprise to him when the teachers told him how often he was late to class or absent. In fact, he would argue with his teachers and tell them they were wrong.

Since it was important that Christopher become aware of his behavior as the first step in modifying it, a strategy was developed that would prove to Christopher just how late he was. When Christopher arrived in each of his classes, he was to look at the clock at the front of the room and write on his chart what time he sat down in his seat. He was very surprised to discover how late he actually was.

Arrangements were made for Christopher to take a city bus that would get him to school on time. After doing a task analysis, Christopher and the counselor developed a checklist of tasks and times that would help him get to school on time. (See Figure 9-10.)

Christopher and his mother also developed a routine that would help him wind down in the evening in order to get to sleep at a reasonable hour. It was hoped that he would now not feel so sleepy in class.

Christopher's school counselor monitored Christopher's program, helped him set goals, and taught him some self-management skills. The principal took an active interest in Christopher and provided an important source of encouragement and reinforcement. The teachers were willing to go the extra mile for Christopher. They cued him to get on task, provided checkpoints for long-term assignments, and reminded him to write down his assignments.

Christopher made good progress the first year on on-time arrival in school and in class. He passed all his classes, although more work needed to be done on homework completion and self-management. During Christopher's last school year, the school provided Christopher with a teacher consultant for 45 minutes a day over a two-week period to provide the structure Christopher needed to successfully complete his (excellent) Senior Paper. As an added incentive, Christopher met with the Marine recruiter once a month to discuss his progress in school. Christopher graduated in June and entered the Marines the following September.

Identifying Christopher's Problem Behaviors

Student: _____   Date: _____

	Number of Times per Week	Comments
• At School		
☒ Absent	1-2 times	
☒ Late to school	3-4 times	Misses bus
☒ Inappropriate behavior: in hallway, between classes, in study hall	2-3 times	Excessive socializing
• With the Teacher		Argues. Unaware of number of absences or lost assignments
☐ Interrupts		
☒ Argues		
• In Class		
☒ Late	Almost always	
☐ Unprepared		
☐ Slow to start work		
☒ Sleeps in class	3-4 times	First class
☐ Gets out of seat		
☐ Talks out of turn		
☐ Uses obscenities, gestures		
☒ Doesn't work, is off task	Every day	OK in some classes
☐ Doesn't finish work		
☒ Very distractible	Every day	
☒ Leaves without permission	1-2 times	Last class
• With Other Students		
☐ Bothers others, makes noise		
☐ Teases or bullies		
☐ Interrupts		
☐ Fights		
• Homework		
☒ Doesn't turn in at all		
☒ Doesn't turn in on time	2-3 times	
☒ Doesn't complete		
☒ Incorrect	3-4 times	
☐ Doesn't start homework in class		
• Other		
☒ Written work: poor organization, illegible writing, often not handed in		
☒ Self-awareness: unrealistic (e.g., He thinks he is doing better than he is)		

Figure 9-8

Strategies for Christopher

1. Design effective learning environment.
- Select Christopher's teachers and courses carefully. First class of the day should be of high interest.
- Ensure continued acceptance by school personnel.
- Select courses at appropriate level of challenge.
- Provide structure: Checkpoints for long-term assignments; checklists for homework completion and writing assignments.
- Help Christopher set up daily "to do" lists.
- Arrange transportation to school in mornings.
- With Christopher, design checklist for on-time arrival.
- Monitor Christopher's assignment book.
- Arrange a place where Christopher can do homework in school.

2. Use recognition and rewards.
- Provide Christopher with intermediary consequences for tardiness to class. No out-of-school suspensions.
- Provide positive social consequence for being on time to school and class (e.g., smiles). Principal greets him at door.
- During the last year of school, arrange monthly contact with Marine recruiters as an incentive.

3. Teach self-management.
- Continue weekly meetings at A.A. and N.A. Increase self-awareness of how ADHD is affecting his academic performance.
- Help him set short-term objectives for his long-term goals (e.g., Marines, graduation).
- Cue him to get on-task using small steps.
- Teach him to self-monitor on-time arrival at school.
- Teach him to use visualization and self-talk to keep himself on task and help him to get to classes on time.

4. Involve parents.
- Investigate sleep problems; an evaluation at a Sleep Disorders Clinic.
- Contact parent whenever more than two assignments have been missed.
- Develop relaxing bedtime routine with him.
- Set up basement study room with no distractions or noise, per his request.

Figure 9-9

Student Checklist: How to Get to School on Time

1. **Answer the following questions:**
   - What time do you have to be in your first class?
   - What time does the school bus come to pick you up?

2. **Time yourself:**
   - If you walk to school, how much time does it take you?
   - How much time does it take you to fix and eat breakfast?
   - How much time does it take you to choose your clothes and get dressed?
   - How much time does it take you to brush teeth, comb hair, wash, shower?
   - How much time does it take you to get up after the alarm rings?
   - What other things do you *have to do* before you go to school and how much time do they take?

     List: _____

     _____

     _____

3. **Make a morning schedule:**
   - Start with the time you have to be in your first class.
   - Next, write the time the bus comes or the time you have to start walking to school to get there on time.
   - Next, write the time you have to start making and eating breakfast in order to be ready to leave on time.
   - Next, write the time you need to get dressed.
   - Next, write the time you have to start your bathroom routine in order to get dressed on time.
   - Figure out when you have to get up in order to do these things.
   - Set the alarm for 5 minutes before you have to get up to begin getting ready for school.

4. **Before you go to bed at night:**
   - Be sure the alarm is set to ring at the right time.
   - Be sure everything you need is in your backpack.
   - Be sure your backpack is next to the front door.

Figure 9-10

A FINAL WORD

Medication for ADHD is an emotional issue. Personal beliefs, attitudes, and values are all brought into play. Teachers, parents, and students often lack adequate information upon which to base a decision. Figure 9-11 lists information parents and teachers can use to help in the decision-making.

Medication is not for everyone. It can play a large part in helping a student focus attention and reduce impulsivity and hyperactivity. By doing this, students can then learn how to function more effectively in school and at home. But some students do not benefit from medication, and some students (and their parents) refuse to take medication.

Medication: Pros and Cons

Pros	Cons
• Research studies over several decades indicate that there are a variety of medications that are safe and effective for relieving the symptoms of ADHD.	• It takes time and patience to identify the most effective medication, dosage, and schedule.
• There are new medications today that can be tried.	• Students may have taken medication in elementary school without results.
• Research studies demonstrate positive results including:	• There may be some side effects for some students for a brief time.
—increased attention	• Some medications may not help some students.
—increased compliance with rules	• Students or adults may be opposed to the idea of taking medication.
—decreased classroom disruptions	• Research studies indicate that medication alone does not lead to improved long-term academic learning.
—decreased hyperactivity, impulsivity	• Students may attribute their improved behavior solely to medication rather than their own effort.
• Positive effects of medication can make the student more available for learning.	• Adults may rely on medication to control behavior rather than teaching the student effective self-management skills.
• Research studies indicate that medication in combination with behavioral interventions can result in both short- and long-term improvements in academic learning and social behavior.	

Figure 9-11

It is important to remember that your role in the decision to try medication is a limited one. At the same time it is also important for you to provide as much reputable information as possible to the parents so that they and the student can make an informed decision.

It can be difficult for you to stand by while a student, who you feel would benefit from medication, doesn't take it because either the student or the parents refuse, for whatever reasons. But stand by you must, once they have made their decision. (See Figure 9-12.)

You must educate yourself regarding medication and its affects on students with ADHD. In addition, your careful monitoring of medication can actually enhance the effects of medication. Monitoring helps the physician adjust the medication until the optimal dosage and type of medication are determined.

If the student is not on medication, your role is to provide the added structure the student might need and to help the student self-manage attention and impulsivity as much as

---

Teacher's Do's and Don'ts about Medication

Do's	Don'ts
• Continue working with the student.	• Give up on the student if the parents refuse to consider medication.
• Tell the parents, "Given my experience, I suggest you consult your physician about the possible use of medication."	• Think parents don't care about the student or his/her education if they decide not to use medication.
• Help monitor the effects of the medication.	• Keep pressuring parents about medication.
• Watch for warning signs.	• Recommend a specific medication or specific dosage.
• Immediately tell the parents of any problems.	• Give the parents the name of another student who is taking medication without permission from that student's parents and the student.
• Continue with your responsibilities under the student's IEP or 504 Plan.	• Tell the parents that the student will fail if he or she doesn't take medication.
• Respect the parent's decision, whatever it is.	
• Respect the privacy of the student.	
• Back off if the parents indicate they are irritated or angry.	
• Tell the parents they must check with a physician on all issues pertaining to medication.	
• Recommend the parents join a parents' group such as CH.A.D.D.	

Figure 9-12

possible. Regardless of the family's decision about medication, you need to continue to use all the strategies in your possession to help the student with ADHD succeed in school.

By refusing medication Christopher took a difficult path toward high school graduation. The fact that he was successful was largely due to his own perseverance and the teachers who were determined to help them.

CHAPTER TEN

Gifted Students with ADHD and/or LD

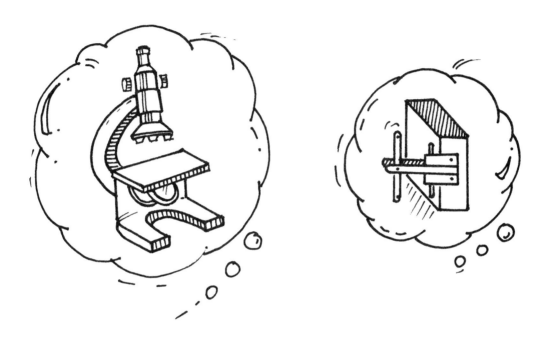

Mike

The first thing you notice about Mike is his thick glossy black hair and his dark eyes. At 15, Mike is a tall, handsome, man-in-the-making. That Mike has ADHD becomes immediately apparent. He constantly walks back and forth exploring everything in his path. As the teacher talks to the class, Mike talks, too, asking questions, blurting out answers. After several sharp glances by the teacher, Mike finally sits down and immediately reaches for a paper clip that he proceeds to bend completely out of shape.

Mike is *not* a behavior problem. He is actually a thoughtful, creative, gifted student. His abilities in reading, math, and vocabulary are extremely high. However, his severe ADHD interferes significantly with his academic success.

Mike's writing is extremely difficult to understand. It is completely disorganized and contains obscure references that appear unrelated to the topic. His handwriting is practically indecipherable. His math papers are full of computation errors although he can solve high-level mathematical problems.

Mike's teachers recognize how bright he is, but this is part of Mike's problem. His teachers expect great things of him and do not understand the role his ADHD plays in his academic behavior. He is in advanced placement classes in all his academic subjects, but his grades hover between D and C, and he is currently in danger of failing his Chemistry course.

Mike feels very badly about school and sometimes gets quite depressed. He feels that the teachers misunderstand him and that he does not deserve the grades he has been given. Sometimes he feels that his teachers are not smart enough to understand him.

He knows the work, even though he generally skips over things he finds "boring." He thinks drills and practice are a waste of his time. He likes to figure out how something works and discover alternate ways of doing things. He loves to read, although not necessarily his textbooks, which he often finds full of "fluff" with little information. His attitude towards school is "parrots seem to win; people who try to understand, lose."

Mike is similar to a "typical" gifted student: highly verbal and well-read. His IQ scores are above 130, but his ADHD throws a monkey wrench into the works. His teachers recognize that he is gifted but often find him very difficult to teach. At other times they think he is lazy and unmotivated. Although his teachers know he has ADHD, they think he gets poor grades because he refuses to follow directions and just whips through his work.

Cory

At eleven years of age, Cory is tall and stocky. Most people picture him as a professional football player. His teachers keep pushing him towards this as a career goal, to the detriment of appropriate educational planning. He *is* good at sports, but he would rather play computer games. A gifted student with learning disabilities in reading and written expression, Cory has a long history of school difficulties.

He can sit in the Language Arts classroom doing essentially nothing for the entire period. He occasionally picks up a pencil and starts to write, but he quickly erases or crosses out everything he has written. He gazes around the room. Sometimes another student will try to help him get started. He begins to read, but then stops after a few paragraphs, a puzzled look on his face. He tries again but soon closes the book, going through the same motions until it is time to get ready for his next class.

Cory's teachers think of him as having low-average intelligence and consider him to be lazy and unmotivated. His teachers say that he doesn't work in class, doesn't participate in class discussions, and doesn't do his homework. His mother is very concerned because she is afraid that Cory will drop out of school. Despite his teachers' assessment, Cory's mother says he is very bright.

"You do have to tell him several times to do something," his mother says, "and he never knows what his assignments are, but he can fix anything that's broken, from a bicycle to a radio. Right now, he is taking apart our cable TV box to see how it works. It's taken him two Sunday afternoons so far. You can't tell me that child isn't bright!

"When he was much younger, he loved to solve mazes. In fact, he got so good at figuring them out that he designed mazes for his friends. He also drew very well, and still does. I have beautiful pictures hanging all over my walls that Cory drew. But he's always had trouble in school. He never learned how to read well. And although he was really good at math, the story problems got him every time. He just couldn't understand them. I blame the school. They never really understood Cory."

Cory's teachers have a hard time believing his mother. Cory began to refuse to go to school. Because the situation was approaching a crisis, the school decided to investigate. When they look at his psychoeducational evaluations (for the first time!), they are shocked to discover that his Performance Score in the WISC-R is 136, well into the gifted range. His Total Score was in the high-average range, due to his low-average Verbal Score. His reading and writing achievement was several grades below grade level. He qualifies for special education services as a student with Learning Disabilities.

Neither Mike's nor Cory's learning problems were understood by their schools. Both were victims of society's stereotypes about gifted students. Mike's ADHD was essentially ignored because gifted people are supposed to be able to overcome all barriers. Cory's intelligence was greatly underestimated because he did not shine in the verbal area.

GIFTED STUDENTS WITH ADHD AND/OR LD

There are many myths and misconceptions about gifted students like Mike and Cory. These myths pose barriers to our identifying and supporting the learning needs of these students. (See Figure 10-1.)

Generally, when we think of giftedness we envision a highly verbal, widely read, and academically successful student. This can be true if the student's strengths are in the verbal area. If the student's giftedness lies elsewhere—in the performance area—we rarely recognize that student as gifted. That is because the school's medium of exchange is language.

In exchange for good grades we require students to express themselves verbally—we ask them to read a great deal, understand and digest what they have read, and be able to talk and write about the ideas they have encountered. A student who cannot do these things well—who may be a gifted visionary or problem-solver, but reads very slowly and painstakingly—doesn't fare well in school.

It is estimated that from 5 to 15 percent of the student population is gifted. There are an estimated 120,000 to 180,000 gifted students with LD. Up to 10 percent of the identified gifted population read two years below grade level.

Gifted Students: Myths and Facts

Myths	Facts
• Students who are gifted are good at everything.	• Most students, including gifted students, have both assets and liabilities, strengths and weaknesses.
• Students who are gifted do not have learning or attention difficulties.	• Students who are gifted may have difficulty reading, writing, speaking, or doing calculations. They may have difficulty maintaining attention, have a slow rate of processing, or poor organizational skills.
• Students who are gifted don't need any help.	• Gifted students with LD or ADHD need support and encouragement. They need to be taught new strategies and skills.
• Unless students have a full-scale IQ over 130, as measured on a standardized test, they are not considered gifted.	• Reliance on the full-scale score may hide gifts when there are significant discrepancies between a low score in one area (e.g., verbal) and a high score in another (e.g., performance).
• All gifted kids are weird or nerds.	• Some students who are gifted have social/emotional problems. Many are well-adjusted.
• Gifted students will automatically be successful in life.	• Gifted or otherwise, student success depends on many factors including: personality, motivation, family support, educational programming, and chance.
• If a gifted student is not working up to potential, he or she is just lazy.	• There are many reasons that account for a student's lack of achievement: boredom, psychological distress, poor instruction, a hidden disability.
• All gifted students speak, read, and write well.	• Many gifted students are very articulate. Others are gifted in other areas.

Figure 10-1

There are many students who are gifted in areas other than language—the artist and the inventor, for example. Students with these gifts may have some surprising difficulty with language and/or may have learning disabilities in the reading/writing area, as Cory does. They do not appear highly verbal. They read very little. They get poor grades. They often grow to hate school.

The intelligence test profiles of these students tend to show low-average Verbal Scores and superior Performance Scores. There is usually a significant discrepancy among the subtest scores. (See Figure 10-2.)

When we look at the other diagnostic tests for these students, we find their weaknesses are in reading decoding, auditory processing, and/or written expression. Their gifts lie in the visuo–spatial areas and/or in the logical/analytical areas.

When we look at Cory's neuropsychological evaluation, we see a significant discrepancy between his Verbal Score and Performance Score. His Performance Score is in the gifted range. His Verbal Score is in the low-average range. His profile is similar to the students in Figure 10-2.

Looking at other test results we see that on the Wide Range Assessment of Memory and Learning (WRAML), Cory scores a 15 on design memory and a 9 on story memory. This means that while his visuo–spatial memory is high, his memory for auditory material dips into low-average. Upon delay, he experiences a more significant loss of information.

Cory's main problem is in the auditory area. In addition, his giftedness in the performance area lies unrecognized.

Other gifted students with ADHD and/or LD have good verbal ability and relatively poor performance scores. (See Figure 10-3.)

Some gifted students have both ADHD and LD. (See Figure 10-4.)

Gifted students with ADHD may have high subtest scores in both the verbal and performance areas. The subtest scores that are most affected by ADHD are Coding, Digit Span, Arithmetic, and Picture Completion. Relatively low scores in several of these areas—coupled with very high scores in other areas—indicate that a gifted student may have ADHD. Additional testing can verify these findings. (See Figure 10-5.)

Gifted students with ADHD, like Mike, have a hard time in school even though they often love to read outside school. Their ADHD can slow down reading comprehension and interfere with writing and test-taking. These students have difficulty getting coherent information from reading material because their eyes skip over words and sentences. They do poorly on tests for the same reason and because they often impulsively select the first answer that is approximately feasible instead of selecting the correct answer.

Mike and Cory illustrate some of the problems of gifted students with ADHD and/or LD. Mike is seen as gifted by his teachers and gets very little help or understanding for his ADHD. His teachers think he is unmotivated and lazy. Cory is seen as a low-average student. His grades are poor but that is what his teachers expect of him. His giftedness has gone unrecognized by his teachers.

Rarely are low-income, "disadvantaged" students' gifts recognized, even if their gifts *are* in the verbal area. These students may be giving sermons in church or writing music, both of which require verbal talent; but in school they may use street language and talk about topics often considered unpleasant or taboo. They may not have been exposed to good reading material. They may be considered Emotionally Impaired because their

Profiles of Gifted Students with LD:
Low Verbal and High Performance Scores

WAIS-R

Student #1:

Scaled Score	TABLE OF SCALED SCORE EQUIVALENTS* RAW SCORE											Scaled Score
	VERBAL TESTS						PERFORMANCE TESTS					
	Information	Digit Span	Vocabulary	Arithmetic	Comprehension	Similarities	Picture Completion	Picture Arrangement	Block Design	Object Assembly	Digit Symbol	
19	—	28	70	—	32	—	—	—	51	—	93	19
18	29	27	69	—	31	28	—	—	—	41	91-92	18
17	—	26	68	19	—	—	20	20	50	—	89-90	17
16	28	25	66-67	—	30	27	—	—	49	40	84-88	16
15	27	24	65	18	29	26	—	19	47-48	39	79-83	15
14	26	22-23	63-64	17	27-28	25	19	—	44-46	38	75-78	14
13	25	20-21	60-62	16	26	24	—	18	42-43	37	70-74	13
12	23-24	18-19	55-59	15	25	23	18	17	38-41	35-36	66-69	12
11	22	17	52-54	13-14	23-24	22	17	15-16	35-37	34	62-65	11
10	19-21	15-16	47-51	12	21-22	20-21	16	14	31-34	32-33	57-61	10
9	17-18	14	43-46	11	19-20	18-19	15	13	27-30	30-31	53-56	9
8	15-16	12-13	37-42	10	17-18	16-17	14	11-12	23-26	28-29	48-52	8
7	13-14	11	29-36	8-9	14-16	14-15	13	8-10	20-22	24-27	44-47	7
6	9-12	9-10	20-28	6-7	11-13	11-13	11-12	5-7	14-19	21-23	37-43	6
5	6-8	8	14-19	5	8-10	7-10	8-10	3-4	8-13	16-20	30-36	5
4	5	7	11-13	4	6-7	5-6	5-7	2	3-7	13-15	23-29	4
3	4	6	9-10	3	4-5	2-4	3-4	—	2	9-12	16-22	3
2	3	3-5	6-8	1-2	2-3	1	2	1	1	6-8	8-15	2
1	0-2	0-2	0-5	0	0-1	0	0-1	0	0	0-5	0-7	1

50th Percentile

Figure 10-2

WISC-III

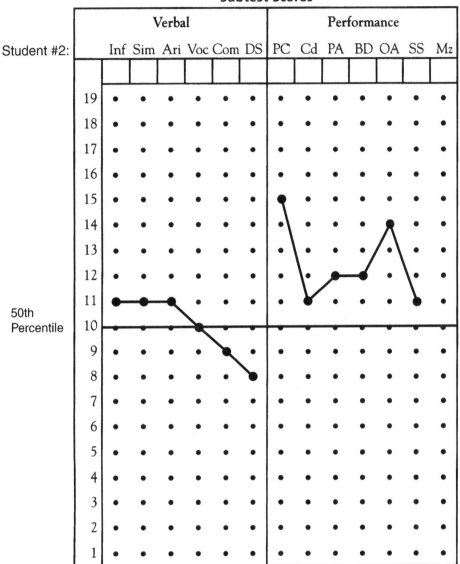

Figure 10-2 *(continued)*

Profile of Gifted Student with LD:
High Verbal and Low Performance Scores

WAIS-III

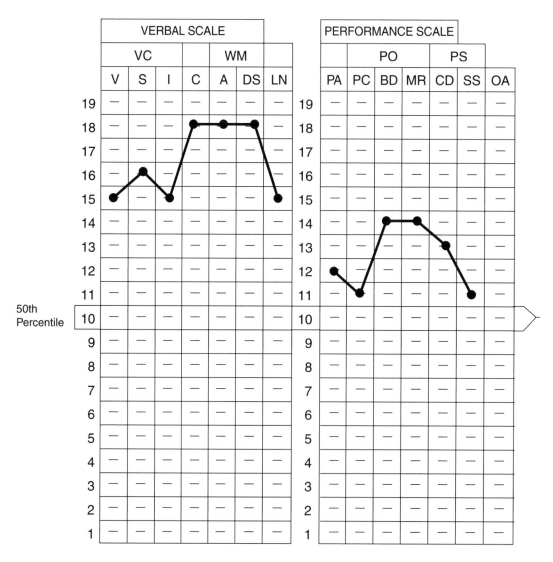

Figure 10-3

Profile of Gifted Student with ADHD and LD

WAIS-III

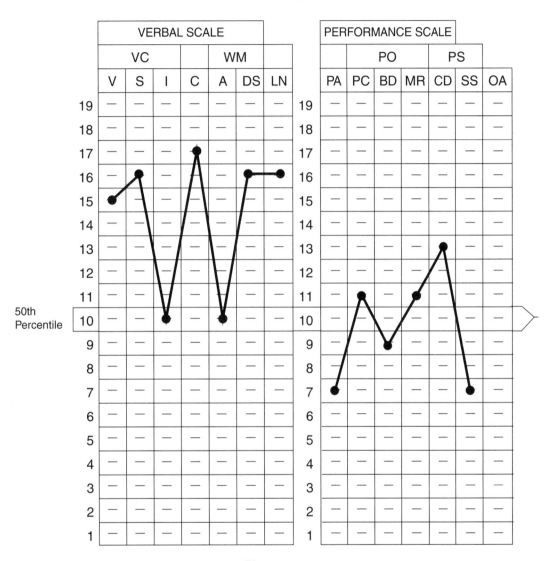

Figure 10-4

Profile of Gifted Student with ADHD

WAIS-III

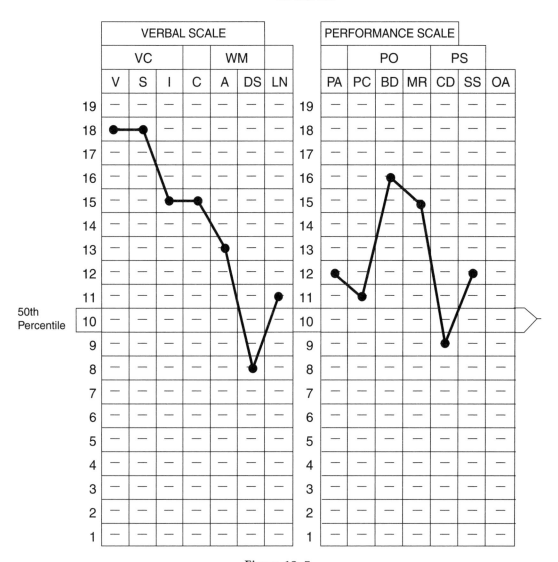

Figure 10-5

behavior can be disturbing at times. It takes a very special teacher to recognize the giftedness of students like these. It also takes an extremely resilient and determined student to succeed against the odds.

SOME DEFINITIONS OF GIFTEDNESS

The four-part federal definition of "gifted" is delineated in the Jacob Javitz Gifted and Talented Education Act of 1988:

- Students with outstanding talent who show a potential for performing at remarkably high levels when compared with others of their age, experience, and environment.
- Students who exhibit high performance capability in intellectual, creative, and/or artistic areas or possess high leadership skills.
- Students who require services or activities not usually provided by the schools.
- These outstanding talents are present in all cultural and socio-economic groups.

This definition eliminates the term "gifted" since it is thought that many students might not be able to demonstrate their giftedness at this time for a variety of reasons. The word "talent" is thought to convey the idea of potential better than the word "gifted."

Other definitions of giftedness refer to the top 1% in general intellectual ability. Still other definitions include the top 10% in the definition of gifted. Some theorists include such things as curiosity, creativity, motivation, and perseverance as part of the definition.

Current research indicates that the definition of giftedness varies from state to state, but generally includes at least two of the following components:

- superior intellect
- demonstrated high-level achievement and performance
- creative artistic abilities

The decision about whether or not a student is gifted or merely above average is a difficult one. Several criteria are used; primary among them is usually IQ scores. However, it is important to bear in mind that IQ test scores for students with ADHD and/or LD are often under representations of the students' true abilities.

When utilizing IQ score as a criterion for giftedness, the focus is on the subtests that measure higher level reasoning, such as Similarities and Comprehension in the verbal area and Picture Arrangement and Block Design in the performance area.

Another component of giftedness may be achievement test scores at or above the 90th percentile. Observations by the student's teachers, parents, and others, and student work samples may also be considered in deciding whether or not a student is gifted. A student interview may be included. Student personality traits such as curiosity, creativity, motivation, and persistence—that are not measured by traditional tests—can be important components of giftedness. (See Figure 10-6.)

Indications of Giftedness

General

- Love to be challenged by difficult problems or concepts
- Prefer to solve problems on their own
- Prefer to work in depth on one project at a time, to the exclusion of others/enjoys conducting scientific experiments
- Unusual comprehension of complex ideas
- Show creativity and imagination
- Are perceptive and insightful
- Display a sophisticated sense of humor
- Combine ideas in unusual ways (divergent thinking)
- See the world differently and have confidence in their perceptions
- Less concerned with order and organization

Verbal Area

- Advanced vocabulary
- Fluency of ideas
- Intellectual curiosity; endless questions
- Rapid grasp of ideas
- Early reading attainment, often before kindergarten
- Remarkable memory for facts and words
- Broad fund of knowledge on many topics, or expert on a particular topic
- Often write poetry, create stories and plays

Nonverbal Area

- Can see the whole, the big picture
- Visualize solutions to complex problems rapidly by using visualization, sometimes without resorting to verbal behavior
- Often like to take things apart, figure out how to operate new equipment or repair machinery
- Create art works, puzzles, dance, musical compositions
- Excel in sports
- Talented musicians
- Invent new ways to do things
- Demonstrate excellent visual-spatial planning

Figure 10-6

Unfortunately, one of the major criteria seems to be student conformity to school norms. Students who are bright and who follow the rules, give teachers what they want, and rarely make waves are much more likely to be seen as gifted than the student who argues with the teacher, interprets things differently, or defends other students if he or she thinks these students are being treated unfairly by the school. The giftedness of divergent thinkers is often overlooked.

INDICATIONS OF GIFTEDNESS AND ADHD AND/OR LD: A PARADOXICAL PICTURE

The first signal you might have that a student may be both gifted and have ADHD and/or LD is the existence of contradictions in the student's performance that are difficult to reconcile. Often teachers assume that a bright student who doesn't hand in homework or gets poor grades on tests is lazy or unmotivated and doesn't study. This may be true, but equally true may be the presence of learning problems that prevent these students from achieving their potential.

A student who grasps ideas quickly but has difficulty noticing or remembering details may have ADHD and/or LD or may just be sloppy. A student who figures out the answers to complex questions, but does not write the computations down, may have ADHD and/or LD or may be cheating.

There are a number of indications that a student may be gifted and have ADHD and/or LD. (See Figure 10-7.)

CURRENT STATUS

The gifted student whose reading comprehension is relatively poor or who processes information slowly may not like to read and may complain that reading is "too slow" a method for getting information. The gifted student with ADHD may complain that the chapter to be read "doesn't get to the point" or is too full of nonessential information to be useful.

These students are not good readers. Their relatively low-level reading and writing ability brings their grades down in many courses. They are often ineligible for traditional gifted programs due to their low grade point averages. If they are admitted to these special programs, they often have a difficult time staying there.

Gifted students with ADHD and/or LD do not fit into traditional programs for students with ADHD or LD either. The students in these programs are generally functioning at a much lower level than the gifted student and the program itself generally progresses slowly.

The gifts and talents of students with ADHD and/or LD are generally unknown or unrecognized by the schools. Their strengths may lie in the nonverbal spheres of intelligence such as visuo-spatial, mechanical, mathematical, or artistic. Because they do not speak well or read well, little effort is made to uncover any hidden strengths.

Giftedness in combination with ADHD and/or LD presents a paradox to the school. Students like Cory and Mike, who are gifted and have LD or ADHD, rarely have appropriate educational programs. They are either in gifted or advanced placement programs with

Indications of Giftedness and ADHD/LD: A Paradoxical Picture

- Gets A's in some courses
- **but** gets D's in others.

- Understands the material
- **but** may not contribute or be involved.

- Is articulate
- **but** has difficulty with written expression.

- Has excellent creative writing skills
- **but** has difficulty with expository writing.

- Excels in one kind of course in an academic area (e.g., geometry)
- **but** does poorly in other courses (e.g., algebra).

- Does well in one aspect of a course (e.g., reading)
- **but** cannot do other aspects (e.g., writing).

- Has broad fund of knowledge, or sophisticated ideas or opinions
- **but** has poor oral expression.

- Gets A's on tests
- **but** fails to hand in homework.

- Demonstrates higher-level thinking skills
- **but** has poor basic skills.

- Shows creativity and inventiveness
- **but** does not complete projects or loses work. Fails to implement ideas.

- Has strong analytical reasoning
- **but** needs more time to process language.

- Is goal oriented, persistent, and motivated in some specific areas
- **but** not in others.

- Works hard in areas of interest
- **but** does not work in areas that he/she feels is boring.

- May have passionate interests outside of school
- **but** does not work in school.

- May act/feel smarter than the teacher
- **but** has low self-esteem or feels stupid.

Figure 10-7

no help for their ADHD and/or LD; or like Cory, they are receiving some help for their ADHD and/or LD but the work they are given is not challenging.

Because these students may have difficulty with introductory courses or lower-level courses and because of the school's insistence on lock-step programs, these students are often stuck in lower-level courses. They are not given the chance to exercise their high-level thinking and problem-solving skills.

The school's future expectations of students like Mike and Cory are often inaccurate. The school's academic expectations for Mike were too high and those for Cory, too low. Students' expectations of themselves are also inaccurate. Many gifted students with LD or ADHD have low expectations of their future. Few people see these students as college material.

SECONDARY EMOTIONAL PROBLEMS

The combination of giftedness and learning disabilities or ADHD can create secondary emotional problems for these students. It is important to note that there is no evidence that giftedness automatically makes a student vulnerable to emotional problems.

Often these students' learning disabilities as well as their giftedness are not identified until high school or beyond. Neither the student, the teachers, nor the parents understand why the student appears so bright, yet does so poorly in school. This can cause the student enormous frustration, especially if parents and teachers believe the student is not trying. The student may feel oppressed by teachers and parents who are constantly trying to get him or her to work harder.

Gifted students with ADHD and/or LD report many negative school experiences with teachers and peers. They are often teased by the other students. They feel that many of their teachers do not understand them. They can challenge their teachers unmercifully and are often persona non grata in several of their classes. They can be disruptive if they feel they are being misunderstood or "wronged."

These students may develop problems with procrastination and perfectionism because they rarely can produce work they feel good about and put off or don't do something they consider second rate. Their self-esteem suffers because they rarely achieve high grades and often fail. They may have few or no friends because it is hard to find peers like themselves who understand them and because they are so different from most of the other students.

CHALLENGES AND OPPORTUNITIES
FOR TEACHERS

Many teachers question both the fairness and the wisdom of providing extra help for gifted students with ADHD and/or LD. "These students already have a leg up," teachers say. "I think it's unfair for me to spend my precious time on them when other students with LD or ADHD need it more." Other teachers believe these students, because of their intelligence, should be able to help themselves.

We have as much responsibility for helping gifted students with ADHD and/or LD as we have for helping average or below-average students with disabilities. It is hard to recognize the subtle but devastating effect ADHD and/or LD can have on these students' academic achievement. The biggest problems these students face are in school, where they are not helped and—according to student reports—are actually turned off.

Helping gifted students with LD and/or ADHD can be very gratifying because they are so smart and can quickly grasp new ideas and strategies. On the other hand, working with a gifted student who hates school, thinks his or her teachers are "dumb," or who is rebelling against parental control can be quite a challenge. One of the major challenges you have is that gifted students—with and without ADHD and/or LD—often think they are exempt from hard work!

The three major qualifications for a teacher of gifted students with ADHD and/or LD are an ability to suspend judgment, a willingness to investigate, and flexibility. As soon as you recognize the contradictory behavior of a bright student who is not achieving, you should question if the student has LD or ADHD. It is important, however, not to dismiss the student as lazy or unmotivated, or the parents as uninvolved or uncaring. When parents, in discussing a student who is having problems in school, tell you that they think their child is very bright, you should question if the student has ADHD and/or LD. If a student is doing poorly in your class but is a shining light in another course, you should consider LD or ADHD.

The first steps you should take are:

- Talk to the other teachers regarding how the student is functioning in their courses.
- Talk to the student about what he or she thinks are the problems.
- Analyze the student's work for any patterns.
- Talk to the parents to find out how the student functions outside of school.
- Refer the student for psychoeducational evaluation.

PSYCHOEDUCATIONAL EVALUATION

In order to design an appropriate educational program for gifted students with ADHD and/or LD, it is very important that these students have a comprehensive psychoeducational evaluation to uncover their areas of strengths and weaknesses. Evaluation can consist of ability testing, achievement testing, teacher and parent checklists and observations, and student self-evaluation questionnaires including learning style inventories. Evaluation of auditory and visual memory, processing speed, executive functioning, and emotional status add important data. When the evaluations are completed, the results can be translated into teaching strategies for the classroom teachers.

Before planning an educational program for one of these students, you must fully understand:

- the student's areas of giftedness and weakness
- the impact of LD or ADHD on the student
- how the student learns best

Accommodations for Gifted Students with ADHD and/or LD

- Provide additional time to complete assignments.
- Develop high-level alternative assignments.
- Provide extra-credit opportunities.
- Provide audio tapes of textbooks, other required reading materials.
- Arrange for enrollment in gifted programs or advanced placement courses.
- Arrange for credit for college courses, mentoring programs.
- Do not remove credit for poor spelling, careless arithmetic errors, poor handwriting.
- Cue student to get on-task, maintain attention.
- Ignore jiggling, other mild hyperactivity.
- Locate quiet nondistracting places for student to work in.
- Develop checklists, graphic organizers.
- Allow students to use calculators and word processors in the classroom.
- Consider foreign language waivers.
- Give students opportunities for physical activity.
- Pair oral with written directions.
- Use computer-assisted instruction.

Figure 10-8

SECTION 504 PLANS AND CLASSROOM ACCOMMODATIONS

Although gifted students with LD or ADHD usually don't qualify for special education services under IDEA, they can qualify for special programming under Section 504. A 504 Plan can ensure that this student receives training in self-management, organization, and time management. The plan also can insure that the student receives the type of accommodations necessary to support his or her progress in school. The 504 Committee should also address the student's giftedness when designing an appropriate educational program for the student. (See Figure 10-8.)

FLEXIBLE PROGRAMMING

Flexible programming may be the key to academic success for these students. This can be accomplished by allowing these students to take:

- higher-level courses out of sequence
- courses in nearby community colleges or universities

- advanced placement courses in high school even though their grade point averages are not very high
- a high-level substitute for a required course in which the student is having great difficulty, such as taking a law course instead of an English course
- independent study courses that can substitute for required courses
- self-paced options

INSTRUCTIONAL PLANNING FOR THE CLASSROOM TEACHER

When planning instruction for the gifted student with ADHD and/or LD, it is extremely important that you address both the student's difficulties and strengths. Remember that the student has a fine mind and that the usual remedial strategies are generally geared for students of lesser intelligence. (See Figure 10-9.)

Additionally, to facilitate these students' learning, you can:

- Provide structure as needed.
- Match their different learning styles.
- Carefully select teachers for compatibility with the student.
- Occasionally arrange for gifted students to work with other very bright students.
- Give students challenging work, assignments, activities.
- Encourage and support divergent thinking.
- Tolerate a certain amount of their challenging behavior.
- Monitor and discourage the teasing of other students.
- Monitor perfectionism.
- Balance difficult courses with easier ones.
- Encourage the student to enroll in extracurricular activities.
- Locate and recommend high-interest summer programs.

THINKING AND SELF-MANAGEMENT STRATEGIES

Many gifted students with ADHD and/or LD have never acquired or practiced effective cognitive and self-management strategies. Being so quick and bright, in elementary school they were able to remember important information and solve mathematical problems without writing them down. They were able to manage the simple reading tasks they were given. They rarely bothered with rules, solving problems in their own way.

However, with the greater challenge of middle school and high school, these students begin to flounder because they don't have the memory and comprehension strategies and organizational skills necessary for them to deal with the increased information load. These

Teacher Do's and Don'ts

- **Do** provide a balanced program so that students can improve and succeed in both academic and social/emotional areas.

- **Do** ask students for their opinions and act upon them if at all possible. Help the students identify what works and what doesn't.

- **Do** leave time for rest or relaxation. Allow time to explore new interests or to socialize and have fun.

- **Do** allow students to drop courses if they are overwhelmed or if failure is due to disabilities. They can elect these courses at a later date.

- **Do** redesign required courses to minimize student weaknesses.

- **Do** find talents: Administer interest surveys, interview, use portfolios, and teacher recommendation or grades.

- **Do** identify stressors and talk to the teenager and a counselor. Provide resources. Modify requirements.

- **Do** show the students how their strengths and weaknesses affect different courses.

- **Do** provide options such as self-enrichment or tutoring.

- **Don't** ignore strengths and interests in an effort to improve deficits. Similarly, don't ignore weaknesses in the face of strengths.

- **Don't** ignore or exclude students' input when planning programs.

- **Don't** overload students with advanced placement courses, tutors, or extracurricular activities.

- **Don't** insist that students take courses they cannot pass because of their vulnerabilities.

- **Don't** insist that students repeat courses they cannot pass.

- **Don't** ignore special talents, interests, or hobbies.

- **Don't** ignore signs of stress and frustration.

- **Don't** assume that students understand their strengths and weaknesses.

- **Don't** require gifted students to teach or assist other students.

Figure 10-9

students need to learn strategies and skills to help them overcome or circumvent their weaknesses, and they need to learn many basic thinking and self-management strategies they never thought applied to them. (See Chapter 6.)

Just like other students with ADHD and/or LD, these students need to learn:

- visualization and self-talk for self-instruction, problem-solving, memory, learning new material

- reading and writing strategies
- memory strategies
- self-monitoring and self-evaluation
- self-management of distractibility and impulsivity
- time management, organization, study skills
- goal setting and long-range planning

Although most of these skills should be taught in the content area classes, these students may also need special education services to:

- Develop the student's self-awareness of his or her own learning style, strengths, as well as problem areas.
- Provide in-depth teaching of learning and self-management strategies.
- Develop checklists and graphic organizers.
- Increase student's social perception and interaction skills.
- Provide consultation to the classroom teacher.

STUDENT INVOLVEMENT

It is imperative that you involve the student every step of the way in educational decisions. These gifted students can help diagnose their problems in school, often with good insight. They can be creative problem-solvers and may arrive at excellent solutions that neither parents nor the teachers have thought of. They may have already developed strategies that you can use for other students. As these students are often opinionated and challenging, unless we involve them in planning and decision-making, our best laid plans are doomed to fail.

You can give these students a self-evaluation questionnaire, such as Levine's Self Administered Student Profile, to help begin defining the problem and developing an appropriate plan.

A FINAL WORD

Teachers of gifted students with LD and/or ADHD have a chance to help create another da Vinci, Einstein, Edison, or Yeats. These four had great difficulty in school because of their ADHD and/or LD. Da Vinci, Edison, and Einstein were visual thinkers with superior spatial ability whose LD was in the verbal area. Yeats and da Vinci had ADHD. You have only to look at some of da Vinci's drawings to see his nimble mind skip from topic to topic. These people succeeded in spite of the schooling they received. But how many others were lost?

There are many potential inventors, artists, poets, and mathematicians in our classrooms today. Some of them will reach their potential, others will not. With appropriate educational programming and strong teacher support, all of them will have a good chance.

Postscript: Pygmalion in the Classroom

Deontray, whose mother was on welfare and who lived in a housing project in the middle of Detroit, had IQ test scores that placed him in the retarded range. He was a shy boy who spoke, read, and wrote very slowly. He was what learning disability specialists call "a slow processor."

Deontray tried very hard in school and never missed a day of class. He seemed to love school. He regularly took books out of the school library that nobody thought he could read. It was assumed he was retarded or certainly not very bright, but he seemed like a sweet kid.

In high school, after being desultorily passed from grade to grade, an English teacher saw something in Deontray that sparked her interest. She arranged to meet Deontray after school once or twice a week to discuss his school work. She discovered that Deontray had some very sophisticated interests and opinions, but that he needed much more time than anyone else to express an opinion, respond to a question, or complete an assignment.

Up to that time, Deontray had hardly participated in class and had rarely handed in any homework. Towards the end of the term Deontray handed the teacher a 14-page report discussing why he wanted to go to college. This was not a topic that the teacher had assigned.

The teacher was astounded. The report was well organized and written at a very high level. The person who wrote that report was definitely college material. It became clear to the teacher that, if given enough time to respond, Deontray could function on a very advanced level. He clearly was a gifted writer.

The English teacher became Deontray's mentor and advocate. She stayed in touch with him all the way through high school and convinced his other teachers to give him the time to demonstrate what he knew—and, given the time, he performed brilliantly. Due to her encouragement and support, Deontray received a four-year scholarship to a nearby college. Deontray's English teacher had truly become his Pygmalion.

CHAPTER ELEVEN

Diversity and Parent Involvement

"It's not right, it's not right! This is not right what they're doing. I walk into that school and they all stare at me. They make me very uncomfortable. You know, the principal never even smiled at me when I said hello. They talk about you as if you're not really there. And then they say to me: 'Who are you to be telling me my job? We are educators!' You know, as parents, we don't have a clue.

"At the IEP the principal asked me 'What about all these other kids in school who can't read?' I told him that's his lookout. I want you to help Clyde!" (Mother of middle school student with LD)

How would you interact with a parent like this? Can you understand what she is saying? Can you handle her anger? Have you heard about this parent through the grapevine? Have they told you she is impossible to deal with?

Teachers often feel unprepared to work with parents of students with ADHD and/or LD. They are not used to sharing decision-making powers. They often feel that parents have nothing of value to offer in the way of suggestions for educating their children. Most teachers do not know how to calm down an angry parent or how to discuss student difficulties so that parents won't become defensive.

Most parents of students with ADHD and/or LD feel unprepared to work with teachers. These parents often feel intimidated by an IEP team. They may feel they have little to offer. They may feel no one is listening to their concerns. They often think of themselves at an IEP meeting as David faced with Goliath.

Some parents of students with ADHD and/or LD want to be very active participants in the education of their child, making suggestions to teachers regarding educational programming and stating their opinions in no uncertain terms. They may not agree with the ways teachers are doing things and may make weekly telephone calls to discuss their child's progress. They, too, may not know how to work with teachers in joint problem solving.

Both parents and teachers want IEP meetings to end harmoniously with all participants agreed on an appropriate educational plan for the child. But many of these meetings end with little accomplished and bad feelings on both sides. Parents and teachers want this to change.

LEGAL UNDERPINNING OF PARENT INVOLVEMENT

Parent involvement has always been a hallmark of special education legislation. In fact, parents were the first ones to pressure state and local governments in the 1960s to pass legislation mandating free, appropriate public education for children with disabilities.

The law makes several assumptions about the benefits of parent involvement for students with disabilities. (See Figure 11-1.)

Research has shown that parent involvement can improve student achievement, improve attendance, create a positive school climate, and prevent school violence. Almost any parent involvement activity has the potential for increasing student achievement. Just having a few parents volunteering in school every day has been shown to improve school safety. For students with ADHD and/or LD, parent involvement in educational planning and working with their child at home can be critical factors in student progress.

Under both state and federal laws, parents of students with disabilities were given the right to be involved in educational decisions affecting their child in several ways:

- As active participants in the IEP process
- As consenters to the evaluation of their child, his or her educational placement, and the services to be provided under the IEP
- As dissenters who may request a hearing or mediation if they disagree with the decision of the IEP team
- As members of state and local advisory committees who review and sign off on state and local plans for the delivery of services

The 1997 amendments to IDEA further strengthened the role of parents and expanded opportunities for parents and school personnel to work in new partnerships at the state and local levels.

- Parents are to have the opportunity to participate in all meetings concerned with the identification, evaluation, and educational placement of the child (not just IEP team meetings).
- The concerns of parents and the information they provide regarding their children are to be considered in developing and reviewing the student's IEP.
- Schools are required to keep the parents informed about their children's progress, in the general education curriculum as well as towards IEP goals and objectives.

IDEA Assumptions about Parent Involvement

- Students will benefit if parents are involved in their education.
- The rights of students will be protected if parents are involved.
- Parent participation in the IEP process will improve the quality of educational decisions.
- Parents will represent the child's best interests.
- Parents are teachers of their children.
- Parents need and want training on how to help their children.
- Parents provide the only continuity in the child's life.
- Parents are prime sources of information.

Figure 11-1

Section 504, with fewer specifics regarding parent involvement, tends to follow IDEA in its requirements.

The laws essentially expect that parents are equal partners with school personnel in the IEP process. Parents are viewed as having an active role in educational decisions affecting their children. Teachers and parents are expected to work together for the benefit of the child.

Teachers have their own set of protections under the law. IDEA says that, if necessary, teachers can ask for additional training and/or an aide to help them in the classroom. Section 504 states that the accommodations given to the student must not be "unreasonable" or cause "undue hardship" to teacher or school. The teachers' union, too, protects teachers from unfair directives.

Although parent involvement has been a part of special education law since 1975, current research shows that most parent involvement continues to be limited to the teacher giving information to the parent and making suggestions to the parent regarding working with the student at home. This is *not* what the laws intend.

DEFINITION OF PARENT INVOLVEMENT

Parent involvement means, essentially, parents and schools working together for the benefit of students. There are several types of parent-involvement activities: Parents can work with their child at home, they can meet with their child's teacher to plan the child's educational program, and they can become involved in the many activities schools offer to parents and the community. There are a variety of possible parent-involvement activities that should be considered. (See Figure 11-2.)

Unfortunately, schools often judge parent involvement on the basis of parents' presence in school. Those not participating in school-related activities are thought of as not caring about their children or the education they receive. In actuality, some of the most important parent involvement occurs in the home where it is not seen by the school.

Parent-Involvement Activities

Work with the child at home

- Provide a safe, caring environment.
- Provide praise and encouragement.
- Stress the importance of education.
- Provide enrichment, recreational, and social opportunities.
- Help, monitor, and supervise the child's homework.
- Follow the teacher's suggestions for helping the student.
- Notify the teacher if the child needs extra help in school.

Work with the child's teacher

- Communicate concerns to the child's teacher.
- Inform teachers of strategies that do and don't work at home.
- Attend parent–teacher meetings and conferences.
- Help to solve the student's academic and behavioral problems.
- Make suggestions to help the student.
- Help make educational decisions.
- Advocate for the student.

Support the school

- Attend schoolwide student performances, sports events, and social activities for families.
- Help raise money for the school.
- Volunteer to work in the school or classroom.
- Become a member of the parent–teacher organization.
- Teach a class in an area of expertise.
- Share the family's cultural traditions with class.
- Attend parent training workshops.
- Serve as a member of the school-improvement advisory committee.

Figure 11-2

Parent involvement is also judged on the basis of student achievement and student behavior. If a student is doing poorly in school, poor parenting is often seen as the culprit. Teachers often think the parents are not providing enough discipline or structure or that parents don't encourage the student to do well in school. This was proven not to be true.

Many of our parent-involvement goals are unrealistic. We want parents to be cooperative, pleasant, and agreeable; to have the time and resources to help each of their children with homework; and to follow through on our suggestions on how to help the child at home. We assume that parents share our values and goals and have the same expectations of the student as we do.

DIVERSITY IN THE SCHOOLS

We often forget that parents and families come in many different sizes, shapes and colors, depending on their culture, their socio-economic status, their life experiences, their communication style, and, of course, their individual personalities. Yet when we talk about parent involvement in the education of children, we tend to forget these differences and make assumptions about our ability to communicate with parents and their understanding of and agreement with what we are saying.

Over 30 percent of our students today are culturally, linguistically, and ethnically different from the dominant culture. Only 10 percent of our teachers come from ethnic minorities. Forty-seven percent of our schools have no minority teachers. Teachers tend to be predominantly female, middle class, and of Anglo–European background.

Over 2,500,000 children in our schools and their parents are nonnative speakers of English. Large percentages of the students in our urban schools are from minority backgrounds. Twenty percent of our school-age children live in poverty, and additional numbers are from low-income families. By 2050 one half of the U.S. population will be a combination of Hispanic, African American, Native American, and Asian/Pacific Islanders.

Involving parents from diverse backgrounds in their children's school can be quite a challenge. In some schools one-third or more of the parents do not attend parent–teacher meetings and sometimes 80 percent do not show up for any school activity. The parents who do show up tend to be those who share the culture of the school and its teachers. The preponderance of parents who don't show up are low income, poorly educated, and those from other cultures.

We may not fully understand how frightening it can be for a parent who speaks little English to come to school to discuss his or her child and not really understand what the teacher is saying. Some of these parents even have difficulty asking where the restroom is.

Socio-Economic Status

Children from low-income families are at high risk for school failure and dropping out. They (and their parents) often find school an alien and unwelcome place. Because their life experiences are very different from mainstream America, they often have difficulty relating what they are learning to their own lives. They do not take vacations with their families.

They do not own bicycles. They may never have been outside their immediate geographical area. They may never have ridden in an elevator.

Children from low-income families may have a history of being misunderstood or stereotyped by insensitive teachers. In one kindergarten class, during show and tell, while most of the students were showing a new toy or game, a low-income student raised his hand and—lacking a toy or game—shared an interesting experience he had that day. He began telling the class about the dead cat he saw in the street while walking to school. He described with great interest the flies and maggots crawling over the body. The teacher interrupted him and told him that this was not a nice topic to be discussing at school and moved on to the next child who talked about her new bicycle.

The parents of these children are also misunderstood by the schools. Most low-income parents work, often at physically demanding, low-paying jobs. Because they usually can't afford a car, they must take public transportation to and from work, shopping, and medical appointments. They often live in gang-infested neighborhoods and cannot help or protect their children as much as they want to. They can be discouraged and depressed and have little energy left over to become involved with their child's schooling.

It is hard for us to comprehend how difficult it is to find a place for a student to do homework at night while living in a single-family house with four other families or living in a two-bedroom apartment with six other family members.

We may not understand how little time single parents may have to help their children with homework while balancing a job, household chores, and the needs of other children in the family. We may not realize that some parents cannot help their child with homework because they themselves cannot read.

Some low-income parents work afternoons or evenings, on shifts no one else wants. Some work two jobs in order to make ends meet. These parents may not be able to meet with the teacher because they are unavailable in the late afternoon or early evening, unless they take off time from work.

Many of these parents have little education. Society often assumes that they are stupid or lazy. They are often not seen as individuals with their own pattern of strengths and weaknesses.

Parents' Own School Experiences

Parents who did badly in school when they were children may feel terribly inadequate when it comes to attending parent–teacher conferences or helping their children with homework. These parents may have difficulty reading or writing. They may have failed and dropped out of school. They may think they do not speak well enough to interact with a teacher. They often cannot read or understand teacher reports or school newsletters.

These parents may themselves have ADHD and/or LD and not received the support they needed in school because ADHD and/or LD were not well understood at the time. Due to their own experiences, many of these parents feel very negative about school.

Some parents like these may feel that the teachers will look down upon them and criticize the way they are raising their children. School staff may have stated or implied that the parent is to blame for the student's problems. No matter how much they deny it or try to hide it, when teachers blame parents for a problem, the parents know it. Parents will not cooperate with teachers or other school staff who feel this way.

Minority Status

African American and Hispanic students are placed in special education classes at a much higher rate than other students. Society tends to believe that minority students from low-income backgrounds have limited abilities, have little support from their parents, and, because of this, there is little that can be done to help these students succeed in school.

Even middle-class African American children often face lowered expectations in school. They and their parents have often been victims of prejudice and stereotyping by society. These parents' feelings about parent–teacher meetings may range from uncomfortable to angry. They may feel patronized by teachers who they think don't respect them. They may feel that teachers are underestimating their children and misunderstanding their behavior. Their distrust of teachers may run so deeply that they may not trust even those teachers who genuinely want to help their children.

Cultural Differences

Many parents from other cultures view education in a different light than we do. Parents from some other cultures wouldn't dream of offering suggestions to teachers or participating in educational decisions that affect their child. Teachers in their cultures are held in such high esteem that it would be rude and presumptuous for parents to collaborate with teachers. They bring the child to the teacher and, in effect, say, "He or she is yours."

Immigrant parents may face severe language barriers when it comes to talking to teachers. Even those who seem to understand what we are saying often miss the subtleties in our language. Serious misunderstandings can occur.

Although all these parents are interested in education for their children, sometimes the needs of the family supersede educational aspirations. If the family is poor and needs another paycheck to survive, a teenager may drop out of school to help.

Concepts such as ADHD or LD don't exist or have different definitions in many cultures. Many parents think that ADHD and/or LD is the equivalent of mental retardation and are very upset when a teacher tells them that their child might have a learning disability.

Communication Style Differences

While we are well aware how difficult it is to communicate with parents who speak a different language, other factors such as culture, socio-economic status, and minority status can affect parent–teacher communication. (See Figure 11-3.)

We often think that parents who interrupt us are rude or disrespectful. However, in "high involvement" cultures, arguing and interrupting are acceptable ways to express feelings and opinions, as are touching and hugging. In these cultures interruption and argumentation

---

Cultural Differences

- Expectations of their child
- Assumptions about schools and education
- Conventions for courtesy
- Directness
- Expressiveness
- Sense of personal space
- Tone of voice
- Nonverbal communication conventions
- Communication style
- Child rearing practices
- Values
- Behavioral norms
- Rules for social interaction
- Gender roles
- Dress
- Religious observances

Figure 11-3

show that a person is really involved in a conversation. Parenthetically, when a student frequently interrupts the teacher and touches or hugs other students, we may see it as a behavior problem.

In "high consideration" cultures, talking softly is a sign of respect. Allowing a person to finish what he or she is saying before the next speaker begins is considered proper manners. Often there is a measurable pause between speakers. In some cultures, serious conversation cannot begin until certain ritual words are exchanged, and it is considered quite rude to immediately plunge into the topic at hand.

Anger and disagreement are expressed differently in different cultures. People from some cultures are more direct. Negative feelings, such as anger, and positive feelings, such as affection, are spontaneously expressed both verbally and nonverbally. In other cultures the expression of both positive and negative feelings is restrained, particularly outside the family setting. The expression of angry feelings can be seen as aggressive and destructive. On the other hand, not expressing angry feelings or hiding them can give the impression of agreement where agreement does not exist.

Communication-style differences also exist between people from different regions of the country, between men and women, and between well-educated and poorly educated people.

Barriers to Collaboration

- Lack of information or misinformation
- Differing expectations of school and schooling
- Differing values and goals
- Different interpretations of legal requirements
- Poor understanding of teacher roles and responsibilities
- Poor understanding of the realities of parents' lives
- Misunderstandings due to differing communication styles
- Inadvertent stereotyping and prejudice
- Low expectations of certain students
- Lack of respect and trust
- Direct or implicit blame
- Myths, gossip, personality clashes

Figure 11-4

When we are speaking to someone with a different communication style, it is as easy to be misunderstood as it is to misunderstand. We often take offense where there is none intended.

Differences in culture, language, social class, life experience, and communication style present subtle barriers to collaboration. These barriers can prevent the development of an appropriate educational plan for a student. (See Figure 11-4.)

An inability to speak English fluently and unfamiliarity with the dominant culture and the culture of the school greatly interfere with parents' ability to participate fully in the education of their child, no matter how strong their desire to do so.

THE INFLUENCE OF ADHD AND/OR LD ON THE FAMILY

Rarely do teachers understand the emotional toll that having a child with a disability can have on a parent. Parents of adolescents with ADHD and/or LD often live lives filled with anxiety and disappointment. They may worry that their child will flunk out or drop out of school, or not get into college. They may become overprotective of a child they think is misunderstood by everyone else. Conversely, they may deny that their child has a problem or blame the child for not working hard enough in school. Fathers may blame mothers for "coddling" the child if the mother seeks support services from the school. These problems may turn a family into a cauldron of frustrated, angry people.

Many parents of students with ADHD and/or LD have a long history of negative interactions with the schools. Clyde's mother had been concerned about him ever since second grade.

"In the middle of third grade, I spoke to the teacher. 'You know Clyde,' I said, 'isn't reading yet.'

"She said, 'We're doing the best we can.'

"But I told her we've got to do something. She said, 'With some kids it just doesn't seem to click. Some kids just doesn't [sic] get it. There's nothing we can do about it.'

"At the beginning of fourth grade, I said to myself, 'What are we going to do with this kid?' First work that came home, no way he was gonna be able to do it. He's getting overwhelmed. He comes home crying and says he feels stupid. Why can't he read?

"I didn't want to cause more waves. They already hated me. But I got in my car and I went to the school and asked for an IEP. At the IEP they said that Clyde wasn't very bright, this 9-year-old boy who could fix his father's tractors when they broke. I really lost it and said, 'You've no right to do this to Clyde! You have no right to treat us like this!' They decided to adjourn the meeting till the next month, I guess because I had really blown my cool."

When we meet parents like Clyde's mother in middle school, they are already angry and distrustful—and they may take it out on us. Do we understand where they are coming from? Do we try to avoid them? Can we weather their attacks as we go about our job of developing an appropriate educational program for their child? It may take a long time to gain parents' trust, but as students like Clyde become more successful in school, trust will grow.

We may not understand how hard many parents of students with ADHD and/or LD must work to keep their children on grade level. They may spend hours with the student every night helping them with homework and teaching them the things they did not grasp in class.

We may consider a parent rude and inconsiderate because he or she is late for a parent–teacher meeting or misses the meeting totally. We may not know that many parents of children with ADHD and/or LD themselves have ADHD and/or LD; they may not know it themselves.

Parents, on the other hand, often do not understand how school systems work. They often have unrealistic expectations of what teachers can accomplish. They do not understand how many responsibilities a teacher has or how many students a teacher may see in one day. They do not understand how federal, state, and local requirements affect what a teacher must teach. They do not understand that although the teacher really wants to help the child, he or she might not have enough time in the day or expertise to do the kind of job the parent would like them to do.

It is no wonder that families of students with ADHD and/or LD often feel very alone. They mistrust school. They feel that the school does not understand them or their child. These feelings are compounded when the parents are from different cultures and/or are members of minority and lower socio-economic groups.

PARENT–TEACHER DISAGREEMENTS ABOUT THE EDUCATION OF STUDENTS WITH ADHD AND/OR LD

It is not uncommon for parents and teachers of students with ADHD and/or LD to disagree about what will work best for the student. These parents are concerned and anxious about their children. They have been frustrated over their child's past failures. They often feel that a redesign of the child's educational program can make the difference between the child's success or failure as an adult. They may even disagree on whether or not the student even has a disability.

Other common disagreements involve:

- The type and amount of special education services the student needs.
- The types of accommodations the general education teacher should provide.
- Whether or not the student belongs in that particular general education class or with that particular teacher.
- Whether or not the teacher really understands how the student's disability affects him or her and knows how to teach the student.
- Whether the student should receive special education help within the general education classroom or outside the classroom for more individualized and more intensive help.
- The amount of responsibility the student is capable of taking for his or her own education at this time.

The underlying cause of all these disagreements is the lack of student success. There is little disagreement on instructional methodology when the student is progressing satisfactorily in school.

Causes of Disagreements

A major cause of disagreements is misunderstanding and miscommunication. Cultural and communication style differences are the causes of some of the miscommunication. But there can be miscommunication and misunderstanding between parents and teachers who share the same culture as well.

Even though we all know that educational jargon is easily misunderstood by parents, we may inadvertently slip into jargon when we explain their child's problem to parents. Although a teacher may feel that he or she has carefully explained a point to a parent, unless that point is couched in terms the parent can comprehend, the point is lost.

Parents and teachers may have different assumptions about a child's educational program, and different expectations of what constitutes student success.

Parents of students with ADHD and/or LD often complain that the general education teacher "just doesn't get it," that the teacher really doesn't understand how ADHD and/or LD affects their particular child. These parents also feel that the general education teacher doesn't understand what to do—and why—to help this particular child. Teachers often feel that parents are asking too much of them or that they are just plain wrong.

Lack of trust between parent and teacher can present an insurmountable barrier to effective communication. Whether based on past history, gossip, or myths that have grown between teachers and parents, distrust must be overcome if parent and teacher are to work together.

Disagreements also occur when financial constraints or administrative arrangements control the amount of services a school district can offer a particular student. This is technically illegal unless the school district has received a waiver from the state of one or more legal requirements. Teachers are sometimes told by administrators to limit the number of services offered to students. This can be a dilemma for some teachers.

Both parents and teachers can be subjective in their judgment and opinions. Teachers' decisions are influenced by the needs of the other students in the class and by their work load. Parents, as the child's advocate, focus on the needs of *their* child, ignorant of other demands on the teachers' time and energy.

Parents are constantly seeking ways to help their children. They may suggest to teachers unproven methods that they read about in the latest magazine or newspaper. Of course, disagreements can also be caused by legitimate differences of opinion. Education is an art as well as a science. There are many theories and hypotheses as to how a student with ADHD and/or LD learns best. It is difficult to reach agreement on what is best for the child if a school or teacher is operating from one point of view and the parent from another.

Disagreements can be overcome when parents and teachers are both committed to do so. Disagreements can also be settled through the mediation or hearing process described in special education law.

A NEW APPROACH TO PARENT INVOLVEMENT

A new approach can be developed that has as its base an understanding of the effects of cultural differences, socio-economic status, language, and communication style, as well as LD and ADHD on parent–teacher communication and parent involvement. This approach is the focus of the system change necessary in order to increase parent involvement.

A Systemwide Commitment

The process begins with a systemwide commitment to work towards the goals of:

- Increased parent involvement
- More effective parent–teacher meetings
- Outreach into the community to involve traditionally uninvolved or underinvolved parents

The principal of the school can provide leadership and encouragement, and commit the resources necessary to achieve the goals.

A committee can be set up, composed of school staff and parents, that can spearhead a needs assessment and report to the staff. Increasing schoolwide parent involvement might mean reallocating a small percentage of the school budget, reevaluating the school climate, and rethinking some current policies and practices. Decisions can be made regarding these and other issues by the entire school staff.

A system commitment begins with an analysis of the current status of parent involvement in the school. Information about the demographics of the community needs to be located. A parent needs assessment should be developed to gather information about how parents view their child's education and the school's responsiveness to parent needs. School policies and practices will also need to be analyzed to determine whether they provide a welcoming environment for students and parents from all cultures and socio-economic classes. (See Figure 11-5.)

Parent demographics are often available from school records. Local governmental agencies can provide additional demographic information. In order to tap into parent attitudes, small representative groups of parents from different community organizations can be assembled to discuss their children's schooling. Asking the parents to fill out a questionnaire will not result in a representative sample of parents, because some parents cannot read or write well enough to answer the questions.

Even without a schoolwide commitment, the planning for increased parent involvement can begin with a single teacher committed to interacting more effectively with the parents of the students in his or her class.

Activities to Increase Parent Involvement

There are many ways to increase schoolwide parent involvement. In fact, there should be a variety of activities offered of interest to a variety of parents. Although our goal is to get parents to attend parent–teacher meetings and otherwise participate in the education of

---

Strategic Planning for Parent Involvement

- Determine specific goals of parent involvement and parent–teacher collaboration.
- Create a committee to study the issue and make recommendations.
- Commit needed resources to committee.
- Analyze the current status of parent involvement, school policies and practices, and parent needs.
- Develop a plan that includes new procedures, programs, and activities.
- Implement the new plan.
- Monitor and evaluate the plan.

Figure 11-5

their children, it is first important to make the school a familiar and enjoyable place for parents to be.

One of the most important things you can do is to welcome parents and inform them about what you expect from the students in your class over the coming year. (See Figure 11-6.)

Written communication with parents as well as notices of school events sent to parents need to be carefully analyzed for readability. Parent materials need to be:

- clear
- short
- to the point
- written in simple, not compound, sentences
- no longer than one page, if possible

Many parent activities are already in place in your school and it is important to build on those that are already working well. However, some parent-involvement activities—especially those activities that can be particularly helpful in involving low-income and minority parents as well as parents from different cultures—are often not in place.

Teacher Training

It is important to provide teachers with information regarding the demographics of their school and give them some insight into the various cultures and socio-economic classes that make up the student body. Inservice training can increase teacher awareness of the effect of attitudes, values, and expectations on interpersonal relations. Not only will teachers become aware of the array of parent values and expectations of school and schooling, teachers will also become aware of their own attitudes, values, and expectations of parent involvement. (See Figure 11-7.)

Specific cross-cultural communication skills can be taught to assist teachers during parent–teacher conferences. Teachers will need to learn how to communicate with parents in ways the parents can understand. In doing this, teachers may need to make adjustments to their usual communication style in order to be fully understood. They may need to communicate through translators. Teachers will need to remember that some parents come from cultures in which disagreements remain unspoken and a smile and a nod may not mean that a parent will do as you ask.

Teachers can learn more about the different cultures in the community by contacting people who are representatives of the individual cultural groups or going to meeting places where members of these groups congregate. For example, the school could call the local Mosque or Korean Christian Church and ask for someone who can provide information regarding Middle Eastern or Korean culture and communication styles. Bringing members of different cultural groups into the school to inform the teachers of cultural and communication differences can greatly enhance teacher understanding of the cultures in general. However, teachers must remember that individual differences exist in all cultures, so each parent must be treated as an individual within a particular cultural environment.

Sample Letter to Parents

Dear Parents,

The new school year has just begun. I want to welcome _____ to my class. I also want to welcome you, the parents. I hope you and I can work together to make this a very successful year for _____ .

I've planned a very interesting and exciting year for the students. This year the students will learn about:

- •   •

- •   •

- •   •

We will be taking _____ one-day field trips during the year. I will let you know as soon as they are arranged.

I am including the school calendar with this letter. It will tell you when school is in session, when the students have vacations, when parent conferences are scheduled, and when other important school events for students and parents are scheduled.

Students will have homework _____
(If the student is spending more than ____ minutes a night on homework from my class, please let me know.)

Students will have tests _____

Students are also expected to _____

Course grades will be based on _____

You are welcome to come to class to see what we are doing. Please call me to make arrangements.

Please call me or write me a note if you have any questions or concerns. The school's telephone number is _____ and my extension is _____ . You can reach me between _____ A.M. or between _____ P.M. At other times leave a message for me with the school secretary.

I look forward to meeting you.

Sincerely,

Figure 11-6

Teacher Checklist: Cultural Self-Awareness

Awareness

☐ Do I understand the affect of culture on a person's attitudes, values expectations, and behavior?

☐ Do I understand the affect of cultural difference on student achievement and parent involvement?

☐ Am I aware of my own attitudes, assumptions, and prejudices regarding students and parents from different cultures, and from different socio-economic groups?

☐ Am I aware that there are different communication styles and do I try not to offend or be offended by the way people express themselves?

☐ Do I understand that all the members of an ethnic or culture group are not alike?

☐ Am I aware of how culturally determined behavior can affect social interaction?

☐ Am I aware of how stereotyping, prejudice, and racism can negatively affect student achievement and parent involvement?

Behavior

☐ Do I actively and consciously try to learn about cultures different from mine?

☐ Do I use language that is free from racial and ethnic/cultural stereotypes and insults?

☐ Do I try to help others recognize and eliminate stereotypical thinking?

☐ Do I try to get to know people who have had different experiences from mine?

☐ Do I try to get to know people who do not think as I do?

☐ Do I attend cultural events put on by ethnic or racial groups other than my own?

Figure 11-7

Teachers will also need information regarding the impact of ADHD and/or LD on the family in order to understand both the involved, overinvolved, and underinvolved parent. If teachers understand where these parents are coming from, it will become easier for them to slough off the occasional criticism and anger that parents might project.

The school can contact local parent groups such as Learning Disabilities Association or CH.A.D.D. to ask them to make presentations to the staff regarding some general parent attitudes towards and expectations of the school. These groups may also suggest strategies for working with the parents.

Outreach

Schools will need outreach programs in order to involve recent immigrants, minority parents, and low-income parents. Cultural groups and churches in the community that serve these parents, as well as health clinics and local social service agencies in the community, need to be identified and contacted. These groups can yield community liaisons who can talk to parents about school involvement and serve as translators and mediators.

Having a parent coordinator on staff can help organize and carry out various parent-involvement activities. The coordinator should be a member of the community with demonstrated skills in relating to parents. The coordinator can meet with individual parents to elicit their concerns and then bring these concerns to the attention of the teacher. The coordinator can also maintain a list of support groups and social service agencies to distribute to all parents in the school.

Holding parent–teacher conferences or school meetings on familiar grounds, such as local churches or community rooms in housing projects, may help these parents take the first steps to parent involvement. (See Figure 11-8.)

The school might call a social service agency that works with new immigrants and ask for people to contact. The school might send one of its teachers to an ethnic celebration that is open to the public to locate a contact person. Teachers can also ask students in their classes for the names of leaders in their communities. These community liaisons can serve as links between the families of children from diverse cultures and the school.

Building Trust

One of the most important building blocks of parent involvement is trust. Trust between parent and teacher must be established if effective communication and problem-solving is to occur. Building trust is not easy, however, especially if the student has long-standing learning problems—but the teacher must actively strive to do so.

Trust is built on understanding and respect. If you understand the parent and respect his or her opinions—and communicate this to the parent—the parent will be much more willing to become actively involved in the child's education. If you also communicate an understanding and respect for the student, the parent will become more trusting. Of course, the more progress the student makes, the more trust will increase.

Outreach Activities

- Hold parent–teacher meetings in apartment complexes, neighborhood churches, shopping malls.
- Encourage community organizations to meet in school.
- Provide ESL and GED classes for parents in the evenings.
- Arrange transportation for parents to school events or parent–teacher meetings.
- Identify community liaisons to help get the parents involved.
- Ensure that posters and pictures that are hung on school walls represent members of diverse cultures.
- Inform parents of your policy of zero tolerance of racial slurs, pejoratives, teasing, put-downs, and exclusions.
- Locate community medical clinics in school.
- Establish a clothing exchange.
- Provide vocational education classes for parents in the evening.
- Conduct phone surveys of parents on school issues.
- Conduct focus groups of parents on school issues.
- Invite parents to some staff-development activities.
- Present cable TV programs of parent interest.
- Conduct schoolwide clean-up/fix-up days for parents.
- Provide a parent "drop in" room staffed by volunteers.
- Provide recreation and sports for parents (e.g., evening basketball).
- Conduct parent interest surveys.
- Provide washing machines and dryers in school that parents can use during meetings.

Figure 11-8

You will need to consider your own attitude toward parent involvement. If you not only accept but value parent participation, this will be communicated to the parent and the parent will respond in kind. Parents can make important suggestions, contribute valuable insights, and provide support for the teacher. A positive attitude towards parent involvement will go a long way to building trust.

Note: If you cannot build trust on your own, there may be someone else who the parent does trust (and with whom you feel comfortable) who can serve as a bridge between you and the parent. This person can be another school employee, another parent, a community liaison, or an outside consultant.

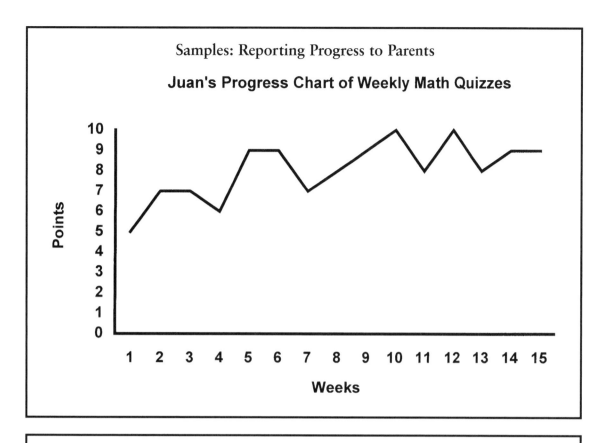

Samples: Reporting Progress to Parents

Juan's Progress Chart of Weekly Math Quizzes

Barbara's Progress on Lab Reports

Laboratory Report #	Number of Points	Comments
1	4/10	No drawing. Incomplete.
2	4/10	Late, messy. See me for help.
3	5/10	More legible but formulas missing.
4	0	Report not turned in.
5	5/10	Report only ½ complete.
6	7/10	Needs a conclusion and more details in the Findings section.
7	7/10	See me for help with the Conclusion and Findings sections.
8	0	Report not turned in.
9	6/10	Still needs work on following directions for Conclusion and Findings.
10	8/10	Keep up the good work. Formulas and findings included. Conclusion and findings good.

Comments: Barbara has made good progress. She is completing more of her lab reports. She is getting better at following directions. It hasn't been easy for her but she's learning how to write reports. She has been working hard.

(continued)

Figure 11–9

Weekly Monitoring Form

Student: Date:
Teacher: Class:

Behaviors	Number of Days	Comments
Arrived in class on time.	M T W Th F	
Handed in homework.	M T W Th F	
Participated in class discussion.	M T W Th F	
Started classwork on time.	M T W Th F	
Other:		

If the parent has a history of not trusting the school, it is often because the parent and/or the student has been blamed for—or perceive that they have been blamed for—the student's learning problems. Blame destroys trust. It is important to communicate to the parents that whatever the student's learning problem, it is a problem to be solved. Blame has no part in the solution.

You can say: "I know your child has had a lot of problems in school in the past, and that must have really upset you. But I'd like to try to make a difference this year. Your son or daughter is a year older, and this is a new semester, a new beginning. It's a good time to try to turn things around. If we work together we can develop an effective way to help your son or daughter become more successful in school."

It is important to tell the parent that there is no miracle cure: Progress may be slow and may not be immediately reflected in the student's grades. Charting student progress for parents can help demonstrate that despite ups and downs, progress is continuing towards the goals you have set collaboratively. (See Figure 11-9.)

EFFECTIVE COMMUNICATION

Before sitting with a parent to discuss a student, it is important for you to realize that you, the parent, and the student all have the same goal: to help the student become more successful in school. Therefore, in order to communicate effectively, you must base your discussions with parents on several assumptions, which you should share with the parents. These are:

- Everyone wants the student to be successful in school, including the student.
- Everyone will feel good if the student is successful.
- Everyone cares about the student.
- Parents want the best for their children.
- Parents want their children to get a good education.
- Parents and teachers are often tired and overworked.
- Teachers, parents, and students all need encouragement and reinforcement.

Unfortunately, much of the communication between parent and teacher regarding a student with ADHD and/or LD is negative. Teachers complain about students; parents are angry with teachers. Although teachers know how important positive communication is when a student is having problems, it is often hard to communicate in a positive way or to figure out what to say to an angry parent.

When working with these parents, it is important that you communicate you really understand the student's strengths and weaknesses and how the student's ADHD and/or LD specifically affects him or her. Say some positive and hopeful things about the child at the onset; however, saying a few positive things about a student is not enough if you imply that the parents are somehow to blame for the student's problems. Even if you do not criticize the parents directly, but make negative comments about the family to other teachers, you can be sure that the negativity will be communicated to the parents at parent–teacher meetings or "through the grapevine."

You must be aware of the implications of your words when you speak with parents. If parents begin to be defensive or if they get angry unexpectedly, you need to back up and analyze what you have just said that the parents may have misunderstood. Then try to restate your message in different terms.

You must become an active listener: Ask questions, restate parent concerns in your own words, and summarize at frequent intervals. Develop rapport with the parents by discussing shared interests, experiences, and problems. You can turn to school social workers and school psychologists for strategies that can help foster rapport.

Parents value direct, open, respectful communication from you, even if you are saying some difficult things. Parents will sense if you are patronizing them or trying to brush them off. If you state the student's problem in a factual, nonjudgmental way and view it as a problem to be solved *jointly* by parent and teacher, parents will be much less defensive. (See Figure 11-10.)

It is also important to keep everyone focused on the *student,* rather than on the problems of the adults. You need to be willing to shrug off most negative things parents might say. If a student is having problems in school, you will need to prepare yourself to respond to being called uncaring, lazy, or incompetent by some parents. You do not have to defend yourself at every turn. After communication is firmly established, you can discuss some of your feelings with the parents.

Talking to Parents about Student Problems: Do's and Don'ts

Do's

- Describe two or three positive behaviors and give examples.
- Describe specific problem behaviors (not more than two or three).
- Describe how you think ADHD and/or LD is affecting the student.
- Communicate an understanding and acceptance of student.
- Communicate enthusiasm and hope.
- Actively listen to parent's questions, concerns, and opinions.
- Ask for parent's ideas about how to solve problem(s).
- Suggest your own ideas and try to mesh your ideas with the parent's.
- Have realistic expectations of the student.
- Anticipate success, but identify possible pitfalls.
- Express positive feelings.
- Be honest and direct.
- Be respectful, caring, and empathic.
- Ask questions.
- Respond constructively to complaints, concerns, and issues raised by parents.
- Ask parents what their goals are for the student this year.
- Summarize and restate important points.
- Use humor. It can be a powerful tool in fostering positive communication and reducing stress.
- Understand how parents may feel (e.g, powerless, overwhelmed).
- Ask parents to help develop a plan of action.
- Describe the types of student support the school will provide.
- Be prepared for disagreements.
- Be willing to compromise.
- Arrange for frequent parent–teacher communication (e.g., phone calls, notes, daily checklist to monitor student progress, e-mail).

(continued)

Figure 11-10

Don'ts

- Judge parents for not being involved in school in traditional and obvious ways.
- Bad mouth the parents when talking to other staff.
- Be defensive when a parent asks questions or is critical.
- Take everything to heart. Be willing to shrug off most negative things parents may say.
- Assume that parents can help students with their homework.
- Assume that parents can make their adolescent children do their homework.
- Respond in kind when a parent is angry.
- Imply in any way the parent is to blame for the student's problem.
- Constantly address what you consider poor parenting.
- Interpret lack of communication on the parent's part as a lack of caring.
- Keep pressing a point if it makes a parent defensive or angry.
- Ask for the impossible from student or parent.

The Teacher Reaches Out to Clyde's Mother

Surprisingly enough, it took very little for the sixth-grade teacher to change Clyde's mother from an angry, frustrated parent to a cooperative, enthusiastic team member. The teacher sent a letter to all the parents welcoming them and their children into a new school for a new year. (See Chapter 3.) The teacher met with Clyde's mother before the first day of class to discuss the types of support she had in place to help Clyde. Clyde's mother felt that the teacher really understood Clyde's needs and strengths and was greatly relieved to give up some of the burden she had been carrying. Remember, teachers can have a positive impact on a parent's life as well as on a student's achievement.

A FINAL WORD

We are all aware of the impact parent involvement has on the achievement of students. We are also aware that a large percentage of parents do not come to schoolwide events and that some parents do not even attend parent–teacher meetings. However, unless they tell us, we do not know what parents may be doing at home to help their children succeed in school. We cannot make assumptions.

In the past we were often not aware of how a parent's cultural and socio-economic background affected their ability to participate in parent-involvement activities. We may not have been aware that prejudice and stereotyping greatly affect both student achievement and the relationship between teacher and parent. We may not be aware of how much time parents of students with LD and/or ADHD need to spend in helping their child keep up with classwork.

The Parent Involvement Checklist*

Directions: Record your YES or NO responses to the following questions. Ideally, a school-based team composed of a teacher, an administrator, and one or two parents should fill out this checklist together. As you fill out the checklist, collect sample material that illustrates the answers (e.g., a copy of the parent involvement plan, a pupil progress report form, an attendance sheet at a school function, etc.). Your school enrollment data will give you information regarding the race and national origin of your student population. Use this information to determine the representativeness of the current parent involvement program at your school and set future goals and objectives.

Parent Involvement Plan

Yes No

☐ ☐ 1. Is there a stated commitment to parent involvement, such as a directive, policy, or guideline?

☐ ☐ 2. Are there adequate resources (i.e., funding, staff) to support parent involvement activities?

☐ ☐ 3. Is there a parent involvement coordinator?

☐ ☐ 4. Is there a written plan for parent involvement?

☐ ☐ 5. Is there provision in the plan for staff training in all aspects of parent involvement?

☐ ☐ 6. Is there provision in the plan for data collection, program monitoring, and evaluation?

☐ ☐ 7. Did parents help develop the plan?

Outreach

☐ ☐ 8. Are special efforts made to involve women and men from different racial and national origin groups in all parent activities?

☐ ☐ 9. Have linkages been made with community organizations and religious groups that serve the families of children enrolled in your school?

☐ ☐ 10. Are liaisons or interpreters available from different national origin groups to help with parent involvement activities if needed?

☐ ☐ 11. Is a particular effort made to involve male family members in school activities?

☐ ☐ 12. Do some parent involvement activities take place out in the community?

School Policy and Procedures

☐ ☐ 13. Is there a parent advisory council? Are parents represented on school advisory council(s)?

☐ ☐ 14. Are members of the advisory council(s) representative of the school population by race, gender, and national origin?

☐ ☐ 15. Are parents trained to be effective council members?

(continued)

Figure 11-11

Yes No

☐ ☐ 16. Are parents involved in developing educational goals and objectives for the school?

☐ ☐ 17. Are parents involved in developing school procedures and rules?

☐ ☐ 18. Are parents involved in developing pupil progress reporting forms and procedures?

School-Sponsored Parent Activities

☐ ☐ 19. Are parents welcomed into the school on a daily basis as observers, volunteers, and resources?

☐ ☐ 20. Is a PTO/PTA active in your school?

☐ ☐ 21. Are parents involved in developing school-sponsored parent and family activities?

☐ ☐ 22. Are there educational activities and training for parents that enable them to work with their own child at home?

☐ ☐ 23. Are there social activities for parents and families?

☐ ☐ 24. Are there ways for parents to help the school (e.g., fundraising, paint up/fix up, etc.)?

☐ ☐ 25. Are there adult education classes for the parents themselves (ESL, GED, exercise classes, etc.)?

☐ ☐ 26. Is there an updated file of community services and resources for parents and families (e.g., health, social services, financial aid, emergency assistance, etc.)?

☐ ☐ 27. Are child-care arrangements made for school meetings and other parent activities if needed?

☐ ☐ 28. Are there parent-recognition programs for service to the school?

Communicating with Parents

☐ ☐ 29. Do teachers make an effort to communicate regularly and positively with parents?

☐ ☐ 30. Is there a regular school newsletter with information for parents?

☐ ☐ 31. Are parent communications written clearly and simply (at a sixth- to eighth-grade level) using language the family can understand?

☐ ☐ 32. Are school procedures and rules clearly communicated to parents at the beginning of each year or when children are enrolled?

Reporting Children's Progress to Parents

☐ ☐ 33. Do teachers make an effort to say positive things about the child and emphasize the child's strengths in their progress reports to parents?

☐ ☐ 34. Are teacher concerns about their child's progress communicated clearly to parents?

☐ ☐ 35. Do parents participate in decisions affecting their child's education (e.g., classroom placement, course selection, etc.)?

☐ ☐ 36. Are all educational options for their child explained clearly to parents?

☐ ☐ 37. Are meetings arranged at the parents' request to discuss parent concerns regarding their child?

(continued)

Yes No

□ □ 38. Are parent–teacher conferences scheduled at times convenient to the parents as well as the teachers?

□ □ 39. Are transportation arrangements made for parents to attend parent–teacher conferences if needed?

Scoring for the Checklist

Three separate scales were used to help you rate your organization on parent involvement.

Program Fundamentals: Count one point for each YES answer you have recorded to questions 1, 3, 4, 7, 8, 13, 16, 21, 29, 35.

7–10 points *Congratulations!* You have a well-planned program in place.

4–6 points You have the elements of a good parent involvement program on which to build a comprehensive program.

0–3 points You are missing the planning needed for an effective parent involvement program. Persuade school officials to commit the resources to begin a comprehensive program.

Equity: Count one point for each YES answer you have recorded for questions 8, 9, 10, 11, 12, 14, 27, 31, 38, 39.

9–10 points *Bravo!* Equity is an important part of your parent involvement program.

4–8 points Although you have considered some equity issues when designing your program, you must do more to address race, gender, and national origin concerns.

0–3 points You need to rethink the equity of your parent involvement program to attract diverse parents to school activities.

Range of Activities: Count one point for each YES answer you have recorded to questions 2, 5, 6, 15, 17, 18, 19, 20, 22, 23, 24, 25, 26, 28, 30, 32, 33, 34, 36, 37.

14–20 points *Melkam serah!* You have an excellent range of parent involvement activities. Monitor them to ensure that they continue to appeal to diverse parent interests.

8–13 points You have some good parent involvement activities in place. New activities should be developed with community input in order to bring additional groups of parents into the school.

0–7 points You need to increase the range of parent involvement activities to bring more parents into the school. Read the recommended resources and the other articles in this issue for suggested parent involvement activities. Form a parent advisory group.

*Reprinted with permission. Judith L. Greenbaum, Ph.D., Project Associate, Equity Coalition, Spring, 1990. Programs for Educational Opportunity. The University of Michigan, Ann Arbor.

It may take a long time for a school to develop and implement a plan to increase parent involvement taking all these factors into account. But you can begin today to increase the involvement of the parents of your own students. It is important, when developing your own plan, to begin with the following cautions:

- Be sensitive to cultural differences.
- Be sensitive to parents who are socially or economically disadvantaged.
- Be sensitive to the feelings of parents of students with ADHD and/or LD.
- Understand parents' opinions and expectations of school.
- Remember that parents who are not visible are not necessarily uninvolved with their child's education.
- Do not interpret a lack of communication from parents as a lack of caring.
- Consider parents to be equal partners in the education of their children.
- Welcome all the parents of your students into your classroom as assistants or observers.
- Invite parents to make presentations in their area of interest or expertise.

The checklist in Figure 11-11 can help you analyze the efforts your school is currently making towards involving all parents in their children's education.

CHAPTER TWELVE

Preparing for the Future: Transitions to Postsecondary Settings

They were all assembling on the sidewalk, jostling and laughing, 200 young adults in caps and gowns. They scrambled to get in line at the introductory strains of "Pomp and Circumstance," hushing each other. Then the first stately chords began. One by one they marched solemnly into the auditorium and stood in front of their seats. Amid a swell of applause, they took their seats after the last chord had rung out. Today they were graduating from high school.

There was hardly a dry eye in the house. Twelve long years of school were over. They had made it. Many parents (and teachers) heaved a collective sigh of relief.

Most of the graduates were planning to go to college. Some were planning to apply for particular jobs. Some had no idea at all about what they were going to do. Students with ADHD and/or LD were a part of all three categories. However, since the high school dropout rate for these students is between 35 and 50 percent, little more than half of them were graduating.

WHY STUDENTS DON'T COMPLETE HIGH SCHOOL OR PURSUE FURTHER EDUCATION

There are several reasons why students with ADHD and/or LD drop out or are "pushed out" of school. These include:

- Excessive absence and tardiness
- Low and failing grades

- Severe behavioral and emotional problems
- Substance abuse
- Weapons offenses

A sizeable percentage of students who drop out of school come from low socio-economic groups. They leave school because of:

- The need to work to help support family
- A lack of information regarding school supports and work opportunities
- An underestimation of their abilities

Approximately 20 percent of students with ADHD and/or LD move on to some type of educational setting: community colleges, technical colleges, and universities. Most of the others will be working in entry-level, low-paying jobs with little opportunity for advancement. A few of them will stay at home, doing nothing.

There are a variety of reasons why students with ADHD and/or LD don't go on to college, including:

- Low aspirations
- Lack of family support
- Lack of information and counseling support
- Need for financial assistance

The reasons for serious unemployment or underemployment of persons with LD are:

- Problems with self-concept
- Poor social skills
- Problems related to academic deficits
- Lack of employability skills

When teaching these students thinking and self-management strategies and providing accommodations for them in your classes, you must keep in mind their future as independent adults. What types of skills will these students need in order to lead satisfactory lives?

We tend to think that the biggest problems students with ADHD and/or LD will have in the future focus on their reading, writing, and math problems. However, most of the problems that get in the way of higher education are the lack of effective learning and thinking skills. Most of the problems that get in the way of employment are the lack of employability skills. Psychosocial problems pose a barrier to both employment and higher education. (See Figure 12-1.)

These problems were thrown into stark relief at a university summer program for high school seniors and juniors with ADHD and/or LD.

Difficulties of Secondary Students with ADHD and/or LD

Psychosocial

- Immature
- Few or no friends
- Anxious/stressed
- Difficulty reading social situations, body language, facial expressions
- Lack self-confidence
- Talking, acting without thinking
- Excessive dependence; learned helplessness
- Follower
- Relatively low aspirations
- Difficulty following rules
- Difficulty focusing/maintaining attention
- Defiant; argumentative
- Poor social judgment

Academics (general)

- Inconsistent
- Short- or long-term memory problems
- Difficulties with oral or written expression
- Difficulty with understanding verbal directions
- Poor organization
- Test anxiety
- Difficulty with planning/maintaining a schedule
- Difficulty with breaking down assignments into small steps
- Frequent tardiness and absences
- Slow rate of processing

Reading

- Low-level reading skills
- Slow reading rate
- Dyslexia
- Poor comprehension

(continued)

Figure 12-1

Writing

- Difficulty with organizing thoughts on paper
- Frequent spelling and grammatical errors
- Slow, messy writing
- Inability to copy correctly from book or chalkboard

Mathematics

- Low-level math skills
- Reverse numbers
- Confuse symbols, such as + and ×
- Copy incorrectly from one line to another

"A TASTE OF COLLEGE," SUMMER 1995

The Taste of College (TOC) program at The University of Michigan was patterned after a program developed by Loring Brinkerhoff at Boston University. Its goal is to give eleventh and twelfth graders a brief experience of college life. Students live in a dormitory, go to classes on campus, attend college social activities, visit the counseling and support offices (e.g., Services to Students with Disabilities), and learn how to use a large university library.

In 1995, the program objectives were to:

- Provide students with information in order to make decisions regarding postsecondary education.
- Teach students strategies to increase reading and writing skills.
- Increase organization and time-management skills.
- Increase student self-awareness of strengths and weaknesses.
- Help students develop self-advocacy skills.

There were 13 students with Full Scale IQ scores ranging from 69 to 114. Two had Full Scale scores above 125, four had Full Scale scores between 110 and 114, and six had scores between 83 and 97. Deontray, who you met in Chapter 10, had a measured IQ of 69 and a teacher recommendation that stated, "Forget his IQ score. This is a very bright, hard working young man. I guarantee you'll agree."

At the end of the program it was clear that three of these students were ready for four-year competitive colleges. This included Deontray. It was suggested to some of the students that they start at the two-year community college level where the standards and the competition are somewhat lower and then consider transferring to a four-year college.

Three or four of the students appeared completely unready to function as adults in whatever postsecondary setting they found themselves.

Some of the negative characteristics of the students who were unprepared for college were:

- Absent or late to classes and activities
- Lack of personal responsibility (e.g., up late at night, skipped meals, ate only junk food)
- Poor social judgment; a follower
- No outside interests
- Lack of motivation

One of the program aides said that the way those students acted was like taking a leash off an untrained dog and seeing it run away.

Some of the positive behavioral characteristics of the students ready for higher education were:

- Determination to learn
- Involvement in extracurricular activities
- High motivation to go to college
- Like school
- Good work habits
- Empathy
- Outside interests (usually music or art)

According to several surveys, the Full Scale IQ scores of students with ADHD and/or LD in college tend to be lower than the Full Scale scores of students without ADHD and/or LD. This is also true for their achievement scores (e.g., seventh-grade reading and math).

Lower IQ and achievement test scores do not seem to stand in the way of college success for students with ADHD and/or LD. This may be because most of the test scores of students with ADHD and/or LD are underestimations of their ability. It also seems clear that other abilities and skills—such as motivation, good work habits, and persistence in the face of challenges—may be more important than measured IQ scores and SAT tests.

CHARACTERISTICS OF SUCCESSFUL ADULTS WITH ADHD AND/OR LD

Several research studies have focused on the characteristics or skills of successful adults with ADHD and/or LD. Many of these characteristics were similar to those found in the students from the TOC program who were ready to enter college. Many of these characteristics and skills are also similar to the goals and objectives of transitioning. (See Figure 12-2.)

Characteristics of Successful
Adults with ADHD and/or LD

- A desire to succeed.
- Motivated.
- Goal-oriented.
- Adaptable.
- Recognize and accept one's weaknesses and able to build on one's strengths.
- Use self-management and cognitive strategies.
- Possess self-advocacy skills.
- Able to anticipate and prevent problems.
- Able to cope with disappointment/failure.
- Use assistive technology to adapt to environment.
- Willing to upgrade skills.
- Able to locate support services.
- Able to design a fit between abilities and environment.
- Aware of accommodations needed.
- Computer literacy.
- Effective study skills.
- Effective time-management/organization skills.
- Able to plan ahead.
- High school work/volunteer experiences.
- High school involvement in extracurricular activities.
- Able to control impulsivity and distractibility.
- General self-sufficiency (e.g., food, clothing, health, safety).
- Able to handle frustration and cope with failure.
- Social problem-solving skills.
- Perseverance.
- Adaptability; learned creativity.
- Able to set realistic goals.
- View ADHD and/or LD as a challenge to overcome.
- Positive outlook.

Figure 12-2

Students with ADHD and/or LD do not develop qualities like these on their own. Parents and teachers need to help these students learn and practice these skills and abilities. However, many students have not developed these skills by the time they enter high school. IDEA recognizes the need for educational services that foster these skills. IDEA states that the IEP team must consider transition issues beginning at age 14.

IDEA TRANSITION PLANNING REQUIREMENTS

Three major transition requirements were incorporated into IDEA 1997. These are:

- Beginning at age 14 a statement of the student's transition service needs must be included in the IEP (e.g., courses required for college, vocational education classes, study skills classes).
- Beginning at age 16 transition services and statement of interagency collaboration must be included in the IEP (e.g., instruction, related services, community experiences, employability skills, adult living skills).
- One year before student reaches the "age of majority" in a particular state, the IEP must include a statement that the student has been informed of rights under state and federal laws. (See Figure 12-3.)

Vocational Assessment

Vocational assessment should be considered at age 15 or 16. Vocational assessment can be an important part of developing transition goals and objectives. Comprehensive assessment can yield information about:

- Student interests, learning style, aptitudes
- Personal and social skills, self-concept
- Values and attitudes toward work
- Career development background
- Accommodations needed
- Student goals for the future

This information can be added to the results of other evaluations and teacher reports to design transition services for high school students with ADHD and/or LD.

The Responsibilities of Classroom Teachers

Although our responsibilities as classroom teachers do not require us to teach vocational skills directly to students with ADHD and/or LD, an awareness of what these

Sample: Transition Plan

Section VII: Transition

Student Name: _____

Beginning at age 14 (consider at age 13), or younger if appropriate, the IEP team determines the need for transition services in one or more of the following areas:

- Instruction: _____
  - ☐ Yes—Describe: _____
  - ☐ No—Explain: _____
- Related Services: _____
  - ☐ Yes—Describe: _____
  - ☐ No—Explain: _____
- Community experiences: _____
  - ☐ Yes—Describe: _____
  - ☐ No—Explain: _____
- Development of employment and other postschool adult living objectives: _____
  - ☐ Yes—Describe: _____
  - ☐ No—Explain: _____
- Acquisition of daily living skills and functional vocational evaluation (if appropriate): _____
  - ☐ Yes—Describe: _____
  - ☐ No—Explain: _____

Beginning at age 16 (or younger age if determined appropriate by the IEP team), a representative from any other agency likely to be responsible for providing or paying for transition services shall be invited to attend:

Agency Contacted: _____ Contacted by: _____

Method of Contact: _____ Date: _____

Agency Contacted: _____ Contacted by: _____

Method of Contact: _____ Date: _____

The student, beginning at 16 (or younger age if determined appropriate by the IEP team), was invited to the transition IEP meeting and provided input regarding preferences and interests. If the student does not attend, describe the steps that were taken to ensure that the student's preferences and interests were considered: _____

Provide a description of each participating agency's responsibilities and/or linkages:

Agency	Statement of Responsibility

☐ Beginning at least one year before the student reaches the age of 18, the student and parent have been informed of their rights under state and federal regulations for special education, if any, that will transfer to the student.

Figure 12–3

(continued)

Office of Instruction and Program Development
Department of Special Education
_____ Public Schools

Individualized Education Program
Transition Services
Confidential

Student Name _____ _____ _____
                    Last   First   MI

Date of Birth _____   ID# _____   Meeting Date _____

Is the student present? ☐ Yes ☐ No   If "No," who is representing his/her preferences and interests at the IEP team meeting?

Name _____   Position _____

PART I: OUTCOME-ORIENTED CONSIDERATIONS: Check any postsecondary school outcomes being considered at the present time.

☐ **Postsecondary Education** University, college, community/junior college, vocational school, technical institute, hospital school of nursing, or other program leading to a degree or career certification.

☐ **Vocational Training** Specific set of activities that enable a person to acquire the skills necessary to obtain and keep employment.

☐ **Integrated Employment** Full- or part-time competitive employment in the open labor market with competitive wages and responsibilities. Includes supported employment provisions for technical assistance or other services (e.g., training, transportation, job coaching) necessary for individuals with disabilities to secure and sustain work.

☐ **Continuing and Adult Education** Instruction that is not college level. Includes, but is not limited to, vocational courses, parent education courses, personal growth and enrichment courses, preparation for GED, and ESOL instruction.

☐ **Adult Services** Postsecondary special services provided to individuals with disabilities after high school that enable the individual to work, live, and/or participate in the community.

☐ **Independent Living** Living options which include the services that enhance the ability of individuals with disabilities to live within their community. Options may include, but are not limited to, living alone, living at home, or living with others.

☐ **Community Participation** Participation in community life activities, including recreation, leisure, volunteer and social activities.

PART II: SECONDARY TRANSITION SERVICE NEEDS AND ACTIVITIES: Check the special education transition services that the student will need **during the next school year** to achieve the postsecondary school outcomes identified in Part I. Include annual goal(s) to reflect the transition service needs. If no transition service needs have been identified, explain the basis for this decision.

☐ **Instruction** Direct teaching by a special or general educator of specific academic or vocational skills that are identified in a course syllabus or on the student's IEP.

☐ **Related Services** Only if needed to benefit from transitions services.

☐ **Community Experience** Direct teaching by a special or general educator of specific academic or vocational skills that are identified in a course syllabus or on the student's IEP that are conducted in an appropriate community setting. Preparation for the activity and follow-up must be provided for all instruction provided in a community setting.

☐ **Employment/Postschool Adult Living** Identification and development of specific skills included in a course syllabus or on the student's IEP that can enhance the opportunities to find gainful employment in a self-selected career when the student leaves the entitlement system and enters adult living.

☐ **Daily Living Skills** Identification and development of specific skills that can promote the highest level of independent functioning in a postschool environment. The diversity of skills required to maintain the highest level of independent functioning impacts on all areas of curriculum and service delivery. These skills may range from, but are not limited to, mathematics (budgeting) to self-help (dressing) and communication (taking or giving directions).

☐ **Functional Vocational Evaluation** Ongoing assessment of the student's interests, aptitudes, learning styles, and skills to enhance successful career development.

☐ **Other**

☐ **No Transition Services** Explain the basis for the IEP team's conclusion: _____

(continued)

277

Office of Instruction and Program Development
Department of Special Education
_____ **Public Schools**

Individualized Education Program
Transition Services
Confidential

Student Name _____ Last _____ First _____ MI _____ Date of Birth _____ ID# _____ Meeting Date _____

Part III: ANTICIPATED POSTSECONDARY SERVICES Identify the student's projected exit day from school and exit category. Check the postsecondary transition services the student may need during the first year following his/her exit from school. See reverse for definitions. Eligibility criteria of the outside agencies will apply. Report annually to SEDS.

A. STUDENT'S PROJECTED EXIT DATE: _____

PROJECTED EXIT CATEGORY: ☐ HS diploma ☐ HS certificate at age 21 ☐ HS certificate prior to age 21

B. POSTSECONDARY TRANSITION SERVICES:

☐ **No Services Needed:** There are no General, Further Education/Training Division of Rehabilitation, Development Disabilities Administration, and/or Mental Hygiene Administration service needs identified.

Development Disabilities Administration (DDA): DDA provides long-term funding for individuals eligible for adult day, residential or support services for individuals with developmental disabilities, such as mental retardation, autism, and cerebral palsy to work and live as independently as possible in the community. Eligibility is based on priority, availability of needed services and funding, and acceptance by the agency of the client's application.

☐ Day Habilitation
☐ Community Residential Services
☐ Supported Employment
☐ Family and Individual Support Services
☐ Behavior/Support Services
☐ Community Supported Living Arrangements

General Postsecondary Services

☐ Public Income Maintenance
☐ Transportation

Further Education/Training

☐ Continuing and Adult Education
☐ Higher Education Support Services per request
☐ Career School Support Services

Mental Hygiene Administration (MHA): MHA provides services through the Public Mental Health System. Individuals and families must meet eligibility criteria.

☐ Mental Health Evaluation and Treatment
☐ Psychiatric Rehabilitation Programs
☐ Residential Rehabilitation Programs
☐ Support Employment
☐ Respite Care

Division of Rehabilitation Services (DORS): DORS provide short-term funding to programs for individuals with disabilities found eligible to meet employment and independence goals. Provision of services is based on funding availability.

☐ Assessment and Evaluation
☐ Vocational Rehabilitation Counseling and Guidance
☐ Job Search, Placement Assistance and Follow-Up Services
☐ Medical Rehabilitation
☐ Vocational and Other Training Services
☐ Rehabilitation Technology Services
☐ Support Services

Part IV: TRANSITION LINKAGES: For students aged **16 years**, or younger, if appropriate, list referrals/applications for postsecondary services and the person(s) responsible for the referrals.

Referral/Application Made to: **Person(s) Responsible for Referral**

_____   _____

_____   _____

skills are can inform our teaching. The previous chapters in this book have already shown how to incorporate the following skills and strategies into the content area:

- Reading and writing
- Planning
- Computer literacy
- Self-management skills
- Study skills
- Time-management and organization skills

Teacher Checklist: How to Prepare Students for College Entry

- ☐ Increase reading and writing skills.
- ☐ Promote independence.
- ☐ Teach/model thinking strategies.
- ☐ Teach/model self-management strategies.
- ☐ Help develop students' interests and strengths.
- ☐ Reward and reinforce effort persistence and progress.
- ☐ Design success experiences.
- ☐ Teach/model study skills and assignment completion.
- ☐ Help students learn how to cope with disappointments and failures.
- ☐ Give assignments similar to college assignments.
- ☐ Promote self-awareness of strengths and weaknesses.
- ☐ Help students maintain motivation.
- ☐ Provide choices.
- ☐ Provide support for risk-taking.
- ☐ Teach students how to learn from their mistakes.
- ☐ Provide new and challenging academic opportunities.
- ☐ Encourage short- and long-term goal setting.
- ☐ Involve students in decision-making and program planning.
- ☐ Teach students to balance personal freedom with academic goals.
- ☐ Teach students how to schedule semester-long projects.
- ☐ Make training in independence part of every activity.
- ☐ Encourage students to use and develop lists and checklists.

Figure 12-4

You encourage self-awareness and self-advocacy when you involve the students in all decisions affecting them. You help students handle frustration and failure by understanding their problems, designing appropriate accommodations, and providing them with encouragement and success experiences. You are encouraging independence when you provide checklists of steps needed to complete specific tasks. You are helping students become independent when you teach them self-management skills.

Special Education Staff Checklist: How to Prepare Students for College Entry

- ☐ Provide information, guidance, and support in developing the IEP.
- ☐ Teach/model social problem-solving and college-level social skills.
- ☐ Teach/model thinking and self-management skills.
- ☐ Help develop and promote self-awareness of student interests and strengths.
- ☐ Help students understand and accept their ADHD and/or LD.
- ☐ Teach self-advocacy and assertive skills.
- ☐ Promote self-esteem and self-confidence.
- ☐ Present role models with ADHD and/or LD.
- ☐ Base postsecondary planning on student skills and interests.
- ☐ Involve students and parents in the planning process.
- ☐ Help develop realistic postsecondary plans.
- ☐ Teach/model how to cope with disappointments and failures.
- ☐ Help locate one-on-one tutoring.
- ☐ Inform students about legal rights and laws governing postsecondary education.
- ☐ Help students develop strategies to adapt to and manage their difficulties.
- ☐ Help make preparations for taking college admissions tests (e.g., timely application for accommodations for ACT or SAT).
- ☐ Teach students how to anticipate and prevent problems.
- ☐ Prepare students for life after high school.
- ☐ Provide information about a "typical" college day.
- ☐ Discuss with parents their concerns about life after high school (e.g., discuss resources at colleges).
- ☐ Encourage involvement in extracurricular activities, after-school clubs, community activities, part-time work.
- ☐ Check that diagnostic evaluations are current.
- ☐ Help students to develop a portfolio of projects, papers, or work samples.
- ☐ Encourage students and parents to maintain a file of school reports, documentation of disabilities, letters of recommendations, résumé, etc.

Figure 12-5

Sometimes you may need to give students a little push in the direction of independence. You can promote independence by gradually releasing some supports you are providing when students demonstrate a readiness to assume responsibility themselves. The key to developing independence is to meet a particular student's need for support at a given time and then provide activities that guide and encourage the student to become an independent learner. (See Figure 12-4.)

Special education staff and school counselors also help prepare the student for college entry. In fact, it is a good idea to have the school counselor attend every IEP team meeting in which transition planning is discussed. The teacher consultant or resource room teacher

---

High School Counselor Checklist: How to Prepare Students for College Entry

- ☐ Help students see the value of good attendance for entering the job market.
- ☐ Help students keep track of their progress toward graduation (e.g., satisfying course requirements).
- ☐ Stress the importance of self-management skills for education and work (e.g., learning to solve problems, make plans, be organized, follow directions, and complete assignments on time).
- ☐ Discuss why grades matter and how colleges or employers use high school transcripts. Describe other important aspects of an application (e.g., letters of reference from employers, volunteer work).
- ☐ Provide an explanation of graduation options (e.g., regular diploma, GED after the age of 18).
- ☐ Discuss why the PSAT, SAT, and/or ACT are important; how to get accommodations; and ways to prepare.
- ☐ Discuss how and why extracurricular activities are beneficial (e.g., fun, learn new skills, socialize, look good on transcript or applications, network).
- ☐ Discuss the pros and cons of applying to college, deferring acceptance for a year to use the time to upgrade skills or to work.
- ☐ Discuss the necessity of applying to several colleges with at least one being a safety net or a guaranteed admission.
- ☐ Discuss how to deal with disappointments and rejections.
- ☐ Discuss whether and when to disclose a disability if the student does not need test accommodations on the SAT or ACT.
- ☐ Identify possible types of, and sources for, financial aid.
- ☐ Help with the identification and selection of appropriate postsecondary educational settings based on the student's interests, abilities, and need for accommodations or other services.

Figure 12-6

do the lion's share of teaching the student employability skills and must coordinate their work with that of the classroom teacher. (See Figures 12-5 and 12-6.)

All students need some insight about the huge differences between high school and college. Too many students fail or fall apart when faced with unexpected challenge and freedom during their first year. (See Figure 12-7.)

Volunteer and Work Experiences in High School

Many educators believe that if a student is struggling in school, an after-school job will just add to the burden. Surprisingly, this is not the case. In fact, students with ADHD and/or LD can learn a great deal from working or volunteering in the community.

Work and volunteer experiences can be very motivating for these students. They receive positive feedback in the form of a paycheck and/or profuse thanks for their help. They

---

**Differences Between High School and
College: What to Expect in College**

- Complete responsibility for independent living.
- Great increase in amount and complexity of reading.
- Increase in length and complexity of writing.
- Longer and more comprehensive examinations.
- Longer and more complex assignments, requiring more extensive planning.
- Less frequent and personal teacher/student contact.
- Less parent support and guidance.
- Much more freedom.
- Much less structure.
- More distractions and temptations.
- Increased academic competition.
- Responsibility for self-identification of ADHD and/or LD.
- Responsibility for requesting and helping to arrange needed accommodations.
- Need for perseverance when problems occur with instructors, finances, illness, etc.
- Larger class size (lectures with 200 students).
- Larger room sizes (auditoriums; difficulty seeing the board, hearing the lecturer, finding equipment in laboratories).
- Teaching assistants may not have teaching experience.
- Lack of awareness of instructional staff about disabilities or the need for accommodations.

Figure 12-7

Parent Checklist:
Helping Teenagers Prepare for College

1. **Act as a model and guide.**
   - ☐ See each family member as a unique individual with his or her own strengths and weaknesses.
   - ☐ Accept your teenager's ADHD and/or LD.
   - ☐ Cope with your own disappointment and failure.
   - ☐ Set realistic goals for yourself and monitor progress.
   - ☐ Change your own goals based on feedback.
   - ☐ Work hard toward a goal, being motivated and persistent.
   - ☐ Use calendars daily to note daily activities and schedule long-term projects.
   - ☐ Use self-talk to solve problems.
   - ☐ Make daily "to do" lists.
   - ☐ Use visualization to help you remember something.
   - ☐ Overcome challenges.

2. **Understand the needs of your teenager.**
   - ☐ Understand his or her needs for physical and emotional independence.
   - ☐ Question your own protectiveness.
   - ☐ Balance controls against freedom to explore.
   - ☐ Ensure your teenager is an active participant in all decisions affecting him or her.
   - ☐ Give your teenager choices.
   - ☐ Allow for changing roles in the family.
   - ☐ Provide opportunities for your teenager to be away from home for periods of time.
   - ☐ Support your teenager's strengths and interests.
   - ☐ Encourage participation in extracurricular activities.
   - ☐ Allow him or her to take risks, make mistakes, self-correct; experience trial-and-error learning.
   - ☐ Foster appropriate social skills.

(continued)

Figure 12-8

3. **Provide information and opportunities for skill development.**
   - ☐ Locate summer remedial or enrichment activities.
   - ☐ Encourage maximum independence in learning, study, and daily living skills.
   - ☐ Provide tutorial help in academic areas.
   - ☐ Give teenager responsibilities at home.
   - ☐ Locate role models/mentors in areas of student interest.
   - ☐ Encourage your teenager to contact community resources such as libraries, recreational facilities, banks, food stores, etc.
   - ☐ Encourage student participation in community activities such as voting in local, state, and federal elections; volunteering in church activities and community action groups; etc.
   - ☐ Share your experience with budgeting; paying local, state, and federal taxes; paying utility bills; etc.
   - ☐ Encourage your teenager to work/volunteer in the community.

4. **Provide information on postsecondary options.**
   - ☐ Have realistically high expectations.
   - ☐ "Lead" to student strengths.
   - ☐ Provide information on college requirements.
   - ☐ Provide information on career opportunities.
   - ☐ Provide information about ADA and other laws.
   - ☐ Encourage teenager to become a self-advocate.
   - ☐ Provide information on community agencies with support services.

5. **Prepare your teenager for adult living responsibilities. Allow your teenager to:**
   - ☐ Prepare meals.
   - ☐ Shop for food, clothing, household goods.
   - ☐ Pay bills.
   - ☐ Keep a budget.
   - ☐ Do laundry and ironing.
   - ☐ Use different types of public transportation.

Student Questionnaire: Preparing for College

Name _____ Date _____

Preparing for College

Think about who you really are.

* What are my strengths? _____

_____

* What are my special interests or hobbies? _____

_____

* What after-school activities do I participate in? _____

_____

* In what courses do I get the best grades? _____

_____

* What do I want to do or be as an adult? _____

_____

Think about your ADHD and/or LD.

* Do I have problems with attention? What are they? How do I overcome them? _____

_____

* Do I have problems with reading, writing, math? What are they? What strategies do I use to compensate for them? _____

_____

* Do I have problems remembering things? What strategies do I use to remember things? _____

_____

* Do I have problems understanding what people (the teacher) are saying? What are they? What strategies do I use to overcome them?

_____

_____

(continued)

Figure 12–9

- Do I have problems getting to class on time? What strategies do I use to help me get to class on time? _____

_____

Think about your academic skills.

- Am I fulfilling the requirements for a high school diploma? _____
- Am I taking courses that are required for college entry? _____
- Is my academic record satisfactory for college admission? _____
- Can I communicate well verbally? In writing? _____
- Is my reading adequate for college-level material? _____
- Have I developed good study habits? _____
- Am I able to work without outside supervision or direction? _____
- Can I take usable class notes? _____
- Am I strongly motivated to go to college? _____

Think about your self-management skills.

- Am I aware of my own pattern of strengths and weaknesses? Describe. _____

- Have I developed strategies to overcome or bypass my weaknesses? Describe. _____

_____

- Do I know what situations to avoid in order to function well? Describe. _____

- Do I know in what situations I do my best work? Describe. _____

_____

- Do I know how to control myself in difficult situations? Describe.

_____

- Do I use a daily calendar to schedule short- and long-term activities?

_____

(continued)

- Can I set realistic goals for myself? _____
- Do I know how to monitor my progress toward a goal? _____
- Do I know how to motivate myself to complete a task? _____

Think about your self-advocacy skills.

- Am I aware of my rights and responsibilities under ADA? What are they? _____
- Am I aware of the accommodations I need in order for me to do my best work? _____ What are they? _____
  _____
- Do I know how to access the community (and college) agencies that help people with different disabilities? _____
- Do I know how to ask an employer or college instructor for accommodations I need? _____

Think about your work-related skills.

- Can I get to work on time every day? _____
- Can I follow verbal directions? _____
- Can I stick to a job until it's done? _____
- Do I ask for help if I need it? _____
- Am I willing to learn new ways of doing things? _____
- Am I willing to work on something even if it's boring? _____
- Can I work well as a member of a team? _____
- Am I able to complete a job without supervision or direction? _____

List any questions or concerns you have.

_____
_____
_____
_____

are able to work on a project until completion, which is also highly motivating. They work with other people and learn a lot about on-the-job social skills. They feel they are an important part of a team and their effort makes a difference. They can learn how to:

- Get to work on time.
- Work independently with little guidance.
- Solve problems.
- Ask for help.

Work prepares these students for all types of postsecondary options.

Vocational Education

There are many benefits for students with ADHD and/or LD to enrolling in vocational educational programs in high school. Since many of these students have problems with reading and relatively high skills in hands-on work, enrolling in these programs can be highly motivating. Students have a good chance of success and are significantly less likely to drop out of school. In addition, the mean income of graduates of high school vocational programs have been found to be 20 to 90 percent higher than students who graduated from regular education programs.

Parent Support

Parents and their teenagers need to sit down and plan for the future. This can involve a lot of soul searching on everyone's part and is not a one-shot affair. There are very important decisions to be made and parents will have to support their teenagers every step of the way. Teachers and counselors can sit down with parents and students and discuss the options that are available, based on the students' goals. They can also suggest the path(s) that can be taken to reach those goals.

Teachers and counselors can send home materials for parents and students to help them begin planning for the future. (See Figures 12-8 and 12-9.)

POSTSECONDARY SUPPORT FOR
STUDENTS WITH ADHD AND/OR LD

The protections of IDEA only extend until the student is 21 or graduates from high school. We often worry what will become of our students with ADHD and/or LD who have not quite achieved what we hoped they would. Are they "all dressed up with no place to go"?

The answer is that there are places for the students to go after high school graduation. There are many supports available for them both at work and when they are in school. The Americans with Disabilities Act (ADA), which is similar to Section 504, protects individuals with disabilities for the life span of the individual in school, at work, and in public facilities and activities. (See Figure 12-10.)

Americans with Disabilities Act (ADA)

- Covers life span of individual.
- Affects education, employment, public transportation, public accommodations (movies, restaurants, recreational activities, hotels, etc.).
- Person who has a physical or mental impairment, has a record of such impairment, or is regarded as having an impairment that interferes with a major life activity, such as caring for one's self, walking, seeing, hearing, speaking, learning, etc.
- The individual must be "qualified."
- Physical accessibility.
- Program accessibility.
- "Reasonable accommodations" not causing "undue hardship."
- Complaints to Office of Civil Rights.

Figure 12-10

An important requirement of this law is that the individual must be "qualified." This means that a student must meet the requirements of the college to which he or she is applying, or be able to meet the requirements of a particular job with "reasonable" accommodations. Some job accommodations might be:

- Job restructuring
- Equipment modification
- Rearrangement of work area

Drew, a high school senior with both LD and ADHD, included a letter to the College Admissions Committee with her formal application. The letter describes her difficulties and the ways she overcomes them. It also describes the accommodations she had in high school and asks for a few necessary accommodations in college. From this letter, it is clear that Drew is ready for college. (See Figure 12-11.)

Vocational Rehabilitation Service

The individual with ADHD and/or LD, age 16 and above, can qualify to receive counseling, training, and other support from the local office of the federal Department of Vocational Rehabilitation. These supports can include:

- Vocational evaluation
- Academic support services
- Vocational training
- Assistance with job placement

Student Sample Letter to
College Admissions Committee

To whom it may concern,

I would like the Admissions Committee to be aware of my learning disability and my Attention Deficit Disorder so that they may understand the effects they have had on my academic performance.

At the end of first grade, when I was seven years old, I was diagnosed with a learning disability that affected my reading and writing skills. This visual perception problem manifests itself in several different ways. First of all, imagine a "word search" puzzle every time you read. This is what I see when I read. I lack the ability to associate letters to create words. I worked one on one with tutors from age seven to twelve to memorize the phonetic sounds and blends of our language. My reading speed and spelling suffer because of this tedious decoding process. With the help of context, I sometimes am able to assume the entire word after figuring out the first one or two syllables and thus am able to read faster.

Second, my visual perception difficulty is similar to dyslexia in that some letters flip-flop in orientation and extra letters appear and disappear with the blink of an eye. There seems to be no consistency and therefore I must rely on my training and studying of our language to get it right.

Because of my determination and desire to overcome my learning disability, I was decertified for the special aid available through the school system in seventh grade. I am able to get my textbooks on audio tape so I can read along for my classes which require extensive reading. I am allowed extra time to complete tests that have longer reading or writing sections. My teachers, fellow students, family and Franklin Speller have assisted me by reviewing my reports and essays.

Latin is the course that was most affected by my learning disability. I had to repeat Latin One in order to review and memorize the phonetic structure of the language. During my three years of Latin, I worked with a tutor.

In fourth grade, I was evaluated and diagnosed with Attention Deficit Disorder with hyperactivity. I have taken medication to control this disorder while studying and attending school. I do not take the medication for sports, social gatherings, volunteer work or my part-time jobs.

I realize both of my conditions likely will not go away. I have engaged the resources available to me to help me cope with my learning disability at a very challenging high school. I plan to continue to do so at the college level without any additional assistance other than requesting extended test time, texts on tape, and proofreading services.

Thank you for your consideration. Should you need any additional documentation of or information about my disabilities, please do not hesitate to contact me.

Sincerely,

Figure 12-11

A counselor from Vocational Rehabilitation Services can be invited to IEP team meetings and 504 planning committee meetings when the student turns 16. This agency can collaborate with the school to provide the student with needed services.

The Carl Perkins Act

The federal Carl Perkins Act ensures that vocational education and the vocational curriculum meet the needs of students with ADHD and/or LD. The Act affects both secondary and postsecondary education. The Carl Perkins Act provides the following services:

- The adaptation of vocational instruction, curriculum, equipment, and facilities to meet the needs of students with disabilities.
- Career development counseling and activities.
- Transition counseling to postschool employment.
- Assessment of vocational interests and abilities.
- Integration of vocational and academic education.

Tech Prep

Tech Prep is authorized by the Carl Perkins Act to help students acquire technically oriented knowledge and skills. The program has several delivery models:

- Two years of high school courses plus two years of higher education or apprentice training.
- Four years of high school plus two years of postsecondary training.
- Four years of high school plus two years of technical college plus two years at a baccalaureate-degree granting institution.

Job Training Partnership Act

The Job Training Partnership Act (JTPA) is a federally funded training program that awards money to Private Industry Councils (PICs) to provide training for entering the labor market. The student's disability must "constitute a substantial handicap to employment" in order to qualify.

POSTSECONDARY OPTIONS

Students with ADHD and/or LD have many options when they graduate from high school. Some are vocational, some are educational, and some are both. There are even second chances for students who have dropped out of high school. (See Figure 12-12.)

Some community colleges allow students without a high school diploma to enroll. Others require at least a GED. Some community colleges give high school credit for such

---

Postsecondary Options

Educational Options

- Two-year colleges, community colleges
- Four-year colleges with comprehensive LD program
- Four-year colleges with academic support services for all students
- Small colleges
- Large universities
- Precollege summer programs designed for LD students
- Summer internships
- Adult education
- General Education Degree (GED) tests for high school completion certificates

Vocational Options

- Trade and technical schools
- Community college vocational and occupational courses
- Apprenticeships
- Entry-level jobs
- Part-time employment
- Volunteer experiences
- Self-employment
- Military service

Figure 12-12

things as work or volunteer experiences, thus enabling students who have dropped out to earn enough credit to cover high school graduation requirements.

It is important to inform students of all postsecondary options so that, according to their circumstances, they can proceed toward their goal of self-fulfillment.

A SENSE OF COMPLETION

Most of the time teachers do not know how their former students are faring after graduation. But sometimes (probably rarely), you get a phone call or a letter thanking you for the support you provided in high school to a student who was struggling. What you don't hear are the many times the adult with ADHD and/or LD says, "If it weren't for my teacher . . . " or " . . . because my teacher believed in me" in casual conversation.

You must take great pride in the fact that they *did* graduate, overcoming great odds. They couldn't have done it without you.

So, what are the teenagers you met in this book now doing?

- Christopher is doing well in the Marines.
- Deontray received a four-year scholarship to a prestigious university. He is the first person in his family to go to college.
- Ophelia was not accepted at the college of her choice so she is planning to go to a two-year college with hopes of transferring to a university at the end of her second year.
- Mike is planning to start at a community college and hopefully transfer to MIT. He wants to study artificial intelligence.
- Brandon stayed in school with the help of his teachers, his mother, and the Special Education Director. He recently graduated from high school. His mother is trying to convince him to take a few courses in the community college.
- Maria is still not sure what she is going to do. Currently she is working as a waitress.
- Frank is still in school and still struggling with his anger, although his self-management has improved.
- Drew was admitted to the competitive four-year university she had dreamed of going to.

Each of these students required a lot of support from their teachers. Some had special education support; some did not. Some had the support of their parents; some did not, not because they didn't want to help but because they didn't know how. Was all the work worth it? Did it make a difference in the lives of these students? Absolutely. Each one of them joined their classmates at graduation to march proudly down the aisle to the majestic strains of "Pomp and Circumstance."

APPENDIX A

Problems and Strategies

Following is a list of 17 problems that you can encounter in instructional settings with adolescents who have ADHD and/or learning disabilities. Solutions to these problems can be found throughout the book. This is a quick reference guide to the most common problems you will encounter in your classes.

1. Hyperactivity, excessive movement, overactivity
2. Impulsivity
3. Acceptance of ADHD and/or LD
4. Focusing and maintaining attention
5. Following directions
6. Remembering new material
7. Coping with frustration and/or failure
8. Disorganization
9. Poor communication between teacher and parents
10. Low motivation
11. Social competence
12. Time management
13. Reviewing and editing work
14. Homework completion
15. Perfectionism
16. Procrastination
17. Poor test-taking skills
18. Noncompliant behavior
19. Disruptive behavior
20. Defiant behavior

PROBLEM 1: HYPERACTIVITY, EXCESSIVE MOVEMENT, OVERACTIVITY

(Students experience difficulty sitting quietly and not disturbing others, e.g., fidgeting, squirming, foot or pencil tapping, rocking, standing, walking around.)

Strategies:

- Focus on academic productivity and ignore other behaviors except when it interferes with the learning of the student or classmates.
- Provide in-seat stretch breaks for the class.
- Avoid lecturing for long periods. Increase "hands-on" activities and discussions.
- Limit amount of seatwork.
- Provide legitimate opportunities for the student to move around the class (e.g., class assistant who hands out papers or resources).
- Request that the student replace annoying behaviors with more tolerable ones (e.g., tap the desk with the eraser portion of a pencil rather than a pen, or tap a leg rather than the desk).
- Reinforce and praise all attempts by the student to self-manage such behaviors.
- Set up a private cueing or signaling system to alert a student if his or her behaviors are interfering with others.
- Reduce unnecessary stress and frustration (e.g., a change in a weekly schedule).
- Allow individual students to stand and stretch occasionally.
- Work with the special educator, social worker, or other specialists to help students to self-manage hyperactivity.
- Understand that some students can listen and learn although they are engaged in such movements.
- Recognize that it is difficult for students to self-manage such behaviors.

PROBLEM 2: IMPULSIVITY

(Students react without considering the consequences of their actions. They blurt out answers, interrupt others, and make inappropriate comments.)

Strategies:

- Give the class a "pep talk." Remind them of the appropriate behaviors before a class activity or discussion.

- Handle inappropriate or disruptive behavior promptly according to preestablished rules.
- Make appropriate class participation skills part of a contract with individual students.
- Establish physical cues to indicate to students that they should "wait." For example, the teacher holds up his hands until a student completes a thought.
- Reinforce students who wait to be called on and do not interrupt.
- Ignore some interruptions unless they affect learning in the classroom.
- Discuss empathy and the need to understand other's feelings.
- Provide adequate response opportunities for all so students know that they will be heard.
- Provide "comment cards" on which students can write their reactions without interrupting others as they speak.
- Involve students in brief, positive one-to-one interactions.
- Reinforce and praise the student for any positive interactions.
- For test taking, remind students to:
  —Read slowly and carefully. Circle key words.
  —Use self-talk (e.g., "Slow down.").
  —Look at all answers before selecting the best one.
  —Check their answers.

PROBLEM 3: ACCEPTANCE OF ADHD AND/OR LD

(Students do not understand their unique pattern of strengths and weaknesses. They do not know how to take advantage of their strengths and talents, how to circumvent difficulties, or how to improve where possible. They want to be "normal." They don't think they have a problem.)

Strategies:

- Inspire. Provide quotes or stories to support the idea that society needs and recognizes strengths of all individuals.
- Use posters and pictures of famous people with learning problems.
- Discuss how everyone has a unique pattern of strengths or weaknesses.
- Discuss that everyone can contribute to society, no matter how large or small the contribution is.
- Demonstrate respect for students with learning or attention problems.
- Discuss ADHD and LD.
- Discuss differences in learning styles.

- Provide older role models—students with ADHD and/or LD who have accepted their disabilities and are advocates for themselves.

PROBLEM 4: FOCUSING AND MAINTAINING ATTENTION

Strategies:

- Organize student workspace to reduce distractions (e.g., papers and books off desk if not needed, seat near teacher if possible).
- Cue student to get on task.
- Seat student away from stimuli that is particularly distracting to him or her (e.g., some students are more distracted by sights than by sounds).
- Keep the physical arrangement of the room as constant and as clutter free as possible.
- Schedule some time for group discussion, hands-on activities.
- Prepare a daily list of activities and a weekly schedule for students.
- Teach self-management strategies, especially for use during unstructured time.
- Give students checklists of tasks during unstructured time.
- Praise students for sustained effort.
- Discover activities that students are interested in and that they are good at. Use these as breaks or rewards.
- Keep up the pace to reduce lag times.
- Model self-talk and self-reinforcement to stay on-task and sustain motivation.
- Provide hands-on materials that help make abstract ideas more concrete and understandable.
- Provide interesting and challenging work.
- Induce curiosity.

PROBLEM 5: FOLLOWING DIRECTIONS

(Students' classwork and assignments are incorrect; test directions are not followed.)

Strategies:

- Give "alerting" messages such as "Please stop what you are doing. Look at me. Listen to the directions."
- Wait until you have their attention before resuming your lesson.

- Check that everyone in the class can hear and see you.
- Face the class or group of students when you are giving directions.
- Keep instructions short. Minimize words and maximize actions.
- Give directions slowly, one step at a time.
- Ask students to repeat or rephrase directions in their own words.
- Separate instructions from other information.
- Provide directions orally and in written form.
- As instructions are given, provide models of what is wanted and what is not.
- Break down larger assignments into steps and write them out as a checklist.
- Provide visuals (e.g., posters, charts, diagrams) around the room to remind students of a sequence of steps, process, or set of rules.
- Provide written agendas and assignments on the board and as handouts. Color code, bold, or highlight the most important points.

PROBLEM 6: REMEMBERING NEW MATERIAL

Strategies:

- Show how each new concept or unit refers to previously learned material.
- Write key concepts on the chalkboard prior to lectures so students know the questions to expect.
- Provide graphic organizers, advance organizers.
- Make new information relevant to students' lives.
- Provide new vocabulary words in context.
- Encourage active participation and active learning.
- Encourage students to discuss new information.
- Break learning material to be memorized into small learning units.
- Provide repeated exposure and multiple repetitions of new material.
- Review and integrate smaller units into larger wholes.
- Make connections explicit by using analogies.
- Describe how information is to be used (e.g., answer test questions, participate in class, solve problems).
- Reduce distractions when providing explanations.
- Provide thinking time.
- Ask students to repeat explanations in their own words.
- Provide additional exercise sheets for practice and review. These can be for extra credit.
- Teach/model SQ4R and KWL (see Chapter 4).

PROBLEM 7: COPING WITH FRUSTRATION AND/OR FAILURE

Strategies:

- Reduce unnecessary stress due to academic demands.
- Alert students of stresses that commonly occur at the beginning of the school year, during holidays, mid-semesters, etc.
- Try to reduce test anxiety (e.g., relaxation techniques).
- Allow students to demonstrate their knowledge and skills in alternative ways (e.g., portfolios, presentations, art projects, video, audio, photography).
- Allow students to use their strengths and interests in class.
- Reinforce progress and effort, especially in difficult courses.
- Discuss how humor helps relieve stress. Give some examples.
- Model patience so that students are more patient with themselves and others.
- Have the class make a list of "stress busters" to use during exams.
- Show enthusiasm for, and appreciation of, student involvement.
- Recognize and reinforce small steps in areas in which students need support. (It is no dishonor to work hard in a course and earn a C if the student is working in an area of weakness.)
- Provide feedback on positive progress as soon as possible.
- Discuss the idea that failures are valuable as learning experiences. This may be difficult for the student to grasp at first, but will be recognized as the student learns from his or her failures.

PROBLEM 8: DISORGANIZATION

(Students lose or misplace assignments, books, materials, keys, etc. They forget appointments and responsibilities.)

Strategies:

- Suggest that students tape schedule(s) on the front covers of their notebooks.
- Tape reminders on classroom doors and on outside of classroom to remind students to bring books and papers to class.
- Increase structure (see Chapter 3).
- Teach students how to organize notebooks, backpacks, and lockers.
- Create memory aids such as rhymes or acronyms.
- Create small checklists so that students can carry them in their pockets.

- Use self-talk and visualization (see Chapter 6).
- Establish a "cut the clutter" time at least once a month so that students will have time to organize materials and throw away outdated papers.
- Suggest routines that students find helpful.
- Model the use of self-stick notes as a memory and organizational aid.
- Help students maintain a three-ring binder that includes labeled and dated handouts, assignments, and tests.
- Establish an end-of-day or end-of-class routine with a checklist (e.g., "Do I have assignment, books, materials? Did I hand in assignment?").
- Model and require students to use individual and class calendars and assignment books.
- Reduce load on memory by providing reminders of schedules and tasks.
- Provide students with checklist to post inside their lockers.
- Help students learn to estimate the time it takes to complete assignments so that schedules will be more realistic.

PROBLEM 9: POOR COMMUNICATION BETWEEN TEACHER AND PARENTS

Strategies:

- Be patient. Try not to overreact.
- Define your role (e.g., "I'm here to help. Please help me to understand. . . .").
- Defuse situations with positive humor.
- Respect differences of opinion.
- Use active listening skills to identify parent feelings and/or concerns.
- Ask for suggestions and feedback (e.g., "Suppose you had the power to change a few things in this classroom. What would you do?")
- Include parents as equal partners when planning for student and making educational decisions (see Chapter 7).
- Expect some short tempers, moodiness, and intense emotions.
- Talk about student behavior rather than the student as a person.
- Prepare for conferences. Have examples of student work and any anecdotal records to show parents.
- Avoid:
  —Blaming the parent or student
  —Lecturing
  —Trying to change parenting styles
  —Pretending to know all the answers

—Judging parents
—Power struggles
(See Chapter 11.)

PROBLEM 10: LOW MOTIVATION

Strategies:

- Involve each student in decisions which affect him or her.

- Discuss the varied interests, hobbies, and special talents of all the students in the class.

- Identify ways that each student would like to contribute to discussions or projects using his or her unique talents (e.g., photography, cartoons, music, jokes, poetry).

- Provide suggestions about how students can do classwork and homework using a learning style consistent with their strengths and interests.

- Encourage cooperative learning for projects or assignments so that all students can contribute by using their strengths and benefiting from others' contributions.

- Avoid insisting that students talk in class or do other tasks that they don't want or can't do.

- Help students set realistic goals and short-term objectives (see Chapter 6).

- Be consistent with your attention and praise. Provide frequent encouragement.

- Counteract "learned helpness." Help students understand or experience the control they can have over their performance (e.g., provide accommodations, checklists).

- Provide direct instruction and model self-management strategies.

- Teach strategies such as self-talk, rehearsal, and self-monitoring to enable students to direct their own learning.

- Provide success experiences.

- Use multiple modalities when new instruction is presented to the student (e.g., provide more visuals, examples, hands-on experiences, or small group discussion).

- Discuss courage and perseverance as an important part of self-motivation.

- Talk about the benefits of patting yourself on the back.

- Provide additional assistance or support (e.g., aids, peer tutors, special educator).

- Give the student responsibilities such as acting as class assistant or tutoring other students.

- Model how to approach and complete "boring tasks."

- Provide more immediate, specific corrective feedback so that students know what to do to improve.

- Provide students with progress charts.

- Consider allowing a student to drop a course that is using all of the student's study time, which the student is failing, and/or which is in the student's area of weakness.

- Consider a waiver or postponement of any course that is in the student's area of weakness.

- Identify areas of interest and/or special talent to use as a "hook" in various courses.
- Explore different types of educational offerings (community college, summer programs, Internet learning, community education) that can be considered for high school credit.
- Involve the student in extracurricular activities if possible, especially those that offer opportunities for success.
- Modify assignments to allow students to use areas of interest to complete assignments.
- Check that the amount of challenge is appropriate to the student's strengths and weaknesses.
- Post photographs to highlight the contributions of students to projects or other assignments.
- Write brief notes of appreciation when students do a good job.
- Ask students to share experiences they are proud of.
- Compliment students when they are doing things well.
- Provide more practice in areas of student weakness.

PROBLEM 11: SOCIAL COMPETENCE

(Students do not know how to positively and productively interact with others. Many students with ADHD and/or LD report feeling isolated, rejected, and humiliated.)

Strategies:

- Establish zero tolerance for teasing and exclusion.
- Establish a cueing system for interactions and class discussion to help students monitor their behavior.
- Give students (with parental permission) a list of phone numbers of every student in the class.
- Establish a reinforcement system to recognize and reinforce students' efforts to improve positive interactions.
- Model social problem-solving. Provide concrete examples of accepting responsibility and resolving conflicts with peers.
- Use peer-pairing in small structured activities, allowing students with ADHD and/or LD to use their strengths.
- Provide directions to the whole class on how to listen, take turns, and not interrupt, even when they have great ideas.
- Refer to school social worker students who need help with pragmatic social skills.
- Provide training in social problem-solving, discussing steps such as:
  —Calm down.
  —Think before speaking or acting.

—Identify the problems.
—Express feelings.
—Think of alternative solutions to a conflict situation.
—Try out the plan.
—Evaluate the effectiveness of the plan.

For Regular Education Social Skills Class or Special Educator, Social Worker, Counselor, Psychologist:

- Observe the student in a variety of settings (e.g., class, cafeteria).
- Use direct teaching to enhance social skills (e.g., respectful greetings, requesting help, complimenting others, receiving negative feedback).
- Try using small groups to provide skill development and practice.
- Work on improving one positive behavior at a time.
- Teach self-advocacy and assertiveness skills.
- Provide direct instruction and practice about:
  —Understanding nonverbal communication
  —Empathy
  —Reading social situations (body language, facial expressions, gestures, voice tone)
  —Respecting another's private space (or time)
  —Seeing another's point of view
  —The importance of paying attention to what someone is saying or doing
  —Responding appropriately to another's negative behavior
  —Initiating social interactions (e.g., greetings, asking polite questions)
  —Preparing for, and adapting to, new situations
  —Managing anger
- Provide videotape situations as triggers for modeling and role playing.
- Watch television sitcoms, addressing questions such as:
  —What are the people thinking or feeling?
  —Why did he or she do that?
  —Why is he or she angry, or sad, or glad?
  —What are some other ways of responding?
  —What would you do or say?

PROBLEM 12: TIME MANAGEMENT

Strategies:

- Discuss the positive consequences of effective time management (e.g., improved quality of work, reduced stress, time saved).
- Model time management by posting daily and weekly schedules.
- Post a monthly class calendar.

- Refer to a large wall clock to indicate when an activity is to end.
- Provide schedules for students to use to plan their day or projects.
- Encourage students to tape a schedule or "To Do" list on their desk or on notebook cover.
- Check activities as they are completed.
- Encourage students to monitor the length of time it takes to complete class assignments.
- Encourage students to estimate the amount of time the next assignment will take to complete.

PROBLEM 13: REVIEWING AND EDITING WORK

(Students do not check work for correctness, completeness, grammar and spelling errors; there are many careless errors on work.)

Strategies:

- Discuss with the class the essential part that checking plays in problem-solving and grades.
- Provide direct instruction on how to check. Show students how they can:
  —Talk aloud as they complete or check a problem.
  —Use a pencil as a pointer, focusing on each item as they check their work.
  —Place a ruler or paper under each line of a direction, problem, or test question.
- Model and reinforce the use of self-instruction and positive self-talk to increase attention to detail and checking work.
- Provide an auditory or visual cue to check work (e.g., use a signal such as a bell or light or announce, "Check work now.").
- Make editing a part of every assignment.
- Use common sense/judgment as a check on work. Ask, "Does this seem to be a logical answer?"
- Encourage students to read papers aloud to themselves to see if papers are readable or if words are omitted.
- Provide short breaks on a regular basis so that students feel refreshed. Ask them to check their work after such breaks.
- Provide specific feedback on progress as soon as possible (e.g., checking work yields "X" points on most tests).
- Provide a proofreading checklist.
- Reduce distractions when checking work.
- Give credit for corrected mistakes.
- Provide examples of work that have many careless errors. Have the class correct them.

- Customize a point system for the student. Identify each step in the editing process (e.g., achieving accuracy, improving legibility, spelling, adding necessary information, attaining completeness).
- Demonstrate going over a test using the COPS system (Capitalization, Organization, Punctuation, Spelling).

PROBLEM 14: HOMEWORK COMPLETION

Types of Problems:	Strategies:
Reading	• Teach reading strategies. • Obtain or make audio tapes of the textbook. • Use supplementary resources (e.g., Cliff Notes). • Have a volunteer read the textbook and other materials to the student.
Writing	• Use computer writing software. • Provide checklists for the writing process and the specific points you want the students to include. • Reduce the amount of writing that is required. • Provide an alternative to writing.
Slow rate of processing	• Relax time constraints on tests. Reduce the pressure to work quickly. • Give the student "thinking" time. • Instruct the student to take the time to work at his or her own pace when completing assignments. • Give the student time to respond to questions.
Poor organization or time-management skills	• Give students homework completion checklist. • Help students schedule intermediary tasks on a calendar.
Distractibility	• Remove nonessential items from the work space; face the student toward a wall; use a cardboard desk carrel. • Create a quiet zone: Use ear plugs, a fan, or other "white noise" or music.
Fidgety, restless	• Work for brief periods (5 to 10 minutes), walk around, stretch. • Use a flip chart or chalkboard for notes.
Problems with motivation	• Provide empathy and support for the challenges faced. • Identify positive consequences of homework completion. • Develop a checklist for self-management.

Types of Problems:	Strategies:
	• Make progress charts. • Shorten assignments; provide recognition and rewards for small steps.
Appears too tired to work	• Help students develop a homework plan. • Suggest a brief rest/break before beginning to work. • Suggest an earlier bed time. • Advise student to work when most alert. • Suggest a visit to physician or to a sleep disorders clinic.

(See Chapter 5.)

PROBLEM 15: PERFECTIONISM

Strategies:

- Discuss the difference between striving for excellence and perfectionism. Distinguish between dreams and reality.
- Model the process of setting fair and realistic expectations.
- Model setting a range of acceptable goals.
- Discuss the negative consequences of being perfectionistic (e.g., always feeling bad, never satisfied with self or others, not attempting new challenges, not doing work or procrastinating, fear of failure, always wanting to be the best).
- Give permission to make mistakes and learn from them.
- Discuss strategies to resist others' pressure to be "perfect."
- Encourage students to allow themselves not to work exceptionally hard *all the time*.
- Discuss concept of "B" as a good grade.
- Discuss how students have handled mistakes and learned from them.
- Discuss how mistakes can be reframed into "lessons learned" (e.g., learn what doesn't work, discover new ways of dealing with difficulties, learn about predictable problems).
- Discuss passive versus active ways of dealing with a mistakes (e.g., do nothing versus asking for help or making a plan).

PROBLEM 16: PROCRASTINATION

(Students have difficulty starting tasks, normally leaving them to the last minute.)

Strategies:

- Discuss with the class what procrastination is and why it occurs (e.g., feeling overwhelmed, unaware of how to start, fatigue, fear of failing).

- Discuss and list situations in which procrastination usually occurs.
- List general strategies to try, including:
  —Make a "To Do" list.
  —Begin with the easiest task.
  —Work for a brief period and take a break.
  —Self-motivate and self-contract.
  —Tell yourself you did a good job.
- Help students break down long-term assignments into "doable tasks."
- Provide checkpoints and feedback.
- Have students identify something reinforcing that can be used to serve as a trigger (e.g., sit in a comfortable chair, listen to favorite music).
- As a class activity, create and use a calendar to schedule and check due dates for sub tasks of longer projects.
- Check that assignment is not too difficult for the student, especially in his or her area of weakness.
- Work with the special educator or counselor. For example, identify the topics or tasks for which the student usually procrastinates. If a student procrastinates only when working in areas of weakness, consider different instructional strategies, remedial strategies, or additional accommodations.
- Contact the school psychologist to review the student's diagnostic report to gain further insights about the causes or solutions for a problem(s).
- Specify what needs to be done to pass.
- Teach homework completion skills.

PROBLEM 17: POOR TEST-TAKING SKILLS

(Students with ADHD and/or LD frequently have trouble scoring well on quizzes and tests. They may not answer questions with the most points, know how to answer different types of questions, or have test anxiety.)

Strategies:

- Provide sample questions and solutions that cover specific concepts (e.g., measurement, sequence of events, punctuation, etc.).
- Give practice tests with different types of questions.
- Type tests. Use bold print or underline directions.
- Read test directions aloud, and discuss.
- Provide review sheets.
- Allow calculators and spell-checkers.

- Allow students to use ear plugs to screen out distractions.
- Illustrate how points are assigned for each type of question on a test.
- Provide model answers for essay questions.
- Schedule brief study sessions in class.
- Allow students to use checklists or study guides during practice tests.
- Allow students to dictate answers.
- Allow students to use computers (if available).
- Allow students to write answers using key terms or phrases rather than sentences and paragraphs.
- Encourage students to take one-minute "mental" breaks during a test.
- Provide a brief pre-test relaxation time. Instruct students to take a few breaths and visualize themselves performing well. Ask if they are ready and then proceed.
- Review higher-level questions (e.g., opinions, analysis).
- Teach:
  —Test-taking skills (see Chapter 4)
  —Study skills
  —Relaxation techniques
  —Homework completion skills

PROBLEM 18: NONCOMPLIANT BEHAVIOR (DOES NOT FOLLOW RULES)

Strategies:

- Clarify and review rules.
- Discuss reasons that each rule is needed.
- Ask student to repeat.
- Post a list of rules.
- Reinforce student when he or she is following rules.
- Devise with the student a point system which reinforces following the rules.
- Help student develop a self-management checklist so that he or she can monitor, manage, and self-reinforce for following rules.
- Request that special educator or social worker work with student on self-management skills.
- Involve student. Discuss or have special educator/social worker discuss underlying difficulties or challenges the student is confronting.
- Write a contract with the student.
- Reinforce other students who follow rules.

- Involve parents.
- Team with another teacher to work on same few rules and routines in each class.
- Seat student near a positive peer model.
- Stay close to the student so that you can cue and reinforce.
- Be consistent.
- Be friendly and fair, empathetic and supportive during times when the student is compliant.

PROBLEM 19: DISRUPTIVE BEHAVIOR

Strategies:

1. Preplan
   - Involve the student. Discuss the problems, your feelings, and the causes and consequences of such behaviors.
   - Work with the social worker, school psychologists and/or special educator to identify triggers and successful interventions.
   - Refer to IEP and Behavioral Support Plan.
   - Involve the parents.
   - Identify with student times and conditions under which difficulties are most likely to occur.
   - Identify a menu of ways that problems should/can be handled.
   - Refer to social worker.
   - Establish a cueing/prompting system to avoid predictable difficulties.
   - Investigate the possibility of social-skills training and role-playing by social worker or other mental health professional.
   - Identify student's "pet peeves" and work on solutions.
   - Recommend a social skills class for teaching student negotiation and problem-solving skills.
2. Act/React
   - Use prearranged interventions/techniques to deal with outbursts, swearing, yelling, etc.
   - Restate the rules or routines that were agreed to by you and student (e.g., "This is one of those times we talked about. So we're going to . . .")
   - Remain calm. Remind yourself that you expected and planned for such occasions.
   - Use a cooling-off period.
   - Ask student to try to control self.
   - Ask the student to stop and think about what he or she is doing or saying.
   - Remind student of possible positive consequences if behavior is more controlled.
   - Allow student time to explain him or herself.

- Provide time to reframe situation.
- Provide empathy and support for the difficulties that the student has when dealing with such situations.
- Remind student of times when he or she did act appropriately.
- Remove student or have removed from class if situation appears to be getting violent.

PROBLEM 20: DEFIANT BEHAVIOR

Strategies:

- Try to assess why and in what situation(s) defiance occurs.
- Develop a behavioral support plan.
- Ignore some mild behaviors.
- Provide clear choices (e.g., "You have three choices. You can sit down and read your book, start on your homework, or leave as we previously arranged.")
- Discuss positive and negative consequences and the active choices the student has.
- Use time-out.
- Reinforce positive behaviors.
- Check the difficulty of the task.
- Disengage from power struggles.
- Remove the audience (e.g., move student out of the classroom).
- Tell the student that you will discuss the problem later.
- Communicate respect for all students.
- Recognize achievement, progress, and effort.

APPENDIX B

Organizations

Association for Supervision and Curriculum
   Development (ASCD)
1703 North Beauregard St.
Alexandria, VA 22311
(800) 933-2723

Association on Higher Education and
   Disability
University of Massachusetts–Boston
100 Morrissey Blvd.
Boston, MA 02125
(617)287-3880

Children and Adults With Attention Deficit
   Disorders (CH.A.D.D.)
8181 Professional Place, Suite 201
Landover, MD 20785
(301) 306-7070

The Council for Children with Behavior
   Disorders (CCBD) of the Council for
   Exceptional Children
1920 Association Drive
Reston, VA 22091
(800) 845-6232

The Council for Exceptional Children
   (CEC)
1920 Association Drive
Reston, VA 22091
(800) 845-6232

Division for Learning Disabilities (DLD) of
   the Council for Exceptional Children
1920 Association Drive
Reston, VA 22091
(703) 620-3660

Education Resource Information
Clearinghouse (ERIC)
(800) 538-3742

Heath Resource Center
Higher Education and Adult Training for
   People with Handicaps
One Dupont Circle, Suite 670
Washington, DC 20036
(800) 544-3284

International Reading Association (IRA)
800 Barksdale Road
P.O. Box 8139
Newark, DE 19714
(302) 731-1600

Learning Disabilities Association (LDA)
4156 Library Road
Pittsburgh, PA 15234
(412) 341-1515

National Association for Gifted Children
1707 L. Street N.W., Suite 550
Washington, DC 20036
(202) 758-4268

National Association of Secondary School
  Principals (NASSP)
1904 Association Drive
Reston, VA 20101
(703) 860-0200

National Attention Deficit Disorder
  Association (ADDA)
5225 Old Orchard Road
Skokie, IL 60077
(847) 432-2332

National Council of Teachers of English
  (NCTE)
11 West Kenyon Road
Urbana, IL 61801
(800) 369-6283

National Council of Teachers of
  Mathematics (NCTM)
1906 Association Drive
Reston VA 20191
(800) 620-9840

National Council on Independent Living
1916 Wilson Blvd.
Arlington, VA 22210
(703) 525-3406

National Information Center for Children
  and Youth With Disabilities (NICHCY)
P.O. Box 1492
Washington, DC 20013
(800) 999-5599

Orton Dyslexia Society
724 York Road
Baltimore, MD 21204
(800) 222-3123

Protection and Advocacy Services
Developmental Disabilities
(Contact the State Department of
  Education)

Recordings for the Blind and Dyslexic
20 Roszel Road
Princeton, NJ 08540
(800) 221-4792

Vocational Rehabilitation Services
(Contact the State Agency)
(800) 605-6722

APPENDIX C

Resources

Books, Technology, and Aids

A.D.D. WareHouse
300 Northwest 70th Avenue
Plantation, FL 33317
(800) 233-9770

ADD Books
P.O. Box 157
Dexter, MI 48130
(734) 662-2778

Franklin Learning Resources
(Franklin S. Peller)
122 Burrs Road
Mount Holly, NJ 08060
(800) 525 9673

Hearit Perfect
www.hearitllc.com
(800) 298-7184

Inspiration Software, Inc.
7412 SW Beaverton, Suite 102
Hillsdale Highway
Portland, OR 97225
(503) 297-3004

WatchMinder
5405 Alton Parkway, Suite 5A
Irvine, CA 92604
(800) 961-0023

Guides

*The K & W Guide to Colleges for the
Learning Disabled*
Educators Publishing Service
Cambridge, MA

*Insider's Guide to Success in the Two Year
College*
G. Sattelyer
Barron's Educational Services, Inc.
New York, NY

Peterson's Guides
Peterson Thompson Learning (New Jersey)
* *Colleges with Programs for Students
  with Learning Disabilities and
  Attention Deficit Disorders*
* *Vocational and Technical Schools (East
  & West)*
* *Guide to College Visits*
* *Guide to Undergraduate Financial Aid*
* *Guide to Sports Scholarships and
  College Athletic Programs*

APPENDIX D

World Wide Web Sites

U.S. Department of Education (Publications for Parents)
http://www.ed.gov/pubs/parents.html

Learning Disabilities
http://www.ldonline.org

International Dyslexia Organization
http://www.interdys.org

HEATH Resource Center
http://acenet.edu/programs/HEATH/home.html

Council for Learning Disabilities
http://coe.winthrop.edu/cld

National Transition Alliance (School to Work)
http://dssc.org/nta/html/index_2.htm

ERIC Clearinghouse on Adult, Career, and Vocational Education
http://ericacve.org/

National Information Center for Children and Youth with Disabilities (NICHCY)
http://www.nichcy.org

Children and Adults with Attention-Deficit/Hyperactivity Disorder (CH.A.D.D.)
http://www.chadd.org

References

Alber, L. *A Teacher's Guide to Cooperative Discipline.* Circle Pine, MN: American Guidance Service, 1989.

American Psychiatric Association. *Diagnostic and Statistical Manual of Mental Disorders, Fourth Edition, Revised.* Washington, DC: American Psychiatric Association, 1994.

Barkley, R. A. *Attention-Deficit Hyperactivity Disorder: A Clinical Handbook.* New York: Guilford Press, 1991.

Barkley, R. A. *ADHD and The Nature of Self-Control.* New York: American Psychiatric Association, 1997.

Barbe, W. B., Allen, H. L., & Sparkman, B. B. *Reading Skills Competency Tests: Advanced Level.* West Nyack, NY: The Center for Applied Research in Education, 1999.

Brinkerhoff, L., Shaw, S., & McGuire, J. "Promoting Access, Accommodations, and Independence for College Students with Learning Disabilities." *Journal of Learning Disabilities,* Vol. 25, No. 7 (1992), pp. 417–429.

Carbo, M., Dunn, R., & Dunn, K. *Teaching Students to Read Through Their Individual Learning Styles.* Needham, MA: Allyn and Bacon, 1991.

Carney, S. B. *The Attention Deficit Disorders Evaluation Scales (ADDES).* Columbia, MO: Hawthorn Educational Services, Inc., 1995.

Conners, C. K. *Conners' Teacher Rating Scale.* North Tonawanda, NY: Multi-Health Systems, 1989.

Cook, D. M. *Strategic Learning in the Content Area.* Madison, WI: Wisconsin Department of Public Instruction, 1989.

———. *A Guide to Curriculum Planning in Reading.* Madison, WI: Wisconsin Department of Public Instruction, 1995.

Deschler, D., Ellis, D., & Lenz, B. K. *Teaching Adolescents with Learning Disabilities: Strategies and Methods,* Second Edition. Denver, CO: Love Publishing Co., 1996.

Dinkmeyer, D. & McKay, G. D. *The Parent's Handbook: Systematic Training for Effective Parenting.* Circle Pines, MI: American Guidance Service, 1982.

Disabled Student Services. *Making the Transition: College and Disabled Students.* University of California, Irvine, 1985.

Flick, G. L. *ADD/ADHD Behavior-Change Resource Ket: Ready-to-Use Strategies & Activities for Helping Children with Attention Deficit Disorder.* West Nyack, NY: The Center for Applied Research in Education, 1998.

Fisher, V. C. & Beckley, R. A. *Attention Deficit Disorder. Practical Coping Methods.* Boca Raton, FL: CRC Press, 1999.

Gartin, B., Rumrill, P., & Serbreni, R. "The Higher Education Transition Model." *Journal of Learning Disabilities,* Vol. 29, No. 1 (1996), pp. 30–33.

Gerber, P., Ginsberg, R., & Reiff, H. "Identifying Alterable Patterns in Employment Success for Highly Successful Adults with Learning Disabilities." *Journal of Learning Disabilities.* Vol. 25, No. 8 (1992), pp. 475–487.

Gillingham, A. F. & Stillman, B. *Remedial Training for Children with Specific Disability in Spelling and Reading.* Cambridge, MA: Educators Publishing Service, 1960.

Groth-Marnet, G. *Neuropsychological Assessment in Clinical Interpretation and Integration.* New York: John Wiley & Sons, Inc., 2000.

Hallowell, E. M. & Ratey, J. J. *Driven to Distraction: Recognizing and Coping with Attention Deficit Disorder from Childhood through Adulthood.* New York: Simon & Schuster, 1994.

Heath Resource Center. *New Resources About Learning Disabilities.* Washington, DC: American Council on Education, 1993.

———. *National Resources for Adults with Learning Disabilities.* Washington, DC: American Council on Education, 1994.

———. *Getting Ready for College: Advising High School Students with Learning Disabilities.* Washington, DC: American Council on Education, 1995.

Jensen, E. *Brain-Based Learning.* Del Mar, CA: Turning Point Publishing, 1996.

"Learning Disabilities Research and Practice." *Special Issue: Risk and Resilience in Individuals with Learning Disabilities.* Vol. 8, No. 1 (1993).

Levine, M. D. *The ANSWER* System: Aggregate Neurobehavioral Student Health and Education Review.* Cambridge, MA: Educators Publishing Service, 1986.

Lyon, G. R. & Krasnegor, N. A. *Attention, Memory and Executive Function.* Baltimore, MD: Paul H. Brooks, 1996.

Mangrum, C. & Strichart, S. *Colleges with Programs for Students with Learning Disabilities.* Princeton, NJ: Peterson's, 1994.

Markel, G. & Greenbaum, J. *Performance Breakthroughs for Adolescents with Learning Disabilities or ADD. How to Help Students Succeed in the Regular Education Classroom.* Champaign, IL: Research Press, 1996.

Mercer, D. C. & Mercer, A. R. *Teaching Students with Learning Problems,* Fourth Edition. Columbus, OH: Merrill, 1993.

National Institute of Mental Health. The NIMH Multimodal Treatment of ADHD (MTA) Study. Washington, DC: National Institute of Mental Health, 2000.

National Joint Committee on Learning Disabilities. *Secondary to Postsecondary Education Transition Planning for Students with Learning Disabilities.* Position Paper. January 1994.

Nichols, P. *Clear Thinking—Clearing Dark Thoughts with New Words and Images: A Program for Teachers and Counseling Professionals.* Iowa City, IO: River Lights, Publishers, 1996.

Parks, S. & Black, H. *Organizational Thinking: Graphic Organizers.* Pacific Grove, CA: Critical Thinking Press & Software, 1992.

Polloway, E. A., Foley, R. M., & Epstein, M. H. "A Comparison of Homework Problems of Students with Learning Disabilities and Nonhandicapped Students." *Learning Disabilities Practice* 7(1992), pp. 203–209.

Rief, S. F. *How to Reach and Teach ADD/ADHD Children. Practical Techniques, Strategies, and Interventions for Helping Children with Attention Problems and Hyperactivity.* West Nyack, NY: The Center for Applied Research in Education, 1993.

Reiff, H., Gerber, P., & Ginsberg, R. "What Successful Adults Can Tell Us About Teaching Children." *Teaching Exceptional Children,* Vol. 29, No. 2 (1996), pp. 10–16.

Robin, A. L. *ADHD in Adolescents. Diagnosis and Treatment.* New York: Guilford Press, 1998.

Schumm, J. S. & Radencich, M. *School Power. Strategies for Succeeding in School.* Minneapolis, MN: Free Spirit Publishing Inc., 1992.

Schunk, D. H. & Zimmerman, B. J. *Self-Regulation of Learning and Performance: Issues and Educational Applications.* Hillsdale, NJ: Erlbaum, 1994.

Shapiro, E. S. & Cole, C. L. *Behavior Change in the Classroom: Self-Management Interventions.* New York: Guilford Press, 1994.

Silver, L. B. *Attention-Deficit Hyperactivity Disorder. A Clinical Guide to Diagnosis and Treatment.* Washington, DC: American Psychiatric Press, Inc., 1992.

Thompson, J. G. *Discipline Survival Kit for the Secondary Teacher.* West Nyack, NY: The Center for Applied Research in Education, 1998.

Walker, H. M. *The Walker Social Skills Curriculum.* Austin, TX: Pro-Ed, 1988.

Wechsler, D. *Wechsler Individual Achievement Test (WIAT).* San Antonio, TX: The Psychological Corporation, 1992.

Wechsler, D. *Wechsler Intelligence Scale for Adults–Third Edition (WAIS-III).* San Antonio, TX: The Psychological Corporation, 1997.

Wechsler, D. *Wechsler Intelligence Scale for Children–Third Edition (WISC-III).* San Antonio, TX: The Psychological Corporation, 1991.

Wong, B. Y. L. *Contemporary Intervention Research in Learning Disabilities. An International Perspective.* New York: Springer-Verlag, 1992.